THE CEDARVILLE CONSPIRACY

D0841367

Lost Ship's Captain Takes
5th Amendment at Inquiry

By STODDARD WHITE
Detroit News Marine Writer

ST. IGNACE, Mich., May 13. —The American captain whose lake freighter sank last Friday in the Straits of Mackinac refused to submit to cross-examination yesterday after telling a board of inquiry that he believes the Norwegian ship that hit his could have avoided the collision

District merchant marine safety officer, said all parties have the right to cross-examine and instructed the captain to answer Keig's first question.

MORE BODIES FOUND

Keenan, in turn, instructed the captain to refuse to answer

Bodies of two more Cedar-

terday in the engine room divers cut open an outsi with a torch. They w bodies of F. Donald chief engineer; and Radtke, the third ass neer, both of Roger This left three m and presume was Charles Conk

2 DEAD, 8 MIS
SINKS IN MACK

THE
CEDARVILLE
CONSPIRACY
Indicting U.S. Steel

L. Stephen Cox

THE UNIVERSITY OF MICHIGAN PRESS ANN ARBOR

A CIP catalog record for this book is available from the British Library.

Library of Congress Cataloging-in-Publication Data

Cox, L. Stephen.
    The Cedarville conspiracy : indicting U.S. Steel / L. Stephen Cox.
        p.   cm.
    Includes bibliographical references and index.
    ISBN 0-472-03063-9 (pbk. : alk. paper)
    1. Cedarville (Steamship)—Trials, litigation, etc.   2. United States Steel
Corporation—Trials, litigation, etc.   3. Trials—Ohio—Cleveland.
4. Liability for marine accidents—United States.   5. Merchant
mariners—Legal status, laws, etc.—United States.   6. Collisions at
sea—Michigan—Straits of Mackinac.   7. Shipwrecks—Law and
legislation—Michigan—Straits of Mackinac.   I. Title.

KF228.C4C69   2005
346.7303'23—dc22   2004020240

To my young bride

Acknowledgments

I wish to express my deepest gratitude to Len and Pat Gabrysiak, and all of the families and crewmen of the SS *Cedarville*. This is their story. Of course, its telling would have been impossible without the generous assistance of Victor Hanson, Chuck Marsh and the good people at Durocher Dock & Dredge. To Pauline, what more can I say? H^2. And finally, to our literary, but bashful, uncle: my regards to the bugling elk.

Contents

Preface

Recounting conspiracies can be tricky business. When I set out to tell the tale of the ill-fated steamship *Cedarville,* I rediscovered the adage that there are two sides to every story. The survivors of the tragedy alleged corporate malfeasance and criminal misconduct. The owners denied all impropriety. The trial court, however, found the company's version to be lacking and sided with the claimants. Eventually, after much research, I too was forced to choose sides. In the end, I adopted the conclusions of the trial judge, as they appeared as clear to me as they had to the court nearly four decades earlier.

How then to paint the portrait of a conspiracy? Many Great Lakes histories have made objective mention of the *Cedarville* incident. But to date, none has explored its deeper themes of heroism and villainy; of betrayal and vindication; of courage and cowardice; of survival and death. Such a story deserves telling in the grandest of maritime traditions—as a historical narrative. As such, I have endeavored to reconstruct the actions and dialogue of crew members, corporate officers, family, friends, rescuers, and those aboard other vessels as accurately as possible from the available record.

Conversations and actions of surviving crewmen and their families are taken directly from the exhaustive personal accounts reflected in their depositions, correspondence, personal notes, hearing transcripts, diaries, logbooks, and press accounts. The remainder of their dialogue was provided by the participants interviewed. The more mundane bridge communications and radio calls (not typically recorded) are portrayed in a manner typical of ships navigating in the various circumstances presented or otherwise prescribed by international law or treaty—particularly with regard to the foreign seamen involved. All judicial opinions and deposition testimony are quoted directly, except when necessary to condense or to correct occasional grammatical errors. Finally, questionable communications of company officials surmised by the trial judge to be in furtherance of the conspiracy are reconstructed in the spirit of the court's factual determinations.

In the face of uncertainty and apparent cover-up, this account makes every effort to shed light on that which can never be fully known. But it is the conflicting nature of the testimony that gave rise to the conspiracy and made this a rewarding and entertaining book to research and to write. That journey began when I chanced to stumble upon an obscure but fiery judgment in a dusty legal text. . . .

Prologue

October 26, 1967
CLEVELAND, OHIO—

This court finds that the conduct of the captain of the Cedarville and his superiors at United States Steel was so oppressively contrary to the dictates of good seamanship, so callously in disregard of human safety, so wantonly careless of the welfare of the crew as to justify the imposition of punitive damages. This court is convinced that the decision to refuse to allow the men to abandon ship was not that of the captain alone, but originated at the corporate office. Indeed, the decisions which condemned these men to death evidence malfeasance of the worst order.

Judge Connell tossed the opinion onto his well-polished desk. As it slid to the far corner, he turned to gaze through the window. Focusing on nothing in particular, Connell made a conscious effort to calm down. He was livid and had been more often than not since this matter first appeared on his docket. Before this complaint was filed, Connell thought he had seen it all, but this was different. This was profoundly disturbing. Senior officers of one of America's largest corporations were implicated in orchestrating the deaths of ten duty-bound seamen while their vessel sank beneath them. Compounding the insult, those officers intimidated witnesses and destroyed evidence to escape civil liability for their actions. But they would not get away with it on his watch.

Running his fingers through his thinning black hair as he faced the window, the senior judge scanned the park below. The Old Federal Building from which Connell and his brethren administered justice was an imposing neo-classical structure originally intended to house offices of the United States Treasury Department and Postal Service. The four-story courthouse was a monument to the ornate pretense common in federal buildings of the late nineteenth century. On either side of the main entrance stood the massive companion marble sculptures entitled "Jurisprudence" and "Commerce." Peering high above these works, Judge Connell's office featured an expansive view of Cleveland's Public Square.

Once a safe and respectable park for casual evening strolls and Sunday picnics, the oasis of green in the central business district known as the Public Square was overrun with long-haired kids in dirty jeans. How one could tell the boys from the girls was beyond Connell's appreciation.

Shaking his head at the thought, Connell sighed and turned his attention back to the matter at hand. Beyond his closed door, the staccato click of his law clerk's typewriter echoed down the hallway.

This case had proven to be an administrative nightmare. Originally filed as a "Limitation of Liability" action by United States Steel not long after the sinking of the steamship *Cedarville* in the Straits of Mackinac, it devolved into a free-for-all as claimants rushed to join the lawsuit, raising accusations of criminal negligence and witness tampering. Before the matter was set for hearing, it had grown to involve thirty-three claimants, three corporate defendants, fourteen attorneys—not including local counsel in Cleveland—and more than 25,300 pages of deposition testimony and other documentary evidence. Because of the exhaustive nature of discovery in this case, live witness testimony was unnecessary, and Connell suffered through the painfully tedious task of reading each and every page in open court for several months before crafting his lengthy opinion.

Connell's high-backed leather chair creaked softly as he leaned to retrieve the thick draft from the corner of his large oak desk. He was surrounded by the history of many years on the bench. The certificates, plaques, mounted gavels, and distinguished photographs on the walls around him reflected an honorable and noteworthy career. Amid these decorations stood his private library, composed almost entirely of *Federal Reporter*s. Finely bound in tan, with black, red, and gold markings, these volumes reflected the opinions of federal judges dating back to the early nineteenth century. Contained therein were Connell's ruminations on justice in numerous cases, including six maritime disputes. Even so, none of those seemed as disturbing as the one at hand. Reclining into the soft leather, he continued his final review.

It seemed as though the vessel was struggling valiantly to keep herself afloat and on an even keel until the last instant so that its loyal crew could be rescued, but the captain was coldly steadfast in his determination that the crew not abandon ship.

The willful and wanton deviations from law and prudence on the part of United States Steel and its captain that caused the collision are dimmed in importance by the outrageous misconduct following the collision. The men in the engine room and on deck stood by their posts. All the crew showed great courage, obedience to duty and dedication to service in the highest traditions of the American merchant marine. However, when he chose to leave, the captain, knowing full well that he had no further need of engine propulsion, stepped out of the pilot house and sent the men below it to their doom, for lack of two words . . . abandon ship.

. . . but it all seemed unreal. Incomprehensible, really. "How could this happen?" Connell mused, allowing his thoughts to return to the lost vessel and her crew. . . .

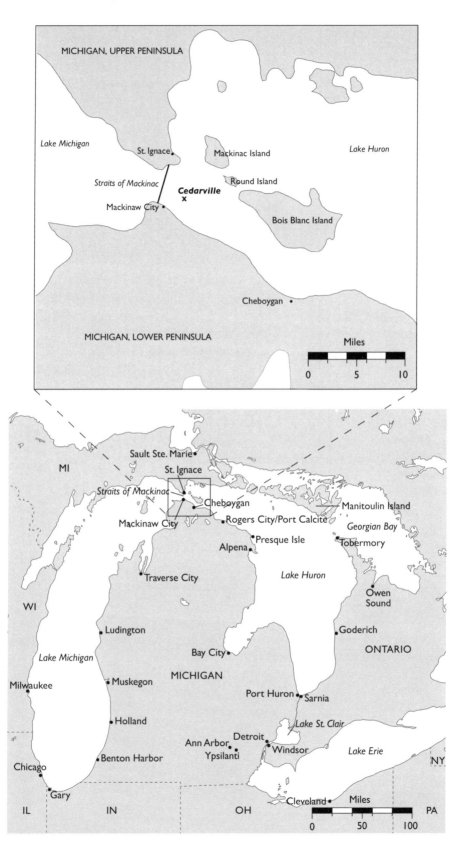

MICHIGAN, UPPER PENINSULA

Lake Michigan

St. Ignace

Straits of Mackinac

Mackinac Island

Round Island

Cedarville
x

Mackinaw City

Lake Huron

Bois Blanc Island

Cheboygan

MICHIGAN, LOWER PENINSULA

Miles

0   5   10

Sault Ste. Marie

St. Ignace

Straits of Mackinac

Cheboygan

Mackinaw City

MI

Manitoulin Island

Rogers City/Port Calcite

Georgian Bay

Tobermory

Presque Isle

Alpena

Lake Huron

WI

Traverse City

Owen
Sound

Ludington

Goderich

ONTARIO

Lake Michigan

Bay City

Milwaukee

Muskegon

MICHIGAN

Port Huron

Sarnia

Holland

Lake St. Clair

Ann Arbor   Detroit

Ypsilanti

Windsor

Lake Erie

Chicago

Benton Harbor

Gary

NY

IL

IN

OH

Cleveland   Miles

PA

0   50   100

I

Return to Rogers City

March 10, 1965
GRAND RAPIDS, MICHIGAN—
0638

Accelerating through the sleepy early morning streets of Grand Rapids, the two-tone Ford LTD turned northeast onto Highway 131 to follow the Grand River for several miles before turning north again toward Cadillac. The six-hour drive would take a series of opposing turns as the car gradually worked its way diagonally across the mitt-shaped land mass that forms the Lower Peninsula of Michigan.

"Slow down, Len. You're going to get a ticket."

The speedometer needle hovered at sixty-two miles per hour. Avoiding the early morning glare, Leonard Gabrysiak—"Len" to his friends—glanced over at Pat and smiled, revealing a mild underbite. Pat was a small, attractive woman in her late twenties, glowing nicely from several months in Mexico. Gabrysiak, on the other hand, was exposed to the sun and wind year-round so never quite lost his tan.

"You worry too much. Go back to sleep." He gave her a sideways wink and tapped the accelerator for good measure. The eight-cylinder engine revved as the car picked up more speed. Pressed back in her seat, Pat suppressed a smile, reclined against the locked door, and turned to watch the sunlight filter between the passing tree-lined hills as her eyes grew heavy once again. Lenny Jr., sleeping soundly in the backseat, barely stirred. Theirs was the only car on the road, and he wanted to make good time while he could.

Gabrysiak was a tall, slender, square-jawed Michigan native of Polish descent with thoughtful eyes, a prominent nose, and a broad and easy smile. He and his family were bound for Rogers City on the northwest shore of Lake Huron for the start of the 1965 shipping season. They had migrated south when the lakes began to freeze the previous winter but were returning for the spring thaw.

Thinking that he needed a cup of coffee, Gabrysiak squinted against the glare on his dusty, bug-spattered windshield as the road, veering eastward into a U-shaped valley, shifted the rising sun into full view. He flipped down his visor in response, feeling under the seat for the sunglasses he had purchased in Brownsville, Texas.

The deeply forested hills and valleys through which the Gabrysiaks sped bore silent witness to the creeping flow of an ancient glacial force that had, over the millennia, repeatedly scoured the southern portion of the granitic Canadian Shield underlying present-day Michigan. Towering more than six thousand feet above the surrounding landscape, prehistoric rivers of ice and debris had once gouged the underlying strata to form and define the topography of much of modern North America.

As the last ice age drew to a close eleven thousand years ago, the ice sheet that had covered the region's expansive basins of deeply carved bedrock melted, leaving behind a series of massive freshwater seas and tributary valleys. In one such valley, the two-lane road onto which Len had just turned wound slowly past the imposing vestiges of glacial rock and silt drumlins in its long descent to Lake Huron.

Gabrysiak was the last of six boys to take to the inland seas and was no stranger to the rigors of the profession. In fact, by the time he started sailing, one of his brothers had already been sacrificed to lake shipping. Len could recall the day, as a seventh-grader, he said goodbye to his brother Frances as he reported to Interlake Steamship Company on Lake Superior. The 602-foot bulk cargo carrier *Edward Y. Townsend* needed deckhands, and Frank filled the billet; but he would soon be lost overboard on a starless night within sight of the Minnesota shore.

On June 27, 1945, the lanky twelve-year-old answered the door to find a uniformed Western Union courier waiting patiently on the front step. Signing the clipboard, Len thanked the courier and stepped back inside. The message was addressed to his father, but he opened it anyway.

Len sprinted across First Street to find the elder Gabrysiak at the pub he co-owned in Rogers City with a curious fellow named Greka. Slamming the screen door, his heavy steps pounded on the wooden floor, disturbing a couple of off-duty Bradley Fleet seamen playing pool in the corner. Breathless, he spotted his father emerging from behind the counter and surrendered the opened telegram. This would ordinarily have earned him a scolding, but Marty Gabrysiak could see that something was wrong. Adjusting his glasses and finding a perch beside the bar, he read the message.

June 26, 1945
Mr. Martin Gabrysiak
Your Son Is Missing from E Y Townsend 5 Hours after Departure from Duluth. Was Going to Watch Station When Lost. Will Keep You Advised.

Frank was never found. A search for his body was fruitless, as he was presumed to have drowned in the frigid waters. Although the family heard rumors that an investigation of his disappearance had taken place, they were never contacted by the Coast Guard, nor ever again by the Interlake Steamship Company. The outcome of the inquiry would remain a mystery.

To his horror, Len later read that the extreme cold and lack of oxygen in the depths of Lake Superior would combine to preserve a human body indefinitely. The thought of his brother Frank drifting pale and wide-eyed along the cold, dark lake bottom would haunt him for the rest of his life. Nevertheless, he too chose to work offshore.

Still blinded by the glare, Len instinctively braked as he followed the curve of the road. Pat had fallen back to sleep, and his only company was the tinny voice of Patsy Cline warbling from the dashboard speakers. As "I Fall to Pieces" reached its crescendo, his mind turned back to the ship that he would call home for most of the season. He wondered how she had fared the winter. Floating empty where he had left her, *Cedarville* was probably home now to countless rats that had braved the frozen mooring lines for shelter from the northern Michigan winter. No telling what they had torn up this year. Pest control was a major fleet issue with the start of each new shipping season.

Len's employer, the Bradley Fleet, was a subsidiary of the United States Steel Corporation. Consisting of seven bulk ore carriers operating from Port Calcite, the fleet supplied limestone to the steel manufacturer from Rogers City quarries, where it was produced in abundance. Ore from the nearby mines was continuously crushed and loaded aboard the vessels, which in turn raced north, through the narrow Straits of Mackinac, then south through Lake Michigan to quickly unload in Gary, Indiana, and return. Although he had worked aboard several of the fleet vessels, Gabrysiak had been assigned to *Cedarville* for over a year.

Originally christened the *A.F. Harvey* in 1927, the 604-foot bulk freighter was eventually converted to a self-unloader and renamed *Cedarville* in a ceremony hosted by her namesake on the Upper Peninsula. After thirty-eight years of service, she continued to be a key component in the chain of production supporting the American industrial machine. Even so, her busy schedule stalled each winter as ice sweeping in from Lake Michigan clogged the Straits, closing it to shipping traffic.

The previous shipping season had ended on December 17, as the vessels of the Bradley Fleet converged at Port Calcite for winter layup.

Adjacent to the Presque Isle County limestone quarry, Port Calcite was a staging area for mountains of colorless limestone surrounding perpendicular shipping terminals, each barely wide enough to accommodate two vessels side by side. The entrance to the port was protected by an equally colorless gray-rock jetty projecting eastward into the sapphire blue waters of Lake Huron. The facility was just large enough to house six of the seven Bradley Fleet vessels for the winter.

Churning the slushy waters of the port, the tugs *Limestone* and *Dolomite* were busy on that early winter day maneuvering the ungainly vessels into their restricted berths when *Cedarville* rounded the jetty. Third Mate Gabrysiak stood on the starboard bridge wing within earshot of the radio, his breath condensing in the chilling air, as he watched the *Dolomite* swing another self-unloader into position before gently guiding it into its berth at the south dock. Without bow-thrusters, the aging Bradley Fleet vessels were unable to turn in close quarters, so tug assistance was routinely needed to approach the pier. This day both tugs would be busy.

A few feet away, the radio crackled to life. "*Cedarville,* this is Tug *Limestone,* approaching from the south. I will push you around for entry into the north terminal and then take a line." Gabrysiak glanced down at the deck crew assembled at the bow, preparing to cast an eight-inch manila hawser to the approaching tug. *Cedarville* would winter in the northern portion of the L-shaped terminal, its fantail almost touching the bow of the *Calcite II,* now doubling up lines in the western terminal. Gabrysiak heard the captain reply, "Roger, *Limestone,* standing by."

Cedarville was the fourth U.S. Steel vessel to pull in for layup and would be the last to occupy a protected berth. In theory, all of the ships would undergo repairs and be ready for the new shipping season as soon as the spring ice conditions would permit.

Earlier that morning, Gabrysiak had packed his belongings for the first time that season. He never took gear home when the ship pulled in for loading because he never knew when, at a moment's notice, she would be underway again. Elsewhere on the ship, most of the crew had also packed, and the hatches and deck gear were battened down for winter storage.

Looking aft, Gabrysiak watched as *Limestone* emerged from behind the fantail and crossed *Cedarville*'s wake at a hundred yards. Turning, the small tug parted the blue waters of the harbor into a white foam as it accelerated to catch up and come alongside the slowing larger vessel.

Unlike most ships, the eighty-foot harbor tug was specifically designed to bump up against other vessels. Protected by rubber fenders and lengths of tattered fire hose, *Limestone*'s bulbous bow was reinforced to withstand the stresses generated by its fifteen-hundred-horsepower engine against the sides of the bulk carriers that she tended. Even so, her bent mast and dented coaming spoke of a thousand previous encounters with the larger craft.

Gabrysiak tracked the tug until it came in contact with his ship.

Almost immediately he felt *Cedarville* swing to the right as she was maneuvered to enter the terminal. With the turn complete, *Limestone* disengaged and came forward. The *Cedarville* deck crew heaved a small line weighted with a heavy knot called a monkey fist. The line draped the tug's deck, with the monkey fist floating in the water on the far side. A tug crewman quickly took up the slack and pulled the smaller cord until an attached manilla line dangled from the ship towering overhead. *Cedarville* paid out the head line while another was secured aft, and *Limestone* was soon ready to guide *Cedarville* to the pier. Positioned so as not to be crushed between the massive ship and the pier, the tug guided *Cedarville* into her winter berth. Gabrysiak walked through the pilothouse to the opposing bridge wing as the ship closed on the wharf. He was joined by Captain Marty Joppich.

From below the starboard bow, the tug gave a single blast of its whistle. "Ahead one-third," Joppich shouted into the pilothouse.

Adjusting the engine order telegraph, Wheelsman Bill Asam answered, "Ahead one-third, aye. Engine room answers ahead one-third." He was anxious to go ashore. He and his girlfriend were planning to tie the knot during the break, and Patricia was probably waiting somewhere on the pier to spirit him away and finalize the wedding plans.

"Very well," Joppich said.

Behind *Cedarville,* limestone silt was churned up by her single four-bladed propeller as she maneuvered alongside the pier. "Left standard rudder. Steady up on three-five-five."

Asam watched the compass swing as he called back, "Left standard rudder, aye. My course is three-five-five."

Joppich allowed his ship to close with the pier for a few seconds before correcting her course once again. "All stop. Come right to zero-zero-four."

Once again Asam answered, "Engine room answers all stop. My course is steady at zero-zero-four."

Lifting his handheld radio, Joppich keyed the microphone. "*Limestone,* she's all yours."

"Roger that, *Cedarville.* Bringing her in."

As *Cedarville*'s forward drift slowed, *Limestone* nudged the ship against the giant fenders lining the west dock. When she came to rest, Gabrysiak and Joppich watched as a flurry of mooring lines shot across the void to workmen waiting on the pier.

With nothing to do for the moment, Len watched the exodus of seamen from the three ships already secured. Opposite *Cedarville* he saw Art Fuhrman jump from the gangway of the *Calcite II*. After waiting on the pier, Fuhrman's wife ran to meet him. Art had been assigned to the deck division of the *Calcite II* but was slated to transfer to *Cedarville* the following spring. The couple would likely celebrate the end of the season with a night on the town. In fact, most of the Bradley Fleet men would flock to local dives, but Gabrysiak was not sure about the other members of his watch team.

Bill Asam was getting married. His bride-to-be doubtless had plans to keep him (and their five children) busy until well after the wedding.

Stan Haske . . . Well, Len didn't know what was wrong with him. The relief helmsman was in a foul temper for most of the last run. Now, leaning against the chart table aft of the pilothouse and holding his lower abdomen, he appeared to be in no mood for postseason revelry. Len had heard First Mate Piechan order Haske to see the company doc as soon as the ship was tied up. "I'll think about it" was the stalwart helmsman's curt reply.

If the rumors about the captain were true, he would likely pass out at home with an open bottle once the ship was secured and turned over to the Bradley Fleet manager for winter repairs.

As for Len, he, Pat, and Lenny Jr. would leave as soon as possible for Tampeco, Mexico, where they would winter for the fifth year in a row. They might even try to catch Mardi Gras in New Orleans on their return trip if the timing worked out. The lunar calculations employed to set the date for Easter and Ash Wednesday had always mystified Gabrysiak, and he could never be sure when Mardi Gras would actually fall. A personnel clerk had long ago told him that he couldn't draw unemployment benefits unless he filled out a work request for winter employment, but he was not interested. With his luck, they just might put him to work and his winter in Mexico would be shot. No thanks!

Now, as the Gabrysiaks continued their descent through the frequently marshy terrain of the Lower Peninsula, Len wondered how his captain and messmates had weathered the harsh Michigan winter.

He would find out soon enough as the *Cedarville* crew reassembled to bring the ship out of winter hibernation.

Reaching up, he touched the windshield with the back of his hand.

Noticing the gesture, Pat asked, "Still cold out there?"

"Yeah. So much for a warm spring."

2

Headquarters

March 15, 1965
PITTSBURGH, PENNSYLVANIA—

Charles Khoury had taken a cab from the Duquesne Club, where he had enjoyed a nice, long breakfast. Founded in 1873, the Duquesne Club was renowned as the oldest and most prestigious of Pittsburgh's clubs, catering to the city's most influential businessmen. Steel chieftains frequented the plush dining and drawing rooms of the exclusive brownstone fortress, and Khoury reveled in the privilege. Tossing a few bills over the seat, he jumped from the taxi, crossed the street to 525 William Penn Place, and entered the towering Mellon Bank Building.

Sweeping aside the heavy glass door, Khoury found the lobby nearly empty. Most U.S. Steel employees had been chained to their desks for more than an hour already, and the random click of leather on marble tile betrayed the presence of only a few well-dressed men, briefcases in hand, each hurriedly pointed for some unknown destination within the building.

Khoury shared the elevator with a runner employed by a local courier service. Bound for the thirty-second floor, the courier carried a bundle of documents to be executed by one of the countless departments packing the overcrowded United States Steel headquarters building.

Stepping to the right, the vice president considered the familiar number panel. Atop the matrix of buttons, "41" illuminated beneath his finger. As the elevator lurched upward, Khoury settled against the back wall and, glancing up, found his reflection in the polished metal doors. Nodding slightly, he gave his reflection a warm and welcoming smile.

The image smiling back was that of an accomplished man in his early sixties, stout, with close-cropped, thinning reddish-gray hair.

Born in New Haven, Connecticut, the soft-spoken Khoury was naturally drawn to the sea. Spurning a private Bostonian education, he joined the Navy as a teen, serving first as a seaman, obtaining a commission and advancing from deck officer to captain. He briefly retired from military service in 1940, only to be recalled with the outbreak of war.

Thirteen years and two wars later, he retired once again, this time at the rank of commodore. The experienced flag officer was quickly recruited by U.S. Steel's Isthmian Steamship Company, where he assumed the mantle of vice president of operations. When the first chair at Pittsburgh Steamship was vacated a few years later, Khoury accepted the position and transferred to his new office on the seventeenth floor of Cleveland's Rockefeller Building, overlooking the Cuyahoga River. There he guided the comings and goings of the Great Lakes ore-carrying division until the corporate shakeup of 1964.

Referred to by Wall Street, the government, and labor as "Big Steel," United States Steel had been the dominant force in American steel production for sixty-three years. Yet, despite its influence on the industry and the national economy, U.S. Steel's market share and profits had dropped dramatically, undercut by competitors and struggling under the weight of its bloated infrastructure.

By 1962, the corporation's leadership was determined to reverse the trend. Helming the eleven-man policy committee, Chairman Roger Blough opted for bold measures. At Blough's direction, U.S. Steel raised prices across the board by more than six dollars per ton. The maneuver backfired. Responding to the obvious market manipulation, President Kennedy and his brother, the attorney general, mustered opposition on Wall Street and Capitol Hill to force Blough to rescind the increase. Thereafter the Justice Department filed six antitrust lawsuits, targeting U.S. Steel. With government harassment preventing the company from raising prices and expanding its markets, Blough had no option but to trim the unwieldy and duplicative management structure beneath which the company was suffocating.

The chairman announced the plan in September 1963, and within four months seven U.S. Steel divisions, including Pittsburgh Steamship, shed their separate identities to merge with Central Operations Division. Overall, the U.S. Steel work force was cut by more than forty thousand as legions of executives converged on Pittsburgh, filling nine local office buildings.

In the course of the consolidation, Khoury's position was upgraded to include management of the newly combined ore- and limestone-carrying divisions of the Great Lakes fleet. The newly promoted vice president for lake shipping was relieved to be joining the fifty-three other vice presidents who had survived the purge.

Nevertheless, survival was not without its price, and the stresses Khoury faced were mounting. Since the beginning of the year, he had come under increasing pressure to push his aging fleets beyond capacity. In regular meetings in the walnut-paneled boardroom, Khoury listened as Blough, U.S. Steel president Leslie Worthington, production manager Ed Gott, R&D head Stephen Jenks, and accountant Bob Tyson plotted a new course for the company. In short, the 1964 reorganization was only the first step in Blough's broader plan to increase market share and to improve the company's profit margin. With the reorganization complete, Blough intended to expand U.S. Steel's presence in the industry.

At that time, United States Steel was the only company in the country producing steel in all grades, including ingots, slabs, plates, bars, tubing, rods, wire, tinplate, and hot and cold rolled sheets and strips. In Blough's estimation, the company should have been dominating the market, but years of slogging through the industry as a top-heavy conglomeration of independently operating production facilities had stifled the company's growth.

Perhaps equally important, U.S. Steel's efforts at employing new technologies developed since the end of World War II were weak at best. On this point, R&D was stepping up to bat. Corporate leadership was beginning to understand that the rebuilding of the decimated industrial infrastructure in Europe and Japan had led to technological breakthroughs with the potential to revolutionize steel production in the United States. The principal advancement, then under development by U.S. Steel's domestic competitors, was the oxygen furnace, which produced molten steel eight times faster than the traditional blast furnace, with the injection of pure oxygen into the mix. Likewise, the introduction of aluminum processing to prevent corrosion of ultralight-gauge tin had the potential to make steel more attractive to food packagers.

Though Khoury had little interest in such matters, he would find that the resulting increase in short-term production goals would impact his fleets substantially. During the previous year, United States Steel facilities operated at less than 70 percent ingot production capacity. Meanwhile, industrywide sales surged by 11 percent due to hoarding by manufacturers in anticipation of labor problems. Sensing an opportunity, Blough was determined to increase ingot production at the Fairless and Gary Works to 122 million tons, creating a tremendous demand for raw materials.

With the increase in production, senior executives were looking to Khoury to keep iron ore and limestone flowing from the company mines and in quantities sufficient to maintain the desired levels of production.

The question was, could his tired old ships hold up under the strain?

With his captains gathering for preseason fit-out, Khoury judged that the time was right to put a little more pressure on the fleets.

Stepping from the elevator, he stormed into his office, barking at his secretary to get the fleet captains on the line.

A few minutes later his phone rang. "Khoury here," he announced without prompting. Joseph Parilla was on the other end of the line. Interrupting his subordinate's greeting, Khoury broke the bad news. Parilla would have to get his fleet fired up. The top floor was putting on the pressure, and he was expected to pick up the deliveries.

Khoury paused while the voice on the other end responded. "No, I don't care how you do it," he interrupted again. The board wanted to go to full capacity. Yes, it would be an almost 50 percent increase in limestone delivered, but the issue was not subject to debate.

With Parilla's reluctant agreement, Khoury hung up. Parilla had better get that limestone moving, he worried, or it would cost Parilla his job.

The phone rang again, breaking Khoury's train of thought. It was Tom Harbottle at Pittsburgh Steamship, no doubt. Reaching across his desk, he lifted the receiver.

"Hey Tom, Khoury here . . ."

PORT CALCITE, MICHIGAN—
1430

"Alright, fellas, we have a new challenge," Joseph Parilla said as he took his seat at the head of the modest conference table. "Admiral Khoury just increased our quota."

His audience collectively groaned. "How much?" one of the captains finally asked.

"Almost 50 percent," Parilla responded, eyeing the room.

The eight men deflating before him commanded the self-unloading bulk freighters of the United States Steel Bradley Fleet. Like migrating geese, these men returned to the port at the same time each year to bring their vessels out of winter layup. Fit-out would begin the next day, and the fleet would be underway within a couple of weeks, weather permitting. During the shipping season they would take their orders from Parilla.

An experienced seaman, Captain Parilla took command of the limestone fleet in 1960, having never sailed the Great Lakes as either master or crew. Instead, Parilla spent his early career with U.S. Steel aboard East Coast "salties." A graduate of the New York Merchant Marine Academy, he had joined the blue-water Isthmian Line as an able-bodied seaman and progressed to master of Isthmian Steamship before transferring to the Bradley Fleet. Now, as manager of operations he answered only to Khoury.

Joppich knew there was no use in complaining. The front office was increasing production, and they needed the raw materials to do the job. Either the captains could ship the extra tonnage with the promise of a nice bonus next Christmas, or the company would find someone else to pilot the ships. Replacement was a serious threat, indeed. For every captain serving aboard a Bradley Fleet vessel, three licensed officers were standing by, equally qualified to take his position.

Sensing that he had made his point, Parilla leaned back in the threadbare swivel chair. "Alright, then, gentlemen. That's settled. Let's get on with the fit-out."

3

Fit-Out

March 16, 1965
SS *Cedarville*—

Don Lamp brushed the dust and soot from his trousers as he emerged from the manhole at the base of the firebrick-lined boiler. As *Cedarville*'s chief engineer, responsibility for the technical aspects of fit-out fell squarely on his shoulders. The combined responsibilities of coordinating the operation and maintenance of the main propulsion plant, the auxiliary systems, the damage control gear, and the ship's self-unloading conveyor system weighed heavily on Lamp, but he had been sailing for United States Steel for over twenty years and was more than qualified to direct the revival of the aging self-unloader.

Coming aboard the previous day to begin fit-out, Lamp had taken the lead in bringing the old girl back to life. For eighteen of the last twenty-four hours he had been opening up the engineering spaces, inspecting the hull and propulsion gear, and supervising the ten engineers, oilers, stokermen, and conveyormen under his charge.

Feeling a draft, he examined a ragged hole in the right knee of his yet unwashed Sears coveralls. Barely a full day back in the saddle and he had already ruined a set of work clothes. Well, this tear could be patched like all the others.

Lamp would spend most of the next few days crawling coal storage, main propulsion, and auxiliary systems spaces; checking miles of steam tubing and associated fittings; inspecting the holds, ballast tanks, and conveyor systems; testing bilge and emergency pumps; and hosting a new crop of Coast Guard inspectors. To his wife's chagrin, his uniforms would likely need several more patches before the ship would be ready to sail.

The son of a retired Bradley Fleet chief engineer, Lamp had been rejected from military service in the early 1940s. Flat feet had kept him out of the war, but he was fit to serve alongside his father in the dark, suffocating engine rooms of company vessels. In 1946 he married Alice Marie Mantych, and of their two sons, one, like Lamp, was forced into orthopedic shoes while the other inherited Alice's hearing impairment. Living in Rogers City, just a few blocks from the quaint, old, white-washed St. Luke's Episcopal Church, the family prospered as Lamp advanced within the Bradley Fleet to become *Cedarville*'s chief engineer.

Having rebolted the boiler access plate into place, Lamp returned the crescent wrench to his tool belt and stood up, his head barely missing a low-hanging pipe. He ducked under the low pressure steam line and, holding the cold-water riser pipes, swung out to the open area in front of the boiler. His aching back reminded him that he was getting older as he climbed the narrow ladder to the starboard cat-walk, heading aft through the engine room to throttle control.

Adjacent to the control panel, a metal desk was mounted to the deck. Most of its original gray-green surface had been worn down to bare metal, and what remained was obscured by decades of accumulated oil and grime. Behind the desk, a threadbare swivel chair creaked as the backrest reclined precariously under Lamp's weight. A stack of paperwork was shoved aside as his utility boots came to rest in the middle of the desk.

Bead-welded into the beam at frame 171 overhead, the vessel's Coast Guard registration number—226492—was visible from his chair. Fingers laced behind his head, Lamp disregarded the familiar inscription and stared at the blackened overhead, obscured with a dusty maze of pipes and wiring, as he mentally retraced the ship's engineering systems.

Cedarville's design was typical of Great Lakes self-unloading bulk carriers. Most of her 604 feet were dedicated to cargo holds beneath which ran a conveyor tunnel. Upon discharge, the limestone cargo sifted downward to hoppers underlying the holds and emptied onto the conveyor belt, which in turn carried the cargo up and out of the tunnel. The smooth deck layout required for this mission was interrupted only by an elevated superstructure forward containing the bridge and other operational spaces and a similar island aft containing the ship's propulsion gear, galley, and engineering crew quarters.

Considering the magnitude of his fit-out responsibilities, Lamp's mind wandered from coal hopper to stoker, through the boilers and their steam tubes, and into the ship's engine. Continuing aft, his thoughts wrapped around the spinning propeller shaft to exit the hull, dodging between the whirling propeller blades, and ended up in the cold, turbulent water beyond.

The echo of footsteps on the starboard catwalk broke Lamp's reverie. He had just lowered his feet from the desk when First Assistant Engineer Walter Tulgetske emerged from behind the throttle control bulkhead. Tulgetske looked at Lamp and struggled to suppress a smile. Square in the middle of Lamp's forehead, an absurd bruise was forming.

Most ships are configured to comfortably accommodate sailors no more than five and a half feet tall. Modern vessel design typically incorporates such obstacles as low overheads; oval-shaped watertight hatches, ladders ascending through intersecting cross beams, and protruding valve handles; and three-foot-diameter rat holes known as "scuttles." While negotiating these hazards can be a challenge for diminutive seamen, it is a near impossibility for taller ones.

Over the years, Lamp's six-foot, five-inch frame had caused him no small amount of difficulty in the confined netherworld of engineering. Weighing in at only 185 pounds, he was capable of maintaining the tightly packed equipment entrusted to his care, but he would regularly visit sick bay to patch the abrasions and contusions suffered to his forehead and bony extremities.

"Give me the rundown," Lamp said, looking up at his assistant.

Tulgetske filled Lamp in on the status of engineering fit-out efforts. As they spoke, Second Assistant Harry Bey was perched precariously above the ship, removing stack covers; Reiny Radke and Mike Idalski were priming and testing bilge and ballast pumps in lower engineering; the oilers, Wingo and Friedhoff, were performing preventative maintenance on the boilers and steam engine; a faulty circuit breaker in the coal stoker occupied Billy Holley and Eugene Jones; and the conveyormen, Ron Piechan and Elmer Jarvis, were busy lubricating roller bearings in the conveyor tunnel.

Having ensured that the engineering crew was gainfully employed, Lamp and Tulgetske briefly reviewed the tasks planned for the day before Tulgetske returned to supervise the crew.

Flipping through the blank pages of the new season's bell book, Lamp was about to prop his feet up again when Captain Joppich emerged from the catwalk, brushing grime from his hands.

There was a natural division between navigational and engineering crew, and Joppich avoided the engine room as much as possible. When in operation, the engine room was as close to the traditional concept of Hell as he could imagine. Located all the way aft and two levels below the weather decks, the temperature in engineering hovered above 120 degrees Fahrenheit, and the boilers and engines emitted a sooty mist of oil that continuously coated the bulkheads, pipes, ladders, railings, chairs, and crewmen. Worse yet, as the engine room was dark, airless, and at the farthest point from the ship's fulcrum, the gut-wrenching ride in heavy weather could nauseate even well-seasoned crew. Even with the fires out, the space was an incomprehensible tangle of blackened tubing and filthy machinery. Joppich found such visits unpleasant.

"Hi, Don. Ready to check the hull?"

As he considered the captain's bulging midsection, receding salt-and-pepper hair, jowls, double chin, and thick unstylish glasses, Lamp thought for the hundredth time that Joppich looked more like an ungainly accountant than a ship captain.

"Sure, Marty, let me grab my notes."

Rising, Lamp led Joppich forward and down to the lower boiler room. Just beyond the boiler, a low access panel in the forward bulkhead opened into the tunnel.

Lamp was the first to stoop down, banging his skull again before pulling himself through and rising to his full height in the shadowy, cavernous tunnel to ascend the easy grade as it slowly veered upward toward the bow.

Joppich followed, stepping to the left of the conveyor. The tunnel was, in fact, a twelve-foot-wide hollow space straddling the centerline beneath the cargo holds. Between two narrow walkways, the elevated black rubber conveyor belt stretched forward and slightly up into the darkness for more than four hundred feet. The tunnel was dimly illuminated by incandescent bulbs mounted at odd intervals along its span. Fifty feet ahead, Joppich could just make out the underside of the V-shaped cargo hold and hopper, through which crushed limestone poured onto the conveyor for discharge.

As the men walked on, their utility boots alternately crunched and slid in the muddy accumulation of limestone silt coating the deck. The slippery sediment was nearly impossible to remove entirely, though a pair of abandoned shovels leaning against the conveyor suggested a recent attempt.

The captain asked how the hull had held up over the winter. Lamp had supervised bow repairs when Joppich had grounded the ship in the St. Marys River the previous October and had sounded the bilge and ballast tanks within an hour of boarding for fit-out. There was still minor leakage in the bow, but that was not Lamp's main concern.

Joppich asked what it was, then, already knowing the answer.

As he walked past, the chief engineer ignored Jarvis and Piechan, who were working on one of the starboard roller assemblies. Lamp resumed the debate the two senior officers held every year at fit-out. *Cedarville* was suffering serious wastage amidships, both port and starboard.

Cedarville's hull was made up of three-eighth-inch steel plate welded to a series of riblike frames, which connected to the keel, or backbone of the vessel. Over the years, her plating had proved susceptible to corrosion, which caused the pitting, thinning, and ultimate weakening of the hull.

In the spring of 1961, Coast Guard investigators had surveyed *Cedarville*'s hull. Finding substantial deterioration of the steel plating, they ordered replacement of the affected areas, starting eighty feet aft of the bow on both sides. Because the cost of the repairs was estimated to exceed $124,000, Captain Parilla convinced Coast Guard officials to defer the replacements to a time "more convenient" to the company. Having gained a deferment, Parilla promptly shelved the repair plans. No action was taken to repair the damage in 1961, nor during the following winter layup period.

Lloyd's Registry of Shipping subsequently prodded the Bradley Fleet on behalf of its insurance underwriters to resolve the issue. However, despite the insurer's demand that Bradley Fleet repair deterioration on both sides, no action was taken during any of the following years, nor when the ship had been forced into dry dock to repair grounding damage the previous October.

Reaching the end of the tunnel where the conveyor veered sharply up, the officers stepped onto the concave rubber belt and balanced with some difficulty as they continued to climb to the first proper platform one level up. Out of breath, Joppich gave him the same answer as before.

Joppich was well aware that Parilla had been sitting on this since 1961. He didn't want another *Carl D. Bradley* incident, but he could not force management to fix the problem. They knew that *Carl D. Bradley*'s hull was the same as *Cedarville*'s, but they weren't going to do anything about it. And if he squealed too much, they would just find a new captain.

The conveyor control shack—complete with a swivel chair, a cot, and a panel with surprisingly few switches, dials, and levers—stood empty as they continued along the catwalk through the mazelike structure. At this point, catwalk and conveyor were woven together as the belt crisscrossed below and above the walkway, ascending to the main deck to join the conveyor boom.

The two officers fell silent as Lamp opened the forward bilge scuttle. Peering through the darkness to examine the bow leakage, they dropped the issue, but Lamp would make sure that the emergency pumps were in good working order before the season started.

1115

Lamp was right, Joppich mused as he strolled the main weather deck, squinting against the sun. During the brief fit-out period Bradley Fleet managers expected Joppich to bring the ship's engineering and operational systems back on-line, to order supplies and replacement parts, to complete paperwork, and to otherwise get things ready for the upcoming biannual Coast Guard vessel inspection. In short, he had ten days to ensure that his ship was seaworthy and ready for the approaching shipping season, but hull repairs, neglected during winter layup, were beyond the limited capability of his small crew.

As he walked, an icy wind tore at the captain's open jacket and stung his hands and face. In the wake of a late season cold front, an arctic air mass had settled down from Canada. The freezing high pressure system brought clear blue skies but threatened to slow the start of the season by prolonging the ice cover in the Straits of Mackinac. Turning from the cold, Joppich zipped his jacket, shoved his fists in the insulated pockets, and crossed to the port side.

Passing between two of the massive cargo hatches, Joppich paused to survey the hold. *Cedarville*'s main deck was long and flat, interrupted at regular intervals by sixteen rectangular hatches that spanned the breadth of the vessel. Most of the hatches were covered by sectional pieces of steel plate that, when pushed aside, stacked neatly out of the way, leaving the hatch opening exposed.

To his right, the cover was open, and Joppich had an unobstructed view into the darkened void below. The cargo hold was not a square box but was constructed in a modified V shape, its sides dropping from the main deck only about twenty feet before angling inward to meet at the center of the ship. Where the two sides came together, a series of gates opened to the conveyor belt below. Overhead, the latticework boom cast an irregular shadow, obscuring detail within the hold.

As he leaned over the waist-high coaming for a better view, the captain's knees weakened. It was more than fifty feet to the bottom of the cavernous void, and he kept a firm grip as he studied the blackened inner wall below and to his left. Above the angle, nothing separated the cargo from the water but steel plate, yet Joppich could see no evidence of hull deterioration in the shadowed gloom of the cargo hold.

Backing away from the imposing drop, Joppich continued to port, where patches of red primer belied recent welds and repairs to the metal decking. Second Mate Rygwelski was busy supervising the deck crew in making the boom, ground tackle, and deck ready for cargo handling operations.

The new welds hinted at the old ship's state of deterioration in burnished red hues. However, Rygwelski's crew would soon apply a fresh coat of paint to erase the visible reminders, and Joppich could once again pretend that his vessel was in prime condition.

An expansive view of the bustling port greeted Joppich at the rail. Port Calcite employed more than six hundred local workers, with another three hundred local seamen manning the fleet's eight huge bulk carriers. The organized mayhem of the port coming to life was a sight to behold.

Movement on the forward ladder caught his eye. Grimacing under the weight of his duffel bag, Helmsman Stan Haske climbed slowly aboard. Though recovering from recent hernia surgery, Haske had been cleared to return to work by his doctor. Joppich was concerned. He didn't need any medical emergencies while underway. He would be keeping a close eye on the helmsman for the first few runs. One more thing to worry about, Joppich mused as he teetered over the lifeline, scanning for rust.

Pushing his glasses into place, he sighed inwardly at the sight. Streaks of red were advancing toward the waterline from bubbles in the aging gray paint as if the tired old girl was slowly bleeding to death. In fact, this was an apt analogy. As the hull plating wasted away, her structural integrity would weaken until the hull would either start to leak or catastrophically fail under the combined forces of water pressure from without and tons of limestone cargo from within. Worst of all, management was standing idly by as the ship deteriorated.

Though Joppich reported to Joe Parilla on operational matters, Clifford Buehrens, a naval architect with no formal training, supervised fleet maintenance. Like Parilla, Buehrens had received notice of *Cedarville*'s hull wastage and had made no effort to implement the recommended hull repairs. Meanwhile, copies of the Coast Guard repair order and the Lloyd's of London maintenance request lay forgotten—tucked away in his filing cabinet.

Confirming that the wastage had not improved over the winter, Joppich turned away, frustrated. Corrosion was just one of his maintenance problems. He was also worried about the metal fatigue and brittleness that had caused the loss of *Cedarville*'s sister ship, *Carl D. Bradley*, only a few years before.

Walking forward in the shadow of the gigantic boom assembly, the captain climbed a series of ladders that wound upward through the forward superstructure, eventually depositing him on the port bridge wing.

Asam was huddled over the navigation table at the far end of the bridge, a shining gold ring gleaming on his left hand.

Standing next to the communications equipment, Third Mate Gabrysiak failed to notice the captain's entrance. "WLC, WLC, this is *Cedarville*. Radio check, over," he broadcast.

Gabrysiak had spent the morning testing the ship's RCA radar, gyrocompass, and radio direction finder. Now he had energized the fifty-watt Lorain–General Electric FM radio and had placed a call to the Bradley Fleet shore-based radio station—WLC. His voice was modulated into a radio signal, routed by coaxial cable to an overhead antenna, transmitted to a tower less than five hundred feet away, and heard quite clearly in the nearby Michigan Limestone radio room.

WLC supervisor Frank Sager took the call. Just as the ships were preparing for a new shipping season, shore-based support personnel were also gearing up. Sager supervised a crew of radiomen who would begin to monitor and provide communication services to the Bradley Fleet as soon as the first ship set sail.

Over the pilothouse speaker, Sager responded, "*Cedarville,* your signal is good."

"Roger that. Stand by for RT," Gabrysiak advised, referring to the 150-watt Lorain radio telephone. Switching the radio telephone to channel 8, Gabrysiak repeated his call, with the same response. Replacing the receiver, he turned to Joppich.

"Hey, Cap, electronics are on-line. Everything checks out OK."

Gabrysiak could not hear the captain's half-hearted reply as he moved past.

"New charts?" Joppich asked Asam as he made his way through the pilothouse.

"Just came in," Asam affirmed before returning to the task of sorting and putting away the oversized sheets that represented the Straits of Mackinac, Soo approaches, St. Lawrence Seaway, and Chicago industrial complex. Prominently displayed on each chart was water depth, known obstacles, recommended shipping lanes, navigational lights and buoys, and shore-based reference points, such as lighthouses and water towers.

"Hmmph," Joppich grunted before moving on.

Asam stared at the captain as he disappeared into the open interior hatch without further comment. "What do you make of that?" he asked, turning to Gabrysiak.

Having sailed as his third mate the previous year, Gabrysiak knew that Joppich could be moody at times. The captain was generally a likeable person, though his curious ascension to command remained a mystery to the crew.

Joppich was first mate when Gabrysiak had reported aboard the previous spring. In the early hours of Good Friday, March 26, 1964, *Cedarville* was loading in Port Calcite when a late winter storm dumped eighteen inches of snow on the deck, halting cargo operations. Captain Elmer Fleming, who had served on previous occasions, reported aboard to start the season. Arriving on deck, he ordered his bags below and stepped ashore to confer with the nearby Bradley Fleet commander. Returning in short order, he stunned the crew when he told the duty watchman to retrieve his belongings and stormed off the ship. Joppich was later summoned by management and returned to announce his promotion. Second Mate Piechan, Third Mate Rygwelski, and Helmsman Gabrysiak, just out of mate's school, each advanced to the next position in the command hierarchy.

Shrugging at Asam, Gabrysiak turned to check out the engine order telegraph.

The small fleet was tasked with supplying the processed limestone needs of the sprawling U.S. Steel Great Lakes industrial empire. Encouraging accelerated limestone delivery, U.S. Steel burdened its captains with overly optimistic shipping schedules while rewarding them for additional tonnage shipped over a certain amount. Using the carrot-and-stick approach, U.S. Steel pressured Bradley Fleet skippers to overload their vessels and offered a bonus for excess limestone delivery. These vessels frequently departed Port Calcite with limestone heaped above the cargo hatch rims and the load lines submerged by several inches in violation of Great Lakes shipping regulations. Beyond the harbor, the crews would assemble on deck and scrape away enough of the mound to slide the stacking hatch covers into place.

The productivity bonus also encouraged captains to depart established shipping lanes to shorten their runs. Despite rules requiring them to slow to bare steerageway and to sound warning signals in reduced visibility, U.S. Steel expected its vessels to keep moving at full speed, regardless of rain, fog, or ice conditions. Never mind the danger of collision, of grounding on a reef, or of piling up on a sunken freighter . . . just to save a few miles.

Joppich made his way down the ladder and through a passageway to his cabin. Slightly more comfortable than the rest, the captain's stateroom was large enough to accommodate a desk and filing cabinet. Muttering as he fumbled for the right key, he turned the knob and wrestled the stubborn door open.

It was almost as if management was *trying* to sink his ship. Discouraged, Joppich slammed the heavy door.

4

Icebound

March 26, 1965
ROGERS CITY, MICHIGAN—

Streams of expletives flowed from the Bradley Fleet office as Parilla cursed the National Weather Service announcer with each new report. An arctic high-pressure system was lingering over the area, and the first week of the shipping season had been a bust. Forecasters were predicting that the Straits of Mackinac would be iced in for at least a few more days.

Parilla was under mounting pressure to get the fleet underway, but this had proven to be one of the most severe winters in recent memory. An early season deep freeze had unexpectedly trapped eighty ocean-going vessels in the St. Lawrence Seaway, and the drift ice that continued to clog the Straits of Mackinac promised to persist well into April.

Portions of the nearby St. Marys Canal, connecting Lake Superior with Lake Huron, were frozen solid, with a twenty-foot ice cap in Whitefish Bay preventing even ice-reinforced vessels from attempting the transit. The weatherman noted that earlier in the day a Canadian vessel, the *Yankcanuck,* had tried to shift position in the St. Marys River, but ice gashed the hull and the ship had to return to port.

In sum, freezing conditions promised to close the shipping lanes vital to Bradley Fleet operations. Even so, Parilla was determined that his ships would be hauling limestone soon, even if they needed ice-breaker escort all the way to Chicago.

Several days later, the weather cleared just enough to tempt the fleet to set out. But not long after, with *Cedarville* in Gary unloading its first load of limestone for the season, a westerly breeze set in, swirling between the monumental pilings of the Mackinac Bridge and driving the brash and drift ice eastward under the span. The freezing wind gently nudged the slushy waves between Bois Blanc Island and Mackinaw City to the south, and the ice started to grind against anchored floes that already clogged the narrow Straits. As the accumulation of brash ice continued, the gap narrowed, and a river of undulating ice spanned the Straits in the predawn darkness. Over a period of several chilling hours, the ice cover had gradually thickened, and the thirty-mile-long Straits of Mackinac was impassable once again.

Having discharged her cargo, *Cedarville* departed early that bright afternoon for the ice-encrusted passage to Lake Huron and Port Calcite beyond. As night wore on, ice patches appeared more frequently, until the dawn broke the next day to find *Cedarville* picking her way through shifting floes as she was piloted north and east toward the Straits of Mackinac. Just before sunset, *Cedarville* had passed Waugoshance Point on the western tip of the Upper Peninsula to starboard and, with a westerly tailwind, was following the current of brash ice to the Mackinac Bridge and the narrowing passage.

Two miles from the bridge, First Mate Harry Piechan piloted the vessel through the shifting floe. Having served for twelve years in the same position, the portly mate had never obtained a masters ticket and could advance no further.

Piechan was on the phone to the forward lookout when the captain strolled into the pilothouse and casually announced that he had the conn. The tops of the bridge's two suspension towers glowed pink with the setting sun before the light faded and twilight settled on the Straits. In the dwindling light, Joppich could see Ed Jungman shivering on the forecastle, his breath floating aft in steamy puffs, as he searched the channel ahead for the thinnest ice concentrations. Seeing an opening just off the port bow, Joppich steered the ship directly under the bridge. *Cedarville* had stumbled upon a channel cleared earlier in the day by the Coast Guard.

"Come left a few degrees, Stan," Joppich ordered. "Steady up in the channel."

Haske gently turned the wheel to port, and the ship slowly responded, swinging into position. *Cedarville* glided toward the center span of the bridge, her bow sweeping the slushy water aside as chunks of ice bounced along the hull. Ten feet to either side, the jagged boundary of solid ice seemed to be closing in on *Cedarville*. Indeed, as the steamer passed beneath the suspended highway, the channel that had promised passage through the Straits abruptly disappeared. The wind that had nudged her along now piled drift ice in on her stern, making retreat impossible. *Cedarville* was stuck.

Joppich knew that tracks cut by icebreakers in the spring were inherently unreliable. Below, the ice field had begun to deteriorate and shift, as thick shore ice drifted into the channel. But in the dark he could not see that the ice before him was more than twenty inches thick and that sections of drift ice recently broken from the nearby shores exceeded that by several feet. Thinking he could push through to a clear channel, Joppich ordered Haske to increase speed.

Still recovering from surgery, Haske was anxious to get home to his wife and their five boys. He swung the brass handle on the engine order telegraph, relaying the command to the engine room.

Five hundred feet astern, the engineering watch officer advanced the throttle. The reciprocating steam engine strained as the six-foot propeller thrashed at one and a half turns per second. Gradually, the thin ice gave way, groaning while being shoved to either side of *Cedarville*'s hull.

The freighter gained speed until, with a tremendous shudder, the ship slammed into a mass of ice, fifteen feet thick. The forward momentum of the eighty-five-hundred-ton vessel was persuasive, and the floe buckled under the force. However, with empty holds, *Cedarville* continued forward until her light bow rode up and over the ice.

Below, a metallic jolt vibrated up the shaft and into the lower engine room. Ice chunks were striking the bronze blades of the spinning propeller. If the ship encountered a large enough chunk, it could detach a blade or twist the propeller shaft. Furthermore, *Cedarville* was not an ice-reinforced vessel, and her deteriorating hull was no match for the frozen Straits. Joppich did not want to push his luck. "Time to call in the cavalry," he said as he tuned the radio to channel 16.

"United States Coast Guard, United States Coast Guard, this is the steamship *Cedarville* transiting eastbound through the Straits of Mackinac, one mile east of the bridge, requesting icebreaker assistance, over."

The petty officer of the watch at Coast Guard headquarters responded. "This is Coast Guard Group Sault Ste. Marie. State your condition, over."

"Roger, Coast Guard. We were following a channel beneath the bridge when the ice just closed in around us. I have tried to break through, but it's too thick. Do you have an icebreaker in the area? Over."

"Negative, *Cedarville*. *Mackinaw* is in Cheboygan and won't get underway until about 0800 tomorrow. I suggest that you drop the anchor and hunker down for the night. Over." Annoyed, Joppich struck the console. He didn't have time for this. Cargo was waiting and he had to keep moving. Still, seeing no option, he composed himself and keyed the microphone. "Roger that, Coast Guard. We'll be standing by. *Cedarville* out." The bridge crew shared a collective thought: "So much for getting home tonight."

A vessel that becomes beset in drift ice will be pulled along by the flow and is vulnerable to grounding on one of the many shoals, reefs, and shallow areas in the Straits. *Cedarville* was only two miles west of Majors Shoal, and the easterly drift of the ice threatened to carry the vessel over the rocks before daybreak. Turning to Piechan, Joppich said, "Harry, go make ready the anchor."

The captain scarcely heard the response before he reached for the radio once again, this time to call home.

WLC Control
PORT CALCITE, MICHIGAN—

Joe Hassett was alone in the WLC control room when the call came in. On the 1600 to midnight watch, he had expected a quiet night and was busy studying the script for a local production of Victor Herbert's musical *Red Mill.* He would be playing the role of Captain Doris Van Damm in a little over a month and was eager to learn his lines. The crackle of an incoming call broke his concentration.

"Hello WLC, Rogers City, this is *Cedarville,* calling on channel 82, over." Hassett reached over to the control board, removed plug 82 from the loudspeaker, and connected the circuit to his headphones. Flipping the transmitter to the matching frequency, he answered, "*Cedarville* from Rogers City, go ahead."

"The vessel is stuck in an ice floe just east of the Mackinac Bridge. I have contacted the Coast Guard for an icebreaker, but they will be unable to get underway until 0800 tomorrow. Looks like we will be spending the night here. Over."

"Roger, *Cedarville,* will advise the office. WLC out." Without taking his eyes from the script, Hassett dialed the number to the Bradley Fleet operations desk nearby, disturbing another watchstander's peaceful evening.

ROGERS CITY, MICHIGAN—

Later that night, Pat was beginning to worry. It was approaching midnight, and Lenny should have been home by now. *Cedarville* was scheduled for a quick turnaround this afternoon, and they had planned to have a family dinner. The meal sat cold and uneaten on the stove as Pat quietly paced the small apartment, peeking periodically into Lenny Jr.'s darkened room. She didn't have far to walk before she found herself back at the front door. It was a small apartment.

With two tiny bedrooms, a kitchen, and a living room, the cozy dwelling was just enough for the young family. Located near Vogelhein Lumber, on the shore of Lake Huron, the air was often pierced by the scream of circular saws during the day. Tonight, however, the lumberyard was quiet and Pat was left alone with her thoughts.

"Where could they be?" she wondered. *Cedarville* was a big ship, but it could sink. That point had been driven home to the small community all too well when the fleet's flagship, the *Carl D. Bradley,* broke apart and sank several years earlier.

There was no support network for Bradley Fleet wives, and Pat was usually in the dark about the ship's movements. She would recognize a few of the other wives while shopping about town, and they would chat for a few minutes, complaining about their husbands' extended absences, but no one thought to organize their group beyond that. The company was even worse. She would hear nothing from the Bradley Fleet unless she placed the call. And then only grudgingly. But there was a way.

In the event of an emergency, Pat knew that she could reach Len by radio telephone through the fleet's communications office, WLC. In fact, that was how Gabrysiak found out he had a son. Pat's sister left the hospital after the delivery to place a call from the Port Calcite office. Len was ecstatic. He had a boy! But he had to wait a few days for the ship to complete her upbound journey before he could hold his namesake.

Pat smiled, remembering the goofy look on his face when the nurse placed the baby in his arms. Shifting aside the curtain now, she stared out the front window. In the morning she would have a beautiful view of the lake from across the park, but tonight it was just dark. No ships gliding past, bound for the company port to the south. Len kept a car at the shipyard, and he should have been home by now. She hated to be a bother, but she needed to know.

Closing the drapes, she turned to the phone, lifted the receiver, and scanned the list of numbers taped to the table. Quickly dialing the number, she was relieved when it was answered after only one ring. "WLC," the voice said on the other end.

"Hello, yes. This is Pat Gabrysiak. I'm sorry to be calling so late, but my husband is on the *Cedarville,* and I was expecting him in this afternoon. Could you tell me when the ship will be in?"

"Yes ma'am," Hassett answered through the line. "They got stuck in the ice, but the *Cedarville* is alright. They should be in tomorrow around noon."

"Thank you," Pat said, returning the receiver to the hook. Too tired to clean the kitchen, she went straight to bed.

USCGC *Mackinaw*—

By 0845 the next morning, the great red hull of the icebreaker was inching southwest toward the stranded freighter, plowing a path as wide as her seventy-four-foot beam. *Mackinaw* had been clearing the

Straits and rescuing vessels in distress since December 1944. Built to ensure the continued flow of iron ore to America's steel mills for war production, *Mackinaw* was especially designed for the hazards of ice clearing in the strategic passage linking the northern lakes. Indeed, in late autumn and early spring, the combined seagoing freight of Wisconsin, Illinois, Indiana, and western Michigan counted on her assistance.

Beneath the waterline beat two massive fourteen-foot steel propellers, with a forward propeller also available for use in more challenging ice-clearing operations. Encased in a protective steel housing, the twelve-foot bow screw was designed to draw water from under the ice, causing it to sag and weaken. This had the further effect of forcing water aft along the sides of the hull, reducing friction between the ship and the ice. When underway in normal conditions, the forward propeller was left to freewheel, but it would likely be employed on this day's patrol.

Generally speaking, the work of an icebreaker is better termed "ice displacement." As an icebreaker searches for the easiest path through the jigsaw puzzle pattern of an ice floe, ice forward of the vessel is pushed aside by its reinforced bow. Where the ice is too thick to permit such displacement, it must be shoved over and under adjacent layers. Only those pieces of ice too big to be shoved aside are broken, and *Mackinaw* had encountered just such a section of ice.

Upon departure from Cheboygan, *Mackinaw* found ice in the wide channel as thick as twenty inches in places. Picking her way through the scattered field, the vessel's imposing bow brushed aside the thinner brash ice as the ship pushed on toward the bridge, now visible on the horizon.

In the light to moderate brash ice near Cheboygan, the ride aboard *Mackinaw* had been pleasant as the heavy bow imperceptibly rode up and through the slushy floes. But deeper in the Straits the ship slowed to a bumpy crawl as the thicker ice closed in.

Joining the officer of the deck on the bridge, Captain Chiswell and his executive officer, Commander Rojeski, reached for the long brass handrail mounted overhead as the vessel jerked abruptly to port. "Captain on the bridge," the boatswain's mate of the watch called out.

"As you were," Chiswell ordered as the bridge crew instinctively tensed in his presence. "Status, Mr. Stewart?"

The young lieutenant reported that he expected to be able to break through about fifty yards ahead. The ship just needed to work through a clump of shore ice that had drifted into the channel.

Chiswell approved and gave him the go-ahead. On the bridge, the watch crew braced for impact.

As the boatswain's mate advanced the large brass throttles on the helm control to the roar of the diesel engines and spinning screws, the ship charged ahead, building momentum until it mounted the offending ice cap. With two inches of steel plate grinding against the hard ice, the ship began to slow, and the large red bow pointed sharply upward as the icebreaker came to rest on the thick floe. On the bridge, the engines were ordered reversed, backing the ship off for another charge. After several runs, the combined forces of impact and cleavage cut the ice, allowing the ship to pass into the widening channel.

In this manner *Mackinaw* worked her way along the lower coast of Bois Blanc, Round, and Mackinac Islands until the icebound *Cedarville* was finally in view, at anchor but dragging eastward nonetheless.

SS *Cedarville*—

"*Cedarville,* this is United States Coast Guard cutter *Mackinaw,* approaching your position one-half mile west of Majors Shoal. Do you read, over?"

Bill Asam was standing the lonely anchor watch when the radio crackled to life. He lifted the transceiver and replied, "*Mackinaw,* this is *Cedarville*. Please stand by."

Coming up the ladder, Joppich heard the call and emerged into the pilothouse to see a bright red ship parting the icy waters, less than a mile distant. No other ships were visible in the ice field, but the distinctive color and telephone-pole mast of the *Mackinaw* were well known to all who regularly sailed these waters.

Taking the handset from Asam, Joppich addressed the cutter. "*Mackinaw,* this is *Cedarville*. Glad you could make it. We were getting a little worried. We are at anchor, but the ice has been trying to pull us into the shallows all night."

"Understood, Captain. If you weigh anchor, we'll get you out of here in no time."

Joppich never ceased to be amused by the Coast Guard's presumptuous habit of addressing anyone making a marine radio call as "captain." Brushing the thought aside, he keyed the mike. "Sound's good. What's the plan?"

By this time, *Mackinaw* had slowed to within a half mile of *Cedarville*'s position and would wait until the older vessel was ready to be escorted from the ice. "I will sweep through the thin patch just to your south. After I pass, you should be able to push through into my wake, and we will lead you out."

Joppich had kept his boilers at pressure through the night in case *Cedarville* was threatened by the approaching shoals, and the ship was now ready for full power. "We will be underway in ten minutes," Joppich said, adding to Asam, "Get Len up here to raise that anchor. I want to get out of here."

An hour later *Cedarville* was trailing *Mackinaw* in the path it had beaten while sailing west from Cheboygan. Farther to the east, the bottleneck loosened and the ice cover was much less severe. At the eastern end of the Straits the ice cap eventually degraded into melting brash, which glided harmlessly along *Cedarville*'s aging hull as alone she turned southward toward Rogers City.

PORT CALCITE, MICHIGAN—
1623

Cedarville's bow rounded the familiar entrance to Port Calcite as the tug *Dolomite* nestled up alongside to nudge her into position along the pier. The declining sun backlit the hoppers on either side of the pier and cast a glare upon the dusty pilothouse windows. With three cargo shuttles on one side of the narrow slip and one on the other, the freighter could be loaded and ready to steam back to Chicago before midnight.

Most of the crew would enjoy an evening at home with the family while the duty section remained behind to supervise cargo placement. Any other night, all hands would have been expected back aboard to get underway as soon as possible, but weather conditions this night would bring a reprieve. Continued freezing conditions threatened to keep the narrow passage into Lake Michigan choked with drift ice, and *Cedarville* could not risk another transit so soon without Coast

Guard support. Instead, with Parilla's grudging approval, the captain would time *Cedarville*'s departure so as to find an icebreaker standing by for escort duty when she entered the slushy channel. Free until 0500, the crew would surprise their families and sleep in their own beds for a change.

5

Topdalsfjord

April 11, 1965
KEFLAVIK, ICELAND—

A high-pitched whine penetrated the ambient clutter of the turbulent sea, drawing the attention of the U.S. Navy watchstanders monitoring the region. Tucked away within the modest confines of the U.S. naval base at Keflavik, Iceland, the top-secret task force detected and tracked every vessel, surface or subsurface, that slipped into the stormy waters of the North Atlantic. The listening post at NAVFAC Keflavik was part of a network of monitoring stations that formed the U.S. Navy's Sound Surveillance System, or SOSUS. Originally code-named "Caesar," the SOSUS network was established in the 1950s to monitor strategic narrows for Soviet submarine movements and was soon tracking the quiet Soviet nuclear ballistic missile submarines that threatened NATO shipping and menaced the eastern seaboard of the United States. SOSUS could easily detect almost every propeller-driven hull afloat in the northern seas.

SOSUS consisted of a series of bottom-mounted hydrophone arrays connected by undersea cables to facilities like the Keflavik SOSUS node. The arrays were installed on continental slopes and seamounts to take advantage of natural shipping choke points and oceanic sound channeling. The combination of location and the sensitivity of the large-aperture arrays created a monitoring system cap-

40

able of detecting radiated acoustic power of less than a watt, several hundred miles distant.

The hydrophone that had detected the new contact was located at the eastern end of an array positioned in the strategic gap between Iceland and the United Kingdom. Located 213 miles to the east-north-east, the contact's propeller was whining at 105 rotations per minute, clearly announcing the vessel's presence to anyone caring to place a microphone in the water. As the ship's screw bit into the water, low-pressure areas formed at the trailing edge of each of the four large bronze blades. As the pressure decreased, water along those edges vaporized, creating microscopic bubbles. When the blade passed, the parcel of water returned to its former pressure, and the bubbles instantaneously collapsed. Individually, the collapsing bubbles created a minute high-pitched pop. Collectively, this phenomena, known as cavitation, generated a continuous swish. Ice damage on one of the blades exaggerated the effect, causing a repetitive chirp in the vessel's sound signature that—along with the cavitation, transient engine noises, and the sound of a creaking hull—could be detected more than 200 miles away.

Water conducts sound four times faster than air, and the cavitation noises generated by the contact raced west-southwest at 3,240 miles per hour toward the waiting SOSUS hydrophone array. At two hundred feet, the thirty-five-degree thermocline acted as a lens to refract the sound waves downward to slam into the shallow floor of the North Sea. Reflecting upward again, the signal ricocheted back and forth in a bottom bounce pattern until its faintest remnant was detected by the SOSUS array.

The contact was soon detected by another hydrophone cluster, and the divergent bearings were transmitted to NAVFAC Keflavik, where a sonarman employed simple trigonometry to calculate the contact's position. As the vessel advanced along its intended track, another fix allowed the petty officer to also determine course and speed. Grease pencil marks on a glowing status board positioned the vessel at latitude 60' 47.3" north, longitude 003' 38.0" west, passing between the Shetland and Faeroe Islands at eleven and a half knots, heading southwest.

Still far off, the contact whined faintly through the ambient din of wave action and the popping of marine life that scoured the rocks of the ocean floor for algae and barnacles, her periodic chirp clearly heard. Undoubtedly, the seaman on watch was under orders to report the unidentified contact to the nearby P-3 reconnaissance squadron for identification. Placing a call on the secured landline, he vectored one of the airborne units to the scene.

M/V *Topdalsfjord*
50 NM NW SHETLAND ISLANDS—

To its master and crew, the contact was known as the Norwegian motor vessel *Topdalsfjord*. Sailing from Denmark to the North American Great Lakes via the St. Lawrence Seaway, *Topdalsfjord*'s ice-reinforced bow pushed southwest at nearly full speed, straining to clear the gates of the tempestuous North Sea before the arrival of a threatening frontal system. That is not to say that the going was smooth in advance of the bad weather. The North Sea was a notoriously rough body of water, and ten-foot northwesterly swells tossed the small freighter broadside like a bath toy.

Second Officer Jan Gronstol lit an American cigarette, his eyes closed to preserve his night vision. Bathed in the dim red light of the bridge electronics, Gronstol stepped from the relative warmth of the pilothouse into the cold night air. Outside, the icy wind whistled past his ears, and the sound blended with the hiss of *Topdalsfjord*'s hull as it sliced through the increasingly undulating ocean.

Off-balance, Gronstol clung to the frozen railing as his vessel lurched to port. Located a little less than halfway along her 423-foot deck, the superstructure upon which the pilothouse stood extended well above the waterline. Minor vessel movements were exaggerated in the lofty pilothouse, frequently causing the bridge watch to scramble for a handhold or better footing.

The watch officer counted as *Topdalsfjord* righted herself. Three seconds. Not too bad, but he would have to keep an eye on her ride if conditions deteriorated. He might have to wake the captain and recommend additional ballasting if the list worsened. *Topdalsfjord* carried an assortment of European goods destined for consumption in the United States and Canada, and she would load up with grain from Port Arthur and Chicago before returning to her home port at Oslo, Norway. Though she was already low, Gronstol could increase draft and stability by filling the ballast tanks.

Built in Göteborg, Sweden, the six-year-old *Topdalsfjord* was owned and operated by Den Norske Amerikalinje, a Norwegian corporation headquartered in Lysaker. With five cargo holds and a deck bristling with cargo cranes, she was powered by a single diesel engine capable of generating up to sixty-five-hundred horses to power the six-thousand-ton vessel and her cargo through the turbulent North Atlantic.

Overhead, the Big Dipper pointed north through scattered clouds to Polaris. Well above the horizon, the North Star was suspended just to the left of *Topdalsfjord*'s wake as the vessel worked its way through the blackened swells. As the ship sailed far to the west of the Shetland Islands, the only lights visible to Gronstol were the stars, the phosphorescent algae churned up by his ship's propeller, the white masthead light above, and the glowing embers of his Marlboro.

To the northwest, an ominous wall of black clouds obscured the stars and raced to catch the westbound *Topdalsfjord*. Tiny sparks of lightning danced at its base, and a flickering glow occasionally illuminated the clouds from within.

"Heavy weather before sunrise," Gronstol thought. "It's good to be heading into open ocean."

Turning, he stumbled into the pilothouse as his ship took another violent list to port. Feeling his way through the darkened bridge, he found the receiver that connected with the engine room. Lifting the handset to his ear, he hesitated, scanning the glowing course and speed displays overhead before quickly dialing the familiar number. After several rings, a tinny voice shouted to be heard over the din of the diesel engine.

"Engine room."

"Yeah, Olaf, how are we doing down there?"

"All systems are fine, but the ride is starting to get rough. How's the weather shaping up?"

"That's why I called. We are rounding the Shetland Islands, and a storm is bearing down on us from the northwest. Do you think we could squeeze a few more knots out of the engine? I want to stay ahead of this storm as long as possible."

"We are turning at 105 rpm's. Give me the order and I'll bump up to 118. That should give us an extra two and a half knots."

"Consider it done. Thanks. Bridge out."

Addressing the helmsman, Gronstol continued. "Kjell, all ahead full." Having served aboard the Royal Norwegian Navy destroyer *Oslo* in the endless maneuvering of NATO and Warsaw Pact forces in the North Sea, Gronstol had left military service for only a few months before reporting aboard *Topdalsfjord*. As a watch officer aboard *Oslo,* he had two engines at his command, and old habits could be hard to break.

Despite the fact that *Topdalsfjord* was a single-engine vessel, Helmsman Kjell Oskarsen knew what the second mate meant and responded correctly, "Ahead full, aye." A few seconds later he added, "Engine room answers ahead full."

"Very well," Gronstol mumbled as he watched the red needle on the speed indicator creep slowly toward fifteen and a half knots.

The contact's speed increase would not go unnoticed.

Silently skimming through the thermocline at two hundred feet, midway between the smooth ocean floor and the choppy, black surface, American fast attack submarines patrolled the Greenland–Iceland–U.K. gap. These platforms were tracking the noisy freighter as a diversion while in search of their primary target: Russian boomers.

By 1965 the U.S. Navy was deploying a new line of ultra-quiet, deep-diving nuclear fast attack submarines to the region. Built of an experimental steel alloy, they could dive to an official depth of four hundred feet and a classified depth of up to thirteen hundred feet. The fast attack boats could make a nearly silent passage at fifteen knots or could double that to race submerged at thirty knots. Designed for prolonged deployments, the fleet's endurance was limited only by the amount of food that could be carried for each boat's 143-man crew.

On the other hand, the prey, Soviet ballistic missile submarines, routinely tried to creep undetected into the open waters of the North Atlantic. While fast attack submarines were designed as hunters to prowl the deep for enemy subs, the missile boats, or boomers, were often dispatched with a simple command: "Find a big piece of ocean and disappear." The strategic value of a boomer lay not in an overt display of force but in the mere suggestion that a nuclear-armed vessel could surface off of a nation's coast and obliterate her capital in less than five minutes.

Unaware of the deadly dance playing out beneath her keel, *Top-*

dalsfjord pressed on into the North Atlantic to turn west for the Americas.

M/V *Topdalsfjord*
45 NM WSW SHETLAND ISLANDS—

Captain Rasmus Hoagland yawned as he peered through the gray squall that had suddenly enveloped his ship. Wipers rhythmically slapped the streams of water from the pilothouse windows as *Topdalsfjord* dipped into a trough, her bow plunging into a wall of green water. He never slept well at sea and was awakened early by the heavy weather.

As quickly as it had appeared, the isolated squall drifted on, leaving *Topdalsfjord* to pitch through the white-capped swells beneath the overcast dawn. The increase in visibility revealed a white, four-engine turboprop aircraft gliding just beneath the cloud cover two miles to the south. No sooner had Hoagland seen the plane when it turned in his direction in a gentle descent.

The U.S. Navy Lockheed P-3 Orion was not the first to conduct a visual reconnaissance of the freighter. *Topdalsfjord* had been under nearly constant surveillance since leaving Danish waters. Before dawn the previous day, a Soviet TU-95 Bear F of the 392nd Maritime Long Range Reconnaissance Regiment had revved its four powerful Kuznetsov NK-12M engines and accelerated down the runway at Kipelovo northeast of Moscow in the Vologda Oblast. Transiting north along the Finnish border, the long-range maritime reconnaissance bomber crossed into international waters, rounded Scandinavia, and began its westward surveillance sweep of the North Sea. With a thirteen-thousand-kilometer range and a belly-mounted radar, the maritime bomber comfortably patrolled the shipping lanes to the southwest for NATO men-of-war, observing and reporting on all vessels in the vicinity, including the insignificant little Norwegian vessel just getting underway.

Topdalsfjord's course would take her through the most active of the cold war battlefields. As she entered the deep blue waters of the North Atlantic, avoiding both the warmer countercurrent of the Gulf Stream to the south and the calving icebergs of the Labrador coast to the north, the ship would likely remain under the watchful eyes of the combined air, surface, and subsurface assets of NATO and Warsaw Pact forces playing cat and mouse in that sea.

Captain Hoagland stepped onto the bridge wing to watch as the white P-3 with U.S. Navy tail and wing markings flew low overhead, circled once, and moved on to the next contact.

KEFLAVIK, ICELAND—
0735

A few minutes later, a red light flashed silently on the sonarman's telephone for several seconds before he noticed. Pulling his earphones off with one hand, he lifted the receiver with the other. "Watch desk."

A voice from the P-3 squadron at the other end of the secure line reported that the surface contact he had called in earlier that morning had been identified as the Norwegian freighter *Topdalsfjord*. "Thank you, sir," he replied before hanging up.

Stifling a yawn, the petty officer checked his watch. His relief was due in just a few minutes, and all he really wanted was a few hours of sleep.

6

Arrivals

April 26, 1965
ROGERS CITY, MICHIGAN—

Cedarville's five-hour turnaround had just begun, and Gabrysiak planned to meet Pat at Karsten's Dairy for a late breakfast. As he crossed the brow with Asam and Fuhrman, the latter returned a wave from his wife, who stood on the pier talking to Patricia Asam and two of their five children.

Turning, Patricia saw Asam step from the gangplank and embraced him at a full trot. Fuhrman crossed the pier and pecked his wife on the cheek. Smiling as he walked past the reuniting couples, Gabrysiak climbed into his dusty LTD, fished the keys from under the seat, and roared off.

Driving north on Third Street a few minutes later, Gabrysiak scanned the busy storefronts, enjoying the occasional glimpse of the white-capped lake between the buildings to the east. Overhead, scattered clouds skidded along the shoreline as he continued on to the rendezvous. Along the way, young mothers peered into boutique windows and old men milled around the barbershop debating politics. An absurdly cluttered movie marquis heralded the debut of the improbably named comedy *It's a Mad, Mad, Mad, Mad World*, and the street was lined with cars in front of the combined city hall and courthouse.

Gabrysiak loved this town. Its broad streets, wide greens, and picket fence–lined walks gave the illusion of a village that had never been touched by misfortune. Church steeples soared above the quaint old homes, and gazebos dotted the lush parks that blanketed the easy slope down to Lake Huron. Old men met for coffee each morning in small cafés, and children played carelessly as they skipped up the hill to the elementary school.

Signs of the community's maritime heritage were inescapable. Anchors, propellers, and lighthouses sprang from the flower beds and gardens of its unpretentious homes. Red and green buoys marked entrances to restaurants and shops, and from nearly anywhere in the city one had a clear view of the lake and its nearby shipping lanes.

Most Rogers City residents had some connection to the U.S. Steel facility. After all, this was a company town. Raised in the shadow of the port's towering hoppers, the children went to school at St. Ignatius and Rogers City Elementary. Teens gathered after school for games in the open-air field on the south side of town. On Friday nights, many could be found huddled in the back of the darkened theater while their parents danced at the Deer Hunt Club or played bingo in the cafeteria at St. Ignatius.

On Sundays, church bells chimed the faithful to worship as parishioners flocked beneath the discerning gaze of the holy family and through the doors of the ornately designed St. Ignatius Catholic Church. A few blocks away, the distinctive cobblestone walls of Westminster Presbyterian filled in quickly, as did the Melvillesque St. Luke's Episcopal on First and Erie. A divine reverence was common among Bradley Fleet sailors, captured well in an oft-quoted psalm: "They that go down to the sea in ships and do business in great waters, these see the works of the Lord and his wonders in the deep."

In sum, with a thriving commercial district, well-kept lawns, beautiful churches, and sparkling new schools, Rogers City was a comfortable and prosperous community. Carved from the woodlands of northern Michigan in the 1870s, the nearby quarry served as a depot for wood-burning tugs transiting the coast with lumber-laden schooners in tow. By 1910, however, the forest was exhausted and the village became a ghost town.

Len's father had come to town as a lumberjack and stayed long after the industry died. He was there when the discovery of commercial-grade limestone revived the community, and he opened Greka's

Tavern on First Street to cater to the new workers. Michigan Limestone Corporation had chosen the site on the sapphire blue waters of Lake Huron to build a crushing plant and loading facility. With industry came rail access, highways, and electricity, and consequently the village grew.

Born in 1930, Len witnessed the expansion firsthand. When he lost his mother as a toddler, his aunts tried to separate the seven children. His father would not allow it, so the children were raised across the street from the establishment, which quickly became known as Rogers City's premier seaman's bar. Over the years the children got to know many of the seamen who were drawn by the high wages promised by the Bradley Fleet. Eventually, each son in turn went offshore.

Under the beneficial influence of United States Steel, the "Nautical City" flourished. Then disaster struck.

On November 18, 1958, *Cedarville*'s sister ship, *Carl D. Bradley*, set out for the return trip to Port Calcite, having delivered her cargo of limestone to the Gary industrial complex. Without benefit of cargo, she was heavily ballasted to reduce freeboard and to maintain steerage control.

Almost immediately after departure, *Bradley* was buffeted by northerly gale-force winds, and heavy seas periodically washed over her bow. While the vessel had weathered many such storms in the past, the swells generated by this tempest would conspire to snap her brittle back. Supported by the displacement of more than three hundred thousand cubic feet of the water upon which she floated, *Bradley* was subjected to a series of undulating stresses that caused the vessel to alternately sag and bend over the waves passing beneath the keel.

Battling a sixty-five-knot head wind, *Bradley* plowed up and over mountains of water piled high by the gale, rivets popping and her tired hull creaking and groaning against the strain. That evening, twelve miles southwest of Gull Island, she mounted a thirty-foot swell. The downward forces of her unsupported bow and stern popped the overstressed hull plating, buckled the frame, and sheared the vessel in two. The two halves settled in 360 feet of water, with only two of the thirty-five-man crew surviving.

Despite the official findings of the Coast Guard investigation,

Bradley Fleet officials refused to publicly acknowledge that *Carl D. Bradley*'s aging hull and keel had failed, asserting that she was simply overwhelmed by the storm. In a single incident, relegated to a mere footnote in most histories of the region, fifty-four children were orphaned. But despite the tragedy, the community pressed on, with brothers, cousins, and uncles of *Bradley* widows and orphans continuing to sail, undaunted, aboard the self-unloaders of the U.S. Steel fleet.

Gabrysiak too had sailed aboard *Carl D. Bradley* and lost many good friends that night. But Len had an independent basis for dark memories of the old ship. As a young deckhand in the early 1950s Gabrysiak often found himself aboard the vessel, working below. On one stormy afternoon he was walking with the conveyorman when a bone-chilling "PING" from the adjacent bulkhead stopped him in mid-stride. "PING . . . P-PING." "What was that?" Len stuttered.

The conveyorman laughed. "Oh, she's just popping some hull rivets. It happens all the time. I wouldn't worry about it."

He could still hear that sound, he mused, as he parked and climbed the short steps to the café entrance. Just inside, Pat was already sipping coffee as Gabrysiak straddled the bar stool next to his wife.

PORT CALCITE, MICHIGAN—

High-quality calcium carbonate limestone drawn from mountainous piles standing about the harbor poured from tandem chutes to fill *Cedarville*'s cavernous belly. *Cedarville* had entered the slip bow first to expose the forward holds to the cargo ramps. Once loaded, tug assistance would be required to swing *Cedarville* around and back her in to load the after holds.

Standing just aft of the number nine hatch, Harry Piechan and his brother Ronald supervised loading operations. A diminutive version of his portly brother, Ron was one of *Cedarville*'s conveyormen, responsible for cargo handling. With his balding head exposed to the sun, he peered through the thick glasses balanced upon his wide nose as he monitored the even loading of *Cedarville*'s cargo bays.

The two watched as rivers of limestone cascaded into the first three holds, emitting billowing clouds of white dust that settled on the deck, in the water, and on the surrounding buildings and vehicles. As the cargo neared the top of the hatches, the flow abruptly stopped. Choking on the chalky dust, Harry stepped forward to peer into the forward hold. He could touch the limestone, but there was room for more. Twirling his fingers in the air, he directed the conveyor operator on the shore rig to resume the flow, and the Piechan brothers stood by as the mound of limestone forming above each hatch started to pour onto the deck. Once underway all hands would turn out to scrape the hatches and deck clear; the volume of cargo loaded was the key to the officers' bonuses.

Loading continued in this manner until the conveyor rig could advance no farther; supervising the watch crew, the first mate then backed *Cedarville* out of the slip to be maneuvered into the secondary load position by the tugs *Dolomite* and *Limestone*.

ROGERS CITY, MICHIGAN—
1245

"Go ahead and give me two cartons," Haske replied to the IGA cashier as she tallied his cigarette purchase. "Oh, can you wait a minute?" he asked, suddenly remembering something.

"Sure," she said, as no one else was in line. "But make it quick."

Darting from the checkout stand, Haske skidded past the aisle before side-stepping back in front of the display. Mother's Day was coming up, and he needed to get a card for Betty. Frowning, he saw that there was not much to choose from. Disappointed, he pulled a small white card from the stack. After all, it's the thought that counts.

The cashier was drumming her fingers on the register when Haske returned, holding the card in his teeth and fumbling with his wallet.

PORT CALCITE, MICHIGAN—

Reporting for duty, Raphael Przybyla arrived at the pier after lunch to find his new assignment in mid-turn. Setting his bags down, he perched upon a bollard to admire the slow dance of the freighter and the tugs. With only a few months' experience on the lakes, he still found the port to be a strange and wonderful place. Casting a cool shadow onto the pier, the loading rig loomed overhead, adjacent to an industrial crane, gray and rusty, jutting into the skyline with its hoist cables separated by an I-beam and dangling in the wind. Dusty mounds of gravel and rock surrounded the port. The combined roar of mining trucks, shoreside generators, and ship engines was deafening, and the smell of burning coal and diesel fuel permeated his senses with every breath.

Przybyla was starting out aboard *Cedarville* as an assistant repairman. He had not been with the Bradley Fleet long. Married to the sister of one of the *Bradley* victims, Przybyla had worked as a mechanic for eighteen years at his father's auto agency. Seeking independence, he had taken a position as an assistant repairman aboard *Rogers City* the previous summer, then transferred to *Cedarville* with ambitions of becoming a licensed engineer.

As *Cedarville* backed into the berth, Przybyla could clearly see that her stern was raised out of the water with much of the rudder exposed and that she had an obvious forward list with her bow noticeably submerged. With the aluminum ladder back in place, he gathered his belongings and climbed aboard as the rocky cargo thundered into the empty holds aft.

Emerging topside, he considered his new assignment. Old, dirty limestone debris caked two to three inches deep where the coaming met the deck. And was that rust dripping down the side of the ship? All the way aft, two characters were fascinated with the incoming cargo. The grossly obese one seemed to be directing the operation, while the funny little man with an oval head, big ears, Coke-bottle glasses, and a rim of dark hair around his sunburned scalp seemed content to watch in silence. Przybyla choked on the white dust as he approached the men. While the big one turned and smiled broadly, the smaller one considered Przybyla out of the corner of his eye with less enthusiasm. Offering his hand to the first mate, the new crewman asked about the chief engineer.

Just around the first hold, outboard of the loading chute, and all the way aft, he was told. He could take the ladder down to engineering, where he would likely find Lamp.

"Thanks," Przybyla replied, continuing on through the billowing dust cloud. Dropping his bag just inside the ladder well, he descended into the moist heat of the dark engine room. At the bottom, he flagged down a crewman and repeated his query, shouting above the din. Without a word, the grimy man pointed down the catwalk and disappeared around the corner.

Winding through the blackened netherworld of *Cedarville*'s engineering spaces, he rounded the control panel to find an engineer recording pressure gauge readings. Przybyla extended a hand to introduce himself. Asking for the chief engineer, he found the second assistant instead.

Harry Bey explained that Lamp was off-duty and that he was keeping the boilers stoked so they could get underway in a few hours. Although Bey held a chief engineer's certificate, he was only the third senior engineering officer aboard *Cedarville*. Having served aboard LSTs during World War II, the Rogers City native stood ready to run his own engine room someday.

Przybyla had not yet officially checked aboard, and his gear was still sitting topside by the engineering ladder. Bey would help him get checked in, but he still had a few things to take care of. In the meantime, Bey had an idea. Rubbing his oil-streaked chin, he called to Wally Tulgetske, who stepped out from behind the engine. Like Bey, the first assistant engineer had served as a machinist during the war. He was just making his rounds and was pleased to give the new wiper the grand tour.

Tulgetske was not a regular watchstander. He was responsible for maintenance and worked primarily during the day to keep the ship's engineering systems in good order. Each day he followed the same routine to inspect and service *Cedarville*'s components. First, he would supervise the assistant in blowing the boiler flues before assigning him a maintenance project for the morning. Having purged the boiler exhaust, he would then start his machinery check, leading from the fantail, through main engineering, lower engineering, the boiler room, and the tunnel, past the switchboard and conveyor rooms, topside to check the boom, and back on the main deck to the engineering spaces aft.

Although Przybyla had spent six months on the *Rogers City* as a helper, Tulgetske launched into a detailed explanation of the ship's engineering systems as he started off on his rounds. This was important, as every ship had its own peculiarities that, if not understood and respected, could endanger the ship and her crew.

The engineering watch section, Tulgetske explained, consisted of three men: an engineer, a stokerman, and an oiler. The engineer maintained throttle controls while the stokerman kept the stokers going, dumped fires, and shot ashes in the boiler room. The oiler made his rounds between the upper and lower engine rooms to keep an eye on water levels in the boiler.

He likened the boiler to a big teapot, converting water to steam to drive the triple expansion reciprocating engine. First, he explained, a fire is lit in the furnace and fed by coal drawn from the bunker. Routing through a couple of thousand steel tubes lining the walls of the furnace, the water would flash to steam, the force of which would create a circulation between the water drum and the steam header. With a steady flow of water through the tubes, steam pressure would build. When it got high enough, the steam would be released to the engine to make turns for about twelve knots.

Przybyla followed Tulgetske, absorbing the tutorial as the first engineer briefed him on the condensers, engines, reduction gears, generators, and pumps that packed the engine room. Continuing the tour, they covered the tunnel and every inch of deck between the fantail and the boom before Przybyla was finally returned to Second Assistant Bey.

The engineering team had been advised that *Cedarville* would get underway in about an hour, so Bey took the opportunity to get Przybyla settled in. "Our berthing and the galley are both aft directly above the fantail spaces," Bey explained. "You came from *Rogers City*, right? Same setup. My room is right over the coal bunker. You'll be next to me. It gets kind of noisy, but you'll get used to it."

Bey asked about his union affiliation as they climbed. Bradley Fleet crew were represented by United Steel Workers Local 14913 out of Rogers City. The local was an autonomous negotiating body but could turn to the district for support if labor problems could not be resolved locally. The crew of each ship elected a "ship's chairman" to take complaints to the captain or mate, who were union members as well but were considered management. Przybyla had signed up with the union aboard *Rogers City* the year before.

Emerging from the engineering ladder, Przybyla snagged his bag and followed Bey up and around to berthing.

"OK. Make sure you check in with Billy Holley," Bey advised. "He's your union rep. You'll be working with him down in the engine room. OK . . . here we are."

Swinging wide the door, Przybyla stepped into the darkened space, blinded by the glare of the sun streaming through the small round porthole opposite the door. With the lights turned on he could see that his room was sparse but adequate. The small bed, writing desk, and combination dresser/closet left just enough room for him to stand and get dressed.

Reaching toward the foot of the bed, Bey pulled a familiar card from a sleeve attached to the bunk. Bradley Fleet vessels maintained a unique "emergency procedures" card for each bunk. The card told the resident of this particular room where to go if an alarm sounded. Seven short and one long bell or whistle blasts meant that there was a general alarm and the crewman was to go topside, don his life jacket, and report to his lifeboat station. One long blast meant fire forward, except when getting underway, and two long blasts meant fire aft. In the event of fire, Przybyla knew that he was to haul back to engineering to look for Bey, Tulgetske, or Chief Engineer Lamp. With a fire at sea, there was nowhere to go. The crew would either put it out or die in the water. Przybyla would study this card soon. But first he needed to stow his belongings.

As Przybyla hefted his bag onto the bunk, Bey stepped to the door and turned. Przybyla was not yet assigned to a duty section. Until he was, he could come back down and observe as *Cedarville* got underway.

Elsewhere aboard *Cedarville,* the crew was trickling back, preparing to make another run to Gary, Indiana. Having enjoyed the day with his wife, Gabrysiak made a point to get back early. He did not want to miss the ship's departure. Len had once missed movement, and it was a nightmare. On that occasion, he had arrived at the pier to find *Cedarville* underway to southern Lake Huron. Embarrassed, he reported to the WLC office to call the ship. He was then forced to drive 266 miles to Port Huron, where he caught a mail boat delivering U.S. Steel documentation out to the *Cedarville*. Gabrysiak did not intend to repeat the experience and was careful to always report back well before the ship sailed.

Gabryziak pulled into the dusty lot just behind Eugene Jones. Rolling up the windows and slamming the door, he greeted his friend with a query. "How's your daughter coming along?"

Known to his shipmates as "Casey," Jones was soon to be a

grandpa. Gena was doing fine, he replied. Reports confirmed that the little guy was jumping all around in there, but she still couldn't hold anything down.

Len chuckled. Better them than us.

Jones shouldered his bag as Gabrysiak turned toward the ship. Scaling the access ladder, Len was dismayed upon his arrival topside to find that Piechan had done it again. Mounds of limestone stood well above the cargo hatch openings, with streams of white pebbles cascading from the sides to cover the surrounding deck. Once underway, he and the rest of the off-duty crew would have to clear the limestone by hand and wash away the debris to get the hatch covers in place. "Wonderful," Len thought as he made his way to his bunk. "More cargo. Extra tonnage. Heap the rock in the holds to overflowing. And oh, by the way, no anchoring, no slowing down. Can't allow the crew to have dinner with their families. You have to keep on going."

"Just wonderful," he mumbled before closing his eyes for a short nap.

Half an hour later, Captain Joppich was the last to come aboard. On the bridge, Harry Piechan reported all hands on board, engine room standing by, and all ready to get underway. On the captain's order, *Cedarville* slipped her lines and surged forward. Above the pilothouse, the ship's whistle sounded one long blast as Joppich switched the radio to channel 51 and keyed the handset.

"WLC, *Cedarville* underway."

Joppich waited for the response before turning to channel 16 for a mandatory security call to announce his entry into the nearby shipping lanes. "Steamer *Cedarville* departing Calcite Harbor. Any ships around, please answer."

"Roger, *Cedarville*, *Munson* here. We are about two miles out inbound from the Soo. Not much traffic out here. See you in a few minutes."

ROGERS CITY, MICHIGAN—

In a ranch-style house on the north side of town, Louella Jane Brege heard the exchange. Married to *John G. Munson*'s first engineer, she routinely listened to Bradley Fleet radio traffic on his Halli-crafters ham radio set in the basement. She had just picked her thir-teen- and sixteen-year-old sons up from school when, standing in the kitchen, she heard the call. Lou hadn't expected Dick home until the next morning, and now she had to worry about dinner.

Without a word, the soft-spoken housewife lit the stove and flew into action.

M/V *Topdalsfjord*
ST. LAWRENCE RIVER—
1938

Just after sunset, Captain Hoagland swiveled in his bridge chair, switched to channel 14, and reached overhead for the handset. To his right the compulsory Canadian harbor pilot he had picked up a few miles downriver was guiding his helmsman through the channel as the ship pushed against the two-and-a-half-knot current.

"Montreal traffic control, this is the motor vessel *Topdalsfjord* five miles out and upbound for Chicago, requesting berthing clearance," he said in English. All ships transiting the St. Lawrence Seaway were required to check in with the appropriate traffic control authority upon arrival at certain checkpoints throughout the system.

Waiting for a response, he took a moment to scan the river. A series of blinking lights, red on the right and green on the left, clearly marked the border between deep water and shallow, their sporadic flashes reflecting on the smooth water and blending with the purples and grays mirrored from the darkening sky. To his left, an American warship passed in the opposite direction, its massive guns silhouetted against the residual glow on the horizon. The St. Lawrence Seaway was one of the world's busiest shipping lanes, and his crew would be on full alert as *Topdalsfjord* worked its way more than two thousand miles west to lower Lake Michigan over the next eight days.

Open for less than six years, the Seaway allowed deep-draft navi-gation between the Great Lakes and the Atlantic Ocean. Under the joint control of the Canadian St. Lawrence Seaway Authority and the U.S. Seaway Corporation, the waterway extended from the St. Lawrence River above Montreal through Lake Ontario, the Welland Canal, Lake Erie, and Lake Huron to terminate in Lake Michigan to the southwest and Lake Superior to the northwest. Along the route, *Topdalsfjord* would pass through two American and thirteen Canadian locks.

With an eighteen-foot draft, *Topdalsfjord*'s keel could easily negotiate the twenty-seven-foot deep channel. In fact, the Seaway and its system of locks were designed for much larger vessels, accommodating ships in excess of seven hundred feet. More than 80 percent of the cargo flowing through the Seaway—commodities such as grain, iron ore, and coal—was transported in bulk form aboard huge carriers that regularly scraped the bottom of the channel. Palletized cargo aboard tramp freighters like *Topdalsfjord* accounted for the remainder of the traffic.

Topdalsfjord would stop briefly in Montreal for unloading and inspection before navigating the locks upriver in the wake of the first Soviet vessel to use the Seaway. On April 19, the ten-thousand-ton freighter *Mitchurunsk* discharged part of her general cargo at Montreal to lighten for transit through the locks. Over the objections of U.S. shipping interests, both the United States and Canada approved the passage, although Canada tightened security to ensure that the vessel could not be used to block the waterway. Hoagland didn't care one way or the other, just as long as this cold war foolishness didn't slow him down.

A French-Canadian accent soon crackled over the radio. "*Topdalsfjord,* this is Station Montreal. Are you precleared for transit? Over."

To avoid bureaucratic delay, ships transiting the Seaway were encouraged to apply for preclearance for passage. This required the vessel's local agent to submit proof of vessel ownership and insurance, a physical description of the vessel, and a security deposit sufficient to cover the fees charged for the ship's registered tonnage, cargo rates, and lockage tolls. Within fourteen days of entering the Seaway, the vessel was also required to submit a Seaway Transit Declaration Form with a certified cargo manifest to confirm the weight of cargo shipped on the waterway.

Hoagland confirmed preclearance, identifying his company's shoreside agent and preclearance approval number. A moment later, the French-Canadian voice returned. "*Topdalsfjord,* you are cleared to proceed immediately to Boucherville Terminal for unloading.

Upon arrival please have all ship's documentation, cargo manifests, and crew passports ready for inspection."

Captain Hoagland was pleasantly surprised. He was under the impression that the port was backed up due to a collision that had recently closed the river and had expected more of a delay. Only a few days before, the West German freighter *Transatlantic* had collided with the Dutch vessel *Hermes* eighty miles downriver. Burning fiercely, *Transatlantic* rolled on her side, killing one crewman and blocking the channel for days. The debris had been cleared by the time *Topdalsfjord* entered the river, but the delay had backed river traffic up for miles, and Hoagland expected to wait at anchor until a berth came available.

Not wishing to question his good fortune, the captain glanced at the river pilot, who only shrugged in return. Confirming his berth assignment, he relaxed in his pedestal-mounted seat as the pilot guided *Topdalsfjord* into the harbor. Unbeknown to Hoagland, Den Norske Amerikalinje's agent in Montreal had been hard at work and stevedores had already been dispatched to the pier to get the vessel unloaded and sent on her way.

7

Passages

April 28, 1965
SS *Cedarville*
GARY, INDIANA—

Elmer Jarvis negotiated the forward maze of ladders leading to the control room at the head of the conveyor. The junior of two conveyormen, Jarvis took his orders from Ronald Piechan, who was on deck in the early morning sun with his brother, preparing to discharge *Cedarville*'s limestone cargo. Climbing into the control booth, he powered up the console and lifted the handset that connected directly with a control station positioned beneath the discharge boom. "Standing by," he said to Piechan on the other end of the line.

"OK. The boom is in position. Start her up."

Jarvis confirmed the order before hanging up. Fumbling with his key ring, he selected a small silver key, which he inserted into the lock and turned. The conveyor system that looped around the control booth roared to life. As the empty belt whizzed by outside of the window, he flipped a switch, activating a servo motor at the base of number one hold. The motor turned gears that opened a chute, and a column of sandy limestone poured onto the moving conveyor below.

Within seconds of flipping the switch, white cargo flashed past Jarvis's position, dumping onto another belt in its upward journey. Forward, the limestone crisscrossed port and starboard toward buckets that lifted the stony cargo to the base of the discharge boom. Meanwhile, in cargo hold number one, the surface level gradually declined as more limestone gushed through the chute onto the moving conveyor.

Walking aft and outboard of the discharge operations, Gabrysiak cleared the superstructure and turned into the galley for some breakfast. Facing the kitchen, the unrated mess stood on the left, while the officers' mess was to the right. The Bradley Fleet preferred to maintain the separation between "management" and the common seamen, though the food was the same.

Glancing left and right, the third mate considered his options.

Gabrysiak started sailing in the summer of 1948 after graduation from Rogers City High School. Initially assigned to *Clymer*, he was soon transferred to *Bradley*, where he served for several years. After briefly being called into active military service, Len returned to the fleet as an unrated deckhand, but, worried about job security, he opted to pursue a third mate's rating in 1959. Having attended the mandatory five-week school in Cleveland, he sat for the weeklong test and earned his license in March 1960.

Now, as a licensed officer, Len was free to eat wherever he chose. "Better company in the unrated mess," he thought as he turned to the left.

On deck, Ron and Harry Piechan stood by as limestone shot outboard from *Cedarville*'s boom, cascading onto the pier in a cloud of dust. As the first discharge mound began to form, the Piechan brothers leaned against the rail, considering the port. Beyond the mountains of iron ore and limestone standing ready for transport to the waiting blast furnaces, the spectral shadows of the Gary Works loomed on the horizon.

Adjusting his thick glasses, Ron Piechan squinted through the haze to make out the rusting towers, mills, and assorted pipes and structures cluttering the landscape. Countless stacks billowed dark brown emissions as sulfur dioxide, carbon monoxide, and countless other pollutants added to the yellow haze blanketing the city. Yet, Gary Works' dreary appearance belied its pristine origins.

Prehistoric marshes and sand dunes once covered the site that bordered the southern shore of Lake Michigan. However, in 1906, U.S. Steel filled the marshes and leveled the dunes to build a plant at the strategic location midway between its eastern coalfields and the northern iron mines. By 1965, the Gary Works occupied almost four thousand acres and was one of the preeminent manufacturing facilities in the highly industrialized Calumet region of the midwestern United States.

Stepping from the side, Harry Piechan watched Ron shift the boom to start a new pile, while below Jarvis activated the flow from hold number two. Before the advent of self-unloaders, shoreside bulk facilities employed expensive unloading rigs like the monstrous Hewlett unloader, whose gigantic claws scooped the holds of visiting cargo vessels. A welcome improvement, *Cedarville*'s boom could be extended outward to allow the ship to discharge her own cargo in only five hours.

Most of the *Cedarville* crew failed to understand the inherent value of the cargo they labored to deliver. Without limestone, modern steel production would become virtually impossible, and many of the skyscrapers jutting across America's skyline, automobiles traveling between them, and steel cans from which their drivers prepared their evening meals were owing to *Cedarville* cargos.

Cedarville's previous delivery, deposited on the same pier, had already been expended to this end. Segregated by type, the Rogers City limestone was shifted to one of several ore storage yards, piled alongside raw iron oxide ore and carbon-rich coke, or processed coal. Individually, these materials were transferred to the nearest stockhouse complex by conveyor belt along one of the hundreds of ore bridges traversing the Gary Works. Deposited into rail hoppers, they were routed through the stockhouse to be weighed, dumped into a skip car, and hoisted on the inclined rail to a receiving hopper atop the furnace. When sufficient load had accumulated, the raw materials were "charged" into the airtight blast furnace.

A blast furnace is designed to remove chemical impurities from iron ore at a high temperature. The furnace into which the *Cedarville* cargo had been dumped was a huge steel stack lined with refractory brick and had been in continuous operation for more than four years.

As a puddle of molten iron accumulated at the base of the stack, super-heated air, or "hot blast," was injected higher up, igniting the newly introduced coke and melting the ores. At 4,200 degrees Fahrenheit, the iron oxides at the top would begin to soften and melt, finally trickling through the burning coke, as oxides were purged from the liquid ore. Likewise, calcium from the melting limestone bonded with the ore's sulfur and silicates to further purify the iron. For more than six hours the *Cedarville* limestone worked its way through the furnace, finally descending with other waste products to form a red-hot slag, which floated upon the heavier liquid iron.

Beneath the furnace, a large bit was eventually swung into place to drill a tap hole through the clay plug that blocked the escape of the accumulating iron. Once the plug was breached, a glowing column of liquid iron and slag filled the trough below. Less dense than iron, the liquid slag floated atop the metallic current until it was diverted by a skimmer and forced off into a slag pit for cooling. The molten iron continued its journey into brick-lined ladles that were taken to nearby steel shops for molding, while the slag was gathered to be processed for landfill or road construction.

As the waste from the Rogers City cargo was heaped in the nearby slag staging area for removal, the *Cedarville* crew, busily discharging their cargo on the adjacent pier, remained oblivious to the workings of the steel manufacturing process that had already consumed previous deliveries.

1350

With empty holds, *Cedarville* rode high in the water as her deck crew singled up all lines in preparation to get underway. On the captain's command, the engineer on duty activated a series of breakers that, in turn, energized the ship's ballast system. Jumping into action, the electric pumps drew massive quantities of water from the polluted harbor.

At a combined rate of almost nine thousand gallons per minute, the oily flow surged through a maze of pipes and valves to be evenly distributed among *Cedarville*'s eight ballast tanks. Numbered from stem to stern, the side and bottom tanks filled uniformly, causing the ship to settle into the murky water on an even keel.

With the ship riding high, its increased freeboard would have made it much more vulnerable to wind action, causing it to skip around off-course. Thus, though *Cedarville* could have negotiated the return trip unballasted, the additional weight actually improved maneuverability and control.

After the ship was properly ballasted, the pumps were secured and the ship was made ready for departure. Outboard from the pier, a single tug stood by to swing the giant self-unloader's bow to the north. Free of her moorings, *Cedarville*'s steam whistle screamed overhead, its message to all within hearing: "Underway."

April 30, 1965
M/V *Topdalsfjord*
LAKE ONTARIO—
1223

As his ship glided swiftly along the Lake Ontario shoreline, Captain Hoagland considered the farms and industry slipping by to port. Dead ahead, the shores of the lake converged, funneling the line of shipping traffic south into the narrow passage.

Running from north to south, the Welland Canal links Lake Erie with Lake Ontario, bypassing Niagara Falls. To climb the 326-foot escarpment separating the lakes, vessels were required to negotiate eight locks along the canal's twenty-six-mile route. Once the ship was approved for passage and queued with other waiting vessels, the transit could be completed in as little as eleven hours, assuming no breakdowns blocked the channel or other problems slowed traffic.

Referring to the well-worn Seaway guide stored within easy reach, Captain Hoagland shifted communications to 156.7 MHz and announced his presence. "VDX22, St. Catherine's Control, this is the freighter *Topdalsfjord* requesting assignment for passage, over."

Also known as Seaway Control Sector 6, St. Catherine's controlled each lock in the canal and ordered the vessels entering the system so as to expedite passage for all. Responding on the working frequency, channel 14, the controller requested the ship's nationality, cargo, port of origin, destination, and specifications.

Hoagland was annoyed at the intrusive query but responded fully. Having checked their records, the controller was satisfied that the

Norwegian vessel was, in fact, precleared by the Seaway Authority, and *Topdalsfjord* was placed in line for entry. In the interim, she was ordered to drop anchor beyond the entrance of the channel to await the compulsory pilot who would guide her through the perfectly straight waterway.

At the nearby pilots' association office, a secretary received a last-minute pilotage request and, checking the roster of available pilots, placed a radio call to the company pier on Lake Ontario. Soon thereafter, a crusty old seaman climbed aboard the crowded boat that would deliver pilots to the transiting vessels.

Compulsory pilotage is an ancient concept that debuted and faded in Roman law, was revived in the fifteenth-century Hanseatic ordinances, and eventually became a well-entrenched feature of modern international maritime law. Mere seamen with specialized knowledge of local conditions and navigational hazards, these pilots are employed to guide vessels through particular channels, rivers, or enclosed bodies of water. The service is "compulsory" when required by law. In this case, the imperative arose by agreement between the United States and Canada requiring foreign vessels transiting the Seaway to engage a pilot to navigate the locks.

Chief Officer Fagerli directed the small deck crew that had lowered a rope Jacob's ladder to starboard. Soon the pilot boat rounded a nearby tanker and turned into view, the large white "P" topside heralding the arrival of the ship's guide. Hoagland bristled mildly at the intrusion. He had taken *Topdalsfjord* up and down through the Welland Canal no fewer than eighteen times and was far more qualified than some old sea dog to maneuver his vessel through the unchallenging passage. Nonetheless, rules were rules, and with the pilot safely aboard and staggering toward the bridge, *Topdalsfjord* weighed anchor.

1550

Having passed the breakwater at the mouth of the canal, *Topdalsfjord* slowed to wait her turn as the bulk carrier ahead entered lock number one. With the gates of the lock closed behind the massive lake vessel, it soon began to rise, its rounded hull peeking over the fifty-foot steel doors. Within a few minutes, smoke billowed from the ship's stack, and it moved on, allowing the lock to empty once again.

Making turns for two knots, *Topdalsfjord* slowly approached the opening gates. Elevating passing ships by forty-six and a half feet, the lock's narrow block-lined walls loomed imposingly above the decks of the tramp freighter. On deck, Seamen Gule and Bergkvist drew lines from the winch drums, leading each through the chocks and up over the lifelines. With sufficient lengths of line available to reach the mooring posts on the lock walls, *Topdalsfjord* proceeded.

As the ship pressed on, the signal at the far end of the lock glowed consistently red, clearly marking the point of maximum advance, beyond which the stem of the vessel was forbidden. On the bow, Gule strained to heave a coil of light line up and over the towering edge of the lock. The spinning bundle sailed over the head of the line handler atop the wall as it quickly payed out. Retrieving the line, the dock worker hauled in the light cord, which was securely fastened to the bight, or loop, at the head of the heavier mooring line.

On the bridge, the pilot spoke briefly with the lock officer, agreeing that *Topdalsfjord* would proceed to the head of the lock and swing into position alongside the wall. When her fantail cleared the gates, Bergkvist let loose his line, which was also received topside and quickly hauled up. Less than a quarter of the way through the lock, the stern line was looped over a large iron bollard, mounted on the pier to secure vessels during the lift.

The pilot ordered the engines cut and leaned out onto the starboard bridge wing. Looking aft, he shouted to Bergkvist, "Take strain on number two."

At the stern, the deckhand quickly wrapped the thick line around a large cleat embedded in the deck. Crisscrossing the mooring line several times upon itself, the line soon took a strain as Bergkvist stood well clear in case the line snapped under the forces generated by the surging vessel. The manilla rope stretched and creaked as *Topdalsfjord* drifted forward, her engines stopped and rudder amidships, the combined forces pulling her into place alongside the wall.

Strolling onto the bridge wing, the motley pilot shouted at Gule and Bergkvist, "Shift the after stern line to the winch and take in slack on one. Let's get those spring lines in place, and be quick about it."

The deck crew grumbled to themselves. Neither spoke English well, but they knew the drill and swiftly secured the vessel for lift.

Astern, just above the fantail, a sailboat mast bobbed from side to side as a forty-four-foot yacht followed *Topdalsfjord* into the lock, the American ensign fluttering beneath her spreaders. As the gaff-rigged ketch cast its lines to the waiting ground crew, the Herculean gates swung shut with a roar.

The Welland Canal made use of water cascading down from Lake Erie to fill the locks. With *Topdalsfjord* and the yacht firmly in place, huge valves located at the base of the lock walls were opened to flood the chamber and lift the vessels. For more than ten minutes, 21 million gallons of water rushed into the narrow lock, swirling about the freighter and the smaller yacht as the two vessels bounced against the walls. Aboard *Topdalsfjord*, Fagerli monitored the winches, which automatically took up the slack as the vessel was raised. Even so, the crew of the yacht kept a wary eye on the six-thousand-ton freighter as she swayed about alarmingly in the swirling current, all the while taking up the slack in their own lines.

Finally, just as the eddied water's surface began to calm, the forward gates opened, and the signal light turned green. Hoagland was eager to move out of the chamber. He knew that if the aft gates failed, his ship would be swept out of the lock like a bath toy poured out of a bucket. Turning his attention to the task at hand, he put the thought out of his mind as the ship prepared to get underway. Meanwhile, the tiresome pilot continued to haunt the deck crew from the bridge wing.

"Hey you," the pilot intoned, "slack off on number one and four. Go ahead and cast off the spring lines and stand by on the bow and stern."

Swinging on her lines, *Topdalsfjord* cleared the wall and drifted aft. Several pairs of eyes widened at the sight of the freighter rotating threateningly close to the yacht's antique wooden bow. Inboard, each line was unceremoniously dropped from the pier and hauled, dripping, aboard the freighter as *Topdalsfjord* accelerated and exited the lock, leaving the yacht crew shaken but untouched.

For the next few hours *Topdalsfjord* motored south through rugged, heavily forested terrain, past rocky escarpments, and through a couple of towns. As the sun set to starboard, the freighter sailed on, casting an expansive shadow across the lush orchards and vineyards lining the canal. By dusk, red and green lights marked the passage beneath the train trestles and drawbridges that crossed the waterway. Pressing on in the dark, *Topdalsfjord* lifted six more times before nearing the end of the passage, the pilot becoming more unbearable with each lift.

May 1, 1965
0608

Overhead, the stars were retreating from the graying eastern sky as *Topdalsfjord* approached the final lock. With Lake Erie in view less than a mile distant, she awaited the passage of a northbound vessel before entering the diminutive lock. Lock number eight served only to adjust for minor fluctuations in the level of the lake, and *Topdalsfjord* was raised only a few inches before clearing the southernmost boundary of the Welland Canal.

Having deposited her unwanted guest at the last lock, *Topdalsfjord* was free to continue the voyage. With the morning sun breaking over the horizon, a weary Captain Hoagland relinquished the conn to the watch officer as the ship rounded the breakwater and accelerated to the west.

8

Turnaround

May 6, 1965
ROGERS CITY, MICHIGAN—

Cliff Buehrens chauffeured the dusty white company sedan north on Highway 23 toward the Presque Isle airfield. Riding shotgun, Joe Parilla flicked the smoldering remains of his cigarette on the passing asphalt and continued to quiz Buehrens on fleet maintenance. He took notes as Buehrens commented on each vessel. Summoned to a production meeting in Pittsburgh, he would be reporting to Admiral Khoury on Bradley Fleet operational readiness, and he wanted to be conversant in the maintenance issues facing his ships. Tucked safely in his briefcase, Buehrens's maintenance report detailed each problem, but Parilla scribbled on. During his absence, Buehrens would be in charge of operations, but Parilla would only be a phone call away.

As the company car turned right onto the gravel parking lot, a small aircraft bearing the United States Steel logo on its tail roared overhead. Watching from the end of the runway, Parilla followed the tiny aircraft as it slowly drifted down to meet the black asphalt, touched down with a puff of smoke, and rolled to a stop at the end of the runway. Proceeding to the taxiway, it turned back toward the administrative building where Buehrens had parked.

The car doors squeaked as Parilla and Buehrens swung wide the doors and stepped out onto the gravel surface. Clouds of dust swirled about their brown leather shoes as Buehrens carried Parilla's overnight bag toward the pavement. Stopping at the warming black-top, Parilla continued his query. "And *Cedarville*?"

Both men had been involved in the decision to defer the expensive hull repairs, and *Cedarville* had become a sore point. Buehrens studied his shoes as he spoke. *Cedarville* was due in from Gary. She still had some minor leakage from her grounding the previous fall, but otherwise she was hanging in there.

Parilla bypassed the small terminal building as the hum of the approaching airplane grew louder. The two watched the company plane taxi forward, then turn and stop twenty yards ahead. Suddenly, the engines sputtered and died, the propellers gradually spinning to a halt. In the relative quiet, the cockpit hatch swung open and the pilot, dressed in dark slacks, a short-sleeved white shirt, and blue tie, stepped onto the wing, jumped to the ground, and trotted to the little building.

Confident that *Cedarville* was holding up OK, Parilla cautioned Buehrens to turn the ships around smartly while he was gone. He didn't want to hear about any more downtime. The fleet captain was under a lot of pressure to keep the limestone flowing, and that is what he intended to do.

Having apparently relieved himself, the pilot reappeared to help Parilla with his bags. The plane's frame tilted as the pilot stepped up onto the low-slung wing root and climbed into place.

With a briefcase in his left hand, Parilla offered his right to Buehrens, turned, and climbed aboard, throwing the rest of his belongings in the back.

Parilla settled into the purple vinyl seat on the passenger side of the gaudy red cockpit. With an array of dials prominently displayed on the black console before him, he was careful not to touch the pedals at his feet or to lean against the space-age steering column that protruded into his lap. He could have shifted to the less comfortable bench seat in the back, but the pilot had already closed the canopy, donned a headset, and, with the press of a button, started the engines.

Two white nose cones spun imperceptibly as the two-bladed props behind them instantly blurred. Moments later, the 235-horsepower engines roared as the small aircraft bumped along, gaining speed over the softly undulating taxiway.

"Papa Zulu Quebec, this is Delta zero niner, request permission to taxi," the pilot said into the headset microphone.

"Roger, Delta zero niner," Presque Isle Control responded. "The runway is clear. You are cleared to taxi and depart. Have a safe flight."

"Roger that, Papa Zulu Quebec. Ya'll have a good one. Delta zero niner out."

Perched at the end of the runway, the pilot set the brake once again to conduct a final systems check. Oil pressure, engine temperature, voltage, and rpm were all normal. The engine was running well. It was time to leave.

The pilot advanced the throttle before releasing the brake. Headed due east on the runway, the wheels, shrouded with teardrop-shaped airfoils, bounced along the pavement as the aircraft accelerated. Having traveled less than a quarter of the length of the three-thousand-foot runway, the aircraft quickly rotated upward, its front wheel leaving the ground an instant before the after gear.

Parilla felt as though the ground had dropped suddenly from beneath the airframe as he was pressed gently into his seat. The fuselage was lifted up and over the raised stadium lights at the adjacent high school field. To the right, a small hillock passed aft as the aircraft continued to climb.

The plane's path took it right over the slate gray quarry, with the dust from a recent excavation billowing below. Beyond that was a miniature version of the Michigan Limestone processing plant and Port Calcite. From eight hundred feet Parilla could still see crewmen walking the deck of *Calcite II* as she took on a load of limestone at the south pier. But he soon lost sight of the ship as she passed beneath the starboard wing. Once over water, the Piper banked southeast and continued to climb as it followed the Michigan coastline toward Pittsburgh.

Parilla felt the decreasing pressure in his ears and the vibration of the engine in his bones as the forested coastline slipped past. Yet, despite the grandeur of the passing scene, *Cedarville* could not fade entirely from his thoughts. Parilla had saved a lot of money by delaying *Cedarville*'s costly hull repairs. Even so, he could not afford another *Bradley* disaster. With an open tunnel and no watertight bulkheads, *Cedarville* would sink like a rock if she breached her hull.

Captain Parilla knew that the repairs would have to be made soon. Budgeting them in would be the challenge.

SS *Cedarville*
STRAITS OF MACKINAC—

Cedarville's gray bow sliced through the frigid Lake Huron waters as she rounded the tip of the Lower Peninsula. A thin afternoon mist that had risen from the surface was swept aside by the passing wall of metal, glided along the slippery hull, and was left to swirl and fade over the ship's turbulent wake.

A fog layer several feet deep was blanketing the channel as if to mock the evaporative forces of the sun overhead. Though it appeared from the bridge that *Cedarville* was sailing on a cloud, the cold air above the layer was clear and visibility was good. At the helm, Bill Asam could see two vessels far ahead where the shores of Bois Blanc Island to the north and Cheboygan to the south threatened to converge. The engine order telegraph confirmed that *Cedarville* was still pressing home at full speed. Good. Asam was looking forward to spending the evening with his bride.

M/V *Topdalsfjord*
LAKE MICHIGAN—

Jan Gronstol had the conn, and less than an hour out of Milwaukee he was already tired. He had spent the last four days supervising the stevedores as they methodically placed the cargo in *Topdalsfjord*'s five holds, while most of the crew enjoyed a little shore leave. *Topdalsfjord*'s first stop was Chicago. She was not the first foreign vessel to reach the Illinois port this season. The Dutch freighter *Prinz Mauritz* held that distinction, arriving several days earlier with a load of tulip bulbs and Holland beers. Arriving shortly thereafter, *Topdalsfjord* discharged the remainder of her European goods and quickly loaded an assortment of general cargo before pushing north to the Wisconsin grain terminals.

The freighter spent three days in Milwaukee as stevedores laboriously loaded pallet after pallet of sacked corn in her holds. *Topdals-fjord's* deck-mounted cranes swung into action to load holds two, three, four, and five nearly simultaneously. A longshoring gang of sixteen men worked each hold—eleven holdsmen below, two on cranes, a gang foreman, and two supervisors—to stow 1,615 long tons of corn.

With the assigned cargo stowed safely aboard, *Topdalsfjord* cast off for Fort William, Ontario, via the St. Marys Canal. She was slated to top off her holds with general cargo in Detroit and Montreal before returning to Europe, and Captain Hoagland was making turns for eleven knots while the visibility held.

Glancing at the bridge chronometer, Gronstol sighed. More than two hours until shift change. Stretching his back, he settled into the captain's chair as the ship continued east toward the Straits of Mackinac.

SS *Cedarville*
PORT CALCITE, MICHIGAN—

It was late when Marty Joppich climbed down the ladder from the main deck to the pier and headed toward the dock office. *Cedarville* was back in for another load, and Joppich needed to check in with Parilla to get his marching orders. Once he knew which grade of cargo to load, he would set the wheels in motion and go home for some rest. A secretary was working late, typing cargo manifests and enjoying the cool lake breeze through an open window, when Joppich walked in. He smiled at the pretty young woman. "Is Captain Parilla in?"

Recognizing the *Cedarville* captain, she replied, "No sir, he's gone to a meeting in Pittsburgh. Mr. Buehrens is watching his desk while he is gone."

"Thanks," he said as he turned toward Buehrens's office. Leaning on the wooden doorframe, he rapped on the opened door. "Mr. Buehrens, do you have a new assignment for me?"

Buehrens looked up from his desk and smiled. "Marty, come on in. I have your paperwork right here."

Joppich took a seat across from Buehrens and studied his ship's new orders.

ROGERS CITY, MICHIGAN—

With the hum of its engine and the crunch of limestone beneath its balding tires, the 1961 Ford pickup rolled into town. Behind the wheel, Art Fuhrman was looking forward to a home-cooked meal. When Fuhrman was not underway or on watch he liked to spend evenings at home. Although Barbara usually met him at the pier when he came in during the day, he kept the truck at the yard in case she was on call at the hospital.

Twenty-nine-year-old Art Fuhrman was raised by his father to be a handyman, but with little interest in plumbing, carpentry, masonry, or car repair, he was now employed as a deck watchman aboard *Cedarville*. His schedule allowed him to see his six-month-old daughter and eighteen-month-old son about twice a week, but tonight he anticipated a more intimate visit with his young wife.

Fuhrman was pleased to catch a glimpse of Barbara through the kitchen window as he pulled into the driveway beside their modest home. With her hair pulled up, she was cooking with purpose, and Fuhrman liked what he saw. His mouth was already watering.

PORT CALCITE, MICHIGAN—

Dodging a speeding forklift, Pat crossed the pier to mount the brow of the ship. She was no stranger to the large ships upon which her husband served, and she climbed the steps with purpose. Scheduled to go on watch at eight o'clock, Len could not leave the ship, so Pat had agreed to meet him aboard for dinner.

"Hey good-looking," a familiar voice called down from above. Pat smiled and waved as Len grinned down from the bridge wing.

"I'll be right up," she called, continuing her climb.

Patricia Mulka was an operator with General Telephone in Rogers City when she met Len at a Christmas party in 1956. He was four and a half years her senior, and although they had both graduated from Rogers City High School, they had not spoken until that night at the Deer Hunt Inn. He asked her out. She said yes. They had been together ever since.

While they were dating, Len spent much of his time on the *Carl D.*

Bradley. When the ship pulled in, he would head straight to the telephone. He had a one-in-three chance.

"Number please," she would answer, plugging the cord into the appropriate line. Alongside two other girls, the operators routed every call in the small community. She always recognized his voice. "You're not supposed to call me here—number please," she would taunt with a smile.

Len soon went into the Army and was stationed at the nearby Nike missile base in Utica, Michigan. Their relationship blossomed, and on Christmas 1958 he gave her an engagement ring. Again, she said yes.

Pat had come from a large family. She was the eighth of nine children—all girls except for Gerald, the baby. Nevertheless, she and Len would only have a single son.

Leaving Lenny Jr. with her sister, she had a dinner date with her husband. She was no longer working. The telephone system was automated, and she had been laid off several years earlier. Now she was free to come and go as she pleased.

Nearing the top, she found Len waiting for her. "Corned beef sandwiches tonight," he told her as he pulled her aboard.

"Sounds good," she replied.

With his arm around her shoulder, the Gabrysiaks turned aft for the galley.

ROGERS CITY, MICHIGAN—

Barb Fuhrman did not like her husband's schedule. He had been sailing with U.S. Steel since he was discharged from the Army in 1959, and she had had enough.

"Maybe I can get on with Michigan Limestone like Dad," he suggested over the remains of a wonderful dinner. He wanted to get off of the water as well. Art was an avid hunter and looked forward to the day when he would have time to take his young son, Jimmy, hunting and fishing in the woods around Rogers City.

"Yeah, well, you need to get out there and finish the cottage too," she said. The Fuhrmans had purchased their home in 1963, but it seemed that he had been working forever with his father and brother on a cottage outside of town.

"Dad and I should be able to wrap it up this year. I promise."

"That's what you said last year. Anyway, I just want you home in the evenings. The kids need you and I need you."

"OK, I'll try," he said, taking her hand and rising from the table with a twinkle in his eye. The kids were in bed, and he had to be back to the ship in just a few hours.

A few streets away, Stan Haske got the rundown as his five sons brooded in their rooms.

"The boys have been giving me problems, and I need your help." Elizabeth was at her wit's end, and she wanted Stan to deal with it.

Lighting a cigarette, he eyed the mother of his children and ran his fingers through his crew cut. "What do you want me to do about it?"

"Lay down the law."

Haske stood carefully, his hernia incision still tender, and reached for his oldest son's school notebook. Ripping a page from the back, he turned to his wife. "What are they doing?"

For several minutes she filled him in as he wrote. When he was finished, he posted the note on the kitchen cabinet. It read:

TO BE DONE EVERY DAY
(To be read every day if it can't be remembered)
(1) Change clothes directly upon entering house from school, unless otherwise directed.
(2) Do your homework pronto. No fooling around.
(3) After supper do the dishes and then back to your homework if not done. Then you can play outside.
(4) Don't leave your underwear on if it's warm outside or if you're not going outside.
(5) Before going outside do any other work you have like garbage, rugs, sink or whatever you are told to do.
(6) Turn off shed light.
(7) Wash face, hands, brush teeth before going to bed (you get 5 min.) When in bed don't talk.
(8) Change underwear every other day unless instructed otherwise.
THE CONSEQUENCES COULD BE PAINFUL!!!

Chuckling as he walked down the hallway, Haske went to talk to the boys. He was an involved father. Firm but kind, he spent most of his time at home mediating disputes between his sons and their harried mother. Knocking, he opened the door to the oldest boys' room.

Calling them all together, he waited patiently as they straggled in. Greg was the oldest, then Ken, Alan, Brian, and little Steven, who had toddled in their wake before Haske closed the door.

"What's going on guys?" he asked, picking up Steven.

Silence.

Stan warned the boys that their mother wanted to conduct business a certain way and that's the way things were going to be done. He told them of the list of instructions that would be posted in the kitchen and assured them that, if their mother had any more trouble, they would be answering to him.

Satisfied that they got the point, he pulled a small envelope from his pocket and handed it to Greg. Mother's Day was coming up that Sunday, and Greg was charged with giving it to his mother.

Taking the card, Greg promised not to forget. With that done, Stan and Steven Haske joined Betty in the living room for a quiet evening.

SS *Cedarville*
PORT CALCITE, MICHIGAN—

The evening's load was nearly complete, with *Cedarville* backed into position alongside *Munson* in the opposite slip. Third Mate Gabrysiak was the officer of the midwatch, keeping an eye on the ship as Ron Piechan directed cargo loading on the main deck.

With only fifteen minutes left on his watch, Gabrysiak was peering over the side when movement below caught his attention. A familiar face ambled leisurely toward the ship, bathed in the glow of the yellow lights that flooded the port at night. A duffel bag slung on his shoulder, the figure mounted the ladder. Charlie Cook. "What was he doing here?" Len wondered.

Charlie Cook was an old-timer who had been sailing with the Bradley Fleet as a "relief man" since 1933. He had taken a season off to build a new home with his eleven-year-old son and had just finished the interior work on the prefab structure. With time on his hands, he had gone back to work. Under union pressure, Parilla had stuck him aboard *Cedarville*.

Of course, this was news to Gabrysiak. "Hi ya, Charlie. What's up?" he asked as Cook crossed the brow.

"Hey, Len, good to see you. I'm coming back to work. Looks like I'm going to be the new third mate."

Gabrysiak examined his paperwork and cringed. With Cook's arrival, Len would be bumped back down to helmsman, with a corresponding reduction in pay. "Well, you'd better get your stuff below and get some shut-eye," he mumbled. "We are getting underway in a few hours."

"Alright. I'll be seeing you on the bridge."

"Yeah, see you there."

No sooner had Cook disappeared when Second Mate Rygwelski arrived to relieve Gabrysiak.

"What a way to find out that you've been replaced," Gabrysiak thought as he made his way to his warm stateroom for a few hours of sleep.

9

Fog

For two days, meteorologists had been tracking a mass of warm saturated air sweeping northward from the Gulf of Mexico, bringing hot, humid conditions to the Mississippi River valley. Continuing north through Tennessee, Kentucky, Indiana, and Michigan, the muggy air flowed over Grand Rapids and Detroit as it fanned out and descended to settle upon the cold waters of Lake Huron, Lake Michigan, and the Straits of Mackinac.

Pushed along by a southwest wind, the tropical air rolled endlessly over the cold water, gradually chilling to dew point. Finally, around midnight, fog began to form in earnest.

In the realm of physics, Charles' law states that, given constant atmospheric pressure, the volume of air decreases with its temperature. As the moist air over the water cooled, its molecules became more densely packed, and the vapor-rich gas was squeezed beyond its saturation point. Suddenly, like a dripping sponge, the excess vapor began to condense on nearby microscopic particles of dust and smoke to hang, suspended, above the wavy surface.

As the tropical air mass advanced through the Straits, the tumbling parcels of chilled air eventually combined to form a dense stratus layer more than a thousand feet thick. Commonly known as "advection fog," this blanket of moisture would likely persist for days.

SS *Cedarville*
PORT CALCITE, MICHIGAN—
0215

As a rule, *Cedarville*'s engineering plant was kept on-line during loading so as to facilitate a rapid turnaround. Under the supervision of the chief engineer and his watch team, the boilers were stoked with coal that was drawn from the coal bunker by screw drive to the hopper, then by gravity onto grates at the bottom of the furnace.

Once ignited, the fuel blazed at more than 2,500 degrees Fahrenheit, generating sulfur dioxides, carbon monoxides, and nitrogen oxides that rushed from the combustion chamber. Swirling upward toward the stack, the burning gases enveloped thousands of steel tubes that lined the furnace walls, transferring thermal energy directly to the exposed metal and heating the water within.

Soon the water expanded and boiled. Becoming less dense, the hot water, mingled with newly formed steam, began to rise toward the collection drum, or header. In the header, the water was separated from the steam and routed back to the boiler, while the saturated steam collected to a pressure of 350 pounds per square inch— sufficient to power the ship's triple expansion reciprocating steam engine.

With the boilers up and running, the engineering team stood by, awaiting the captain's order to get underway.

On deck, Stan Rygwelski shivered in the damp cold of the night. Although he had not given it much thought, the second mate sensed that the relative humidity was increasing. As his watch wore on, light patches of mist began to drift in from the lake, wafting over the deck before disappearing into the darkened quarry. Finally noticing the change, Rygwelski watched as the ship was gradually blanketed by the wall of fog that swept in from the water, obscuring the port. In the muffled silence of the foggy spring night, the yellow lights of the pier glowed dimly through the stratum, reminding the deck crew that the ship was still moored.

Rygwelski thought nothing of the fog. The lakes were shrouded most of the spring and a good part of the summer, and he was well accustomed to steaming full speed through the soup. Disregarding the mist, he turned his collar up against the chill and continued to pace, counting the minutes until his relief.

M/V *Topdalsfjord*
MACKINAC APPROACHES, LAKE MICHIGAN—
0230

Fog had been building for the past two hours, and First Officer Larsen strained to scan the shipping lanes for the lights of oncoming traffic as his ship continued east-northeast at ten knots. Adjacent to the helm, the faint green sweep of the Decca radar repeater cast its glow across the bridge. Set to scan the sea lanes up to twelve nautical miles distant, the display indicated a rough line of shipping traffic apparently steaming toward the Mackinac Bridge and Lake Huron beyond. Falling in line with this procession, *Topdalsfjord* would make the Straits in about seven hours.

Despite periodic clearings, *Topdalsfjord* was increasingly plagued by sporadic patches of fog, and Larsen decided to set the fog watch. Activating the automatic fog signal, he sent Seaman Bjornoy to the bow with orders to report any contacts. As Bjornoy took his place forward, bundled in a peacoat, wool watch cap, and leather gloves, a blast of steam issued from the ship's whistle over the pilothouse. The signal echoed between the coalescing clouds, its shrill pitch lingering in the air above the advancing ship.

Without warning, the air before the ship cleared, and less than a mile ahead, Bjornoy, Larsen, and Helmsman Finn Skauen beheld a solid fog bank towering overhead and extending to the horizon in either direction. Lifting the telephone receiver, Larsen dialed Hoagland's cabin. Apologizing for waking him, the first mate briefed Hoagland on the developing conditions as *Topdalsfjord* disappeared into the wall of fog.

SS *Cedarville*
PORT CALCITE, MICHIGAN—

Cecilia Bredow drove her husband, Wilbert, to the pier, her blue hair glowing in the artificial light. Bredow had been sailing as a steward with the United States Steel fleet since 1936, and Cecilia was accustomed to the early morning departures.

On the road from Rogers City, she was troubled by the reduced visibility but had no concerns for her husband. Since the *Bradley* disaster, she had grown to fear the violence of Great Lakes storms, but tonight Lake Huron was calm and the breeze was mild.

Pulling into the parking lot adjacent to the pier, she hunched over the steering wheel, squinting to see the ship through the fog. Kissing her on the cheek as she looked on, Bredow said, "Take care, sweetie. I'll see you in a few days." With that, he opened the door, stepped out toward the ship with his bag over his shoulder, and was soon enveloped by the swirling mist.

M/V *J. E. Upson*
STRAITS OF MACKINAC—
0325

Damaged and flooding, *J. E. Upson* limped through the fog to drop anchor in the relative safety of Old Mackinaw Point. A few hours earlier, the five-hundred-foot freighter was steaming from Chicago to Silver Bay, Canada, when she encountered dense fog in the Straits. With practically no visibility, *Upson* inched along through the channel. Ahead, Gray's Reef lighthouse, a narrow tower built upon a wide concrete base, loomed out of the darkened waters, its light and signal horn dampened and obscured by the fog.

Unable to see the lighthouse, *Upson*'s officers steered the vessel on a collision course. Suddenly, the beacon's brilliant beam pierced the shroud, blinding the bridge crew. By then, disaster was imminent. With a crunch, *Upson*'s bow smashed into the rocky station, crushing handrails, chipping cement, and jolting the three-man Coast Guard maintenance team from a sound sleep.

Startled to find their crow's nest rammed by a confused ship, the senior watchman placed an immediate call to Coast Guard group headquarters at Charlevoix to report the incident. Upon inspection, the team found no appreciable damage to the lighthouse, and the vessel, taking water in a forward compartment, was ordered to shore for a safety inspection at first light.

As *Upson's* master awaited the dawn, he supervised the damage control crew as they contained the flooding. Meanwhile, most of her crew went back to sleep as the tethered vessel swung slowly through the blinding mist.

PORT CALCITE, MICHIGAN— 0347

Kissing Elizabeth as she slept, Haske slipped out and climbed into his 1955 Oldsmobile. He was assigned the 0400 to 0800 deck watch and would be on duty when *Cedarville* cast off. At the pier, he recognized Don Lamp's distinctive International Scout, and if he was not mistaken, the car next to it looked like Charlie Cook's 1959 Rambler. "Is Charlie working again?" he wondered. "If he came back aboard as third mate," he mused, "Len will not be happy."

Disregarding the dew on the wet gangway, Haske made his way aboard just in time to assume the watch.

Less than a minute later, deckwatchman Ed Brewster and his wife pulled into the same gravel lot. At thirty-three, he had been sailing for nine years, and Jean was used to early-morning good-byes. Holding his boyish face and smiling into his blue-gray eyes, she kissed him as he climbed from the driver's seat. "Be careful out there," she said as he disappeared into the mist. "I will," she heard in casual reply.

M/V *Topdalsfjord* 0400

As the watch shifted aboard *Topdalsfjord,* Larsen briefed the bleary-eyed chief officer, Karl Fagerli, on weather conditions and nearby shipping traffic as Willy Knutson took the helm and Idar Hansen relieved a grateful Bjornoy from his frozen perch. Throughout the handoff, the ship's automatic foghorn blared away, its signal echoing and mimicking similar blasts from the vessels fore and aft of *Topdalsfjord* in the eastbound procession.

PORT CALCITE, MICHIGAN—
0440

Half an hour before sailing, Joppich arrived at the port. Unable to see his ship in the haze, he stopped in at the dock office to sign for the bills of lading that had been drafted late the previous evening. Taking a moment to review the documents, he found that his holds were burdened with over fifteen thousand tons of open hearth limestone, well beyond lawful capacity. Even so, the increased load would help to pad his bonus this year. Thanking the night clerk, he folded the bills and passed back out into the moist early-morning air.

On the pier, Joppich bypassed the boarding ladder and continued forward to check the draft marks on the hull. Also known as "Plimsoll marks," load line markings were devised to prevent overloading and to ensure sufficient reserve buoyancy for safe sailing.

Coast Guard regulations governing Great Lakes merchant vessels required bulk freighters to maintain at least ten and a half feet of freeboard, as measured from their load lines, but Bradley Fleet vessels were routinely loaded far beyond that limit. In fact, *Cedarville*'s load line was submerged by six and a half inches. "Yep," Joppich thought, "that extra thousand tons of rock makes a difference."

0501

Climbing aboard, the captain headed straight to the bridge, where he was met by First Mate Piechan. "Morning, Harry, how are we doing?" Joppich inquired as he sat in the pedestal-mounted captain's chair.

"Ready to go, Cap. All hands are aboard and watches are set. Engineering reports ready to get underway. The boom is secured, and we managed to close the hatch covers with a little extra cargo onboard."

"OK. I have the bills of lading, and it looks like we are ready to shove off. Let's take her out, Mr. Piechan."

The 604-foot SS *Cedarville*, owned by U.S. Steel.
Courtesy Historical Collections of the Great Lakes, Bowling Green State University.

The bulk carrier *Cedarville* operated out of Rogers City with a crew of thirty-five.
Courtesy Historical Collections of the Great Lakes, Bowling Green State University.

The *Cedarville* was loaded with about 15,000 tons of open hearth limestone when she left Port Calcite for Gary, Indiana on the morning of May 7, 1965.

The 423-foot Norwegian freighter *Topdalsfjord* would carry European goods to the United States and return to Norway with grain.

Arthur and Barbara Fuhrman on their wedding day, January 26, 1963. Art, a deck watchman, had recently transferred to the *Cedarville*.

Charles and Jean Cook at their 25th wedding anniversary, 1961. Charles rejoined the crew of the *Cedarville* the day before the collision.

Stanley and Elizabeth Haske after a Christmas meal, 1955. Stanley, a 19-year veteran of the Great Lakes, had planned to retire from shipping in June to spend more time with his family.
Courtesy National Archives and Records Administration, Great Lakes Region.

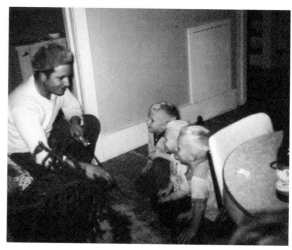

(Above and left) Stanley Haske spends time with his sons Greg, Kenny, and Allen, in 1956. Stanley and Elizabeth would have two more sons.
Courtesy National Archives and Records Administration, Great Lakes Region.

Donald Lamp with his son Stuart, January 1959. Don served as Chief Engineer on board the *Cedarville*.
Courtesy National Archives and Records Administration, Great Lakes Region.

At sea for long stretches, the crew valued their time at home with family. *Above,* Donald Lamp with Alice, his son Malcolm, and nieces Linda and Donna. *Right,* a successful catch ice fishing, November 1961.
Courtesy National Archives and Records Administration, Great Lakes Region.

Eugene "Casey" Jones
with his daughter Rosie,
Christmas 1963.
Courtesy National Archives
and Records Administration,
Great Lakes Region.

The bodies of two crewmen
are draped in flags as they
are transferred from the
Weissenburg to the Coast
Guard Cutter *Mackinaw*,
May 7, 1965.
News clipping from the *Cheboygan
Tribune* courtesy Len and Pat
Gabrysiak.

Survivors were rescued
from the cold water by the
Weissenburg and cared for
before transferring to the
cutter *Mackinaw*.
News clipping from the
Cheboygan Tribune courtesy
Len and Pat Gabrysiak.

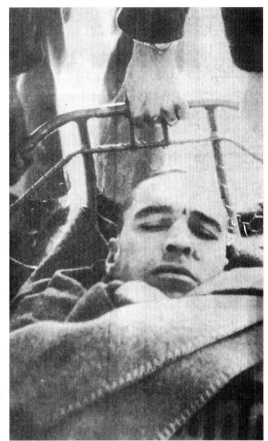

Leonard Gabrysiak is taken aboard the *Mackinaw* on a stretcher. He, with four others, would be hospitalized following the collision.
News clipping from the *Cheboygan Tribune* courtesy Len and Pat Gabrysiak.

Damage to the *Topdalsfjord*. There were no injuries to the crew of the *Topdalsfjord,* and the ship was able to continue on to Sault Ste. Marie for repairs.
Courtesy Historical Collections of the Great Lakes, Bowling Green State University.

Bow of the *Topdalsfjord* showing damage from the collision.
Courtesy Historical Collections of the Great Lakes, Bowling Green State University.

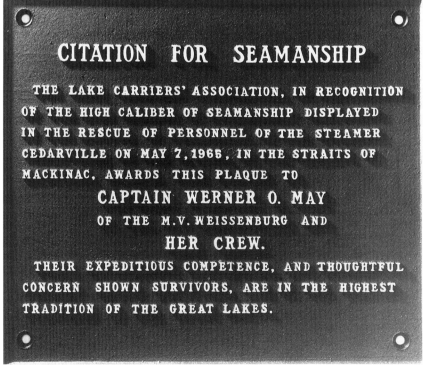

CITATION FOR SEAMANSHIP

THE LAKE CARRIERS' ASSOCIATION, IN RECOGNITION
OF THE HIGH CALIBER OF SEAMANSHIP DISPLAYED
IN THE RESCUE OF PERSONNEL OF THE STEAMER
CEDARVILLE ON MAY 7, 1965, IN THE STRAITS OF
MACKINAC, AWARDS THIS PLAQUE TO
CAPTAIN WERNER O. MAY
OF THE M.V. WEISSENBURG AND
HER CREW.
THEIR EXPEDITIOUS COMPETENCE, AND THOUGHTFUL
CONCERN SHOWN SURVIVORS, ARE IN THE HIGHEST
TRADITION OF THE GREAT LAKES.

Courtesy Historical Collections of the Great Lakes, Bowling Green State University.

"Aye, sir" was the response as Piechan switched the RCA radar set from standby to active and radioed Rygwelski on deck to single up and cast off all lines. That done, Piechan gave the order. "Bill, ahead slow."

Bill Asam advanced the engine order telegraph, and engineering soon responded. "Engine room answers ahead slow," he said.

"Very well. Take her out nice and easy."

Cedarville would not require tug assistance, as she would advance from her backed position straight into the channel. Nevertheless, *Dolomite* bobbed gently in the wide man-made harbor, standing by in case of emergency.

Just aft and starboard of the twenty-two-hundred horsepower engines, Don Lamp stood before the wall-like control panel and advanced the throttle control approximately one-third of its length. With the opening of the valves, steam rushed from the header into the chambers of the triple expansion reciprocating steam engines. The flood of steam introduced residual moisture that provided critical lubrication to the moving pistons and joints as, with a groan, the engines sprang to life.

The rotary power from the main engines translated to the wildly spinning shaft that exited the machine housing, traveled aft, and connected to the main reduction gear. The gear, in turn, converted and reduced the high-speed rotation with a corresponding increase in torque.

Exiting from beneath the securely bolted cast-iron cover, the main gear was linked, via coupling, to the propeller shaft. Suspended upon well-lubricated bearings, the twelve-inch shaft ran the length of lower engineering to become the focus of the converted energy. With the engines operating at less than one-third capacity, the shaft exited the hull at a watertight seal, turning the ship's four-bladed propeller once every three seconds.

Beneath the ship, the accumulation of limestone silt was churned to a milky consistency as the massive bronze blades swept clockwise, pushing the overloaded freighter from her berth.

Piechan stepped to the starboard bridge wing to watch the pier slip by. He shared the view with Ed Jungman, who was condemned to spend the next few hours battling the chill as topside lookout. He was old for a deckwatchman but had endured the cold with the Bradley Fleet for eight years to support his wife, Jennie, and their three teenaged children.

Leaning against the rail, Jungman mumbled calmly, "We're going to hit."

It took a moment to register Jungman's warning, and Piechan glanced aft just in time to see the old hull scrape against the pilings at the end of the pier. The hands who were securing their lines on the main deck chuckled and pointed over the side.

The squeal of wood against the metal hull was interminable, and the first mate cringed until, with the passing of the ship, the grating stopped. Turning, he shouted into the pilothouse, "Asam, mind your helm!"

An unconcerned "aye, sir" was his only response.

Cedarville soon cleared the harbor and turned north on its eleventh run of the season. Out of habit, Joppich reached for the radio handset and called in on channel 51. "WLC, *Cedarville* is underway," he said, before switching to channel 16 for a security call. "Steamer *Cedarville* departing Calcite Harbor. Any ships around, please answer." Hearing nothing but static, Joppich returned the microphone to its cradle.

"Let's make some time," he said to his first officer. "Ahead full."

Answering the captain, Haske acknowledged the command, as the propeller speed increased fourfold. Gradually accelerating to more than twelve knots, *Cedarville* sliced through the mist, her automatic fog signal blaring into the night.

0558

Four thousand yards abeam of Forty Mile Point, *Cedarville* was poised to enter the shipping lanes that would carry her through the narrow Straits of Mackinac. Dozing in his chair, Joppich was awakened with the position report. Standing, he crossed the bridge to check the radar.

Short for "radio detection and ranging," radar generates a directional radio wave that travels at the speed of light and, upon striking an object, is reflected back at the same velocity. At that instant,

Cedarville's transmitter, located just aft of the bridge, generated an electromagnetic pulse. A hollow steel waveguide attached to the transmitter carried the radiation aloft.

High atop the pilothouse, an RCA three-centimeter-band radar antenna scanned the horizon. As the rectangular waveguide reached the base of the rotating equipment, the microwave pulse routed upward to be transmitted through the antenna on a discrete compass bearing. As the focused pulse cut through the fog, it sped north-north-west above the water until, five miles distant, it encountered the wall-like hull of a Chicago-bound freighter. The vast majority of the microwave energy that painted the side of the ship was scattered, to be absorbed by the water and atmosphere. A tiny portion of the signal reflected directly back to the antenna and was received before the next pulse could be generated.

Following the same waveguide, the faint radar return was carried below to a receiving unit that amplified the back-scattered radiation, converting it to a low-frequency signal for visual display. This signal was routed via coaxial cable to the bridge, where it was processed by the radar repeater, appearing on the cathode ray tube as a glowing blip behind the green sweep of the antenna. This process repeated for other shore and lake contacts as the antenna completed its 360-degree circuit.

Joppich considered the eight-mile sweep, noting the outline of the passing shoreline and two ships several miles ahead. Glancing over his shoulder, he found Piechan resting his massive bulk over the chart table in the predawn twilight. "What's the recommended course?" he asked.

To promote safety of shipping, the Coast Guard had established shipping channels along the major trade routes and approaches of the Great Lakes. These were clearly delineated on the charts Piechan studied. Tracing the line that paralleled the coast from Forty Mile Point, his finger came to rest beneath the annotation.

"Coast Guard says three-zero-one true," Piechan replied, not looking up.

"Alright, let's make it three-zero-five and shave a few miles off of the trip."

"Aye, sir. Helm, come left to three-zero-five."

Asam was spinning the wheel before the order was given. "Coming left to three-zero-five, aye." The helmsman kept a steady eye on the compass before him as it turned slowly through three-four-zero, three-three-zero, three-two-zero, three-one-zero. Asam corrected the helm, and the compass slowed, stopping exactly at three-zero-five, four degrees north of the track designated by the Coast Guard. "Steady on three-zero-five."

Though Piechan had the conn, he allowed the captain to reply. "Very well," Joppich said as he returned to his swivel chair.

With that simple command, *Cedarville* joined the line of ships bound for the Straits, charging through the early morning fog at full speed.

ROGERS CITY, MICHIGAN—

Louella Jane Brege woke up two minutes early. The alarm clock ticking on her nightstand was poised to emit a clatter sufficient to wake the dead. Preempting the obnoxious alarm, she switched it off and rolled back over. Dick would be coming home today. He had missed her birthday on May 3. This was an error he would soon regret. She had listened to the company radio frequency for the past four days, hoping for a message, but none came. Dick would certainly have some explaining to do this afternoon, but she had too much to do this morning to worry about that now. It was time to get the boys up for school.

Relishing the warmth of the double mattress for just another moment, she finally gave in to her responsibilities, switched on the light, rolled out of bed, and started the day.

Approaches

LAKE HURON—
0700

As *Cedarville* approached the Straits of Mackinac from Forty Mile Point, she passed the vessels Joppich detected on radar and fell in behind the coal-bearing freighter *George M. Steinbrenner*. At twelve and a half knots, *Cedarville* would continue to gain on the slower *Steinbrenner* as the two swept through the Straits and neared the Mackinac Bridge.

West of the bridge, on a reciprocal heading, another line of ships would soon enter Lake Huron. Led by M/V *Benson Ford*, the convoy included the German tramp freighter *Weissenburg* and the Norwegian freighter *Topdalsfjord*, taking up the rear. *Topdalsfjord* had been overtaking *Weissenburg* and would soon pass to bear down upon *Benson Ford*.

As the sun rose above the thick fog layer, the ships steaming blind in the mist below were bound for a catastrophic meeting.

SS *Cedarville*—

The Great Lakes "rules of the road" required fog-bound vessels to slow to moderate speed, sound fog signals, set a fog watch, and otherwise navigate with caution. Though not defined, "moderate speed" was generally understood to be somewhat less than twelve and a half knots. Even so, speeding through fog was routine for *Cedarville*.

Resting at the corner of the chart table, the ship's log reflected that, despite limited visibility, the captain had long since ordered the engines to full and that the ship's speed remained unchanged as she passed one ship after another in the murky blindness. No matter. Just like every log before it, this record would be reviewed by Captain Parilla for speed of delivery, not prudence of operation. Over the years Bradley Fleet officers had been conditioned to disregard the dictates of good seamanship in favor of the company imperative: No slowing down!

ROGERS CITY, MICHIGAN—

With the flip of a switch, the glowing vacuum tubes in the ham radio came slowly to life. Soon the hum of the set filled the Brege basement, and Lou dialed in channel 51 as Bradley Fleet shipping traffic crackled through the speakers.

". . . understood *Munson*. Be careful through the Straits. The weatherman says it's not likely to let up today. Will report conditions to the office. WLC out."

Munson was upbound from Chicago! Satisfied that her husband would, in fact, be home today, she returned to the kitchen.

The boys had scarfed down their eggs and were nowhere to be seen. With a few minutes to kill, she refilled her coffee and opened the *Presque Isle Advance*.

Lou planned to take care of groceries this morning; skimming past the articles on politics and declining polio rates, she scanned for IGA specials. Steak, thirty-nine cents a pound; eggs, three dozen for a dollar; chicken, fifty-five cents a pound. She ripped the ad from the paper, folded it neatly, and tucked it away in her purse on the floor.

Continuing through the newspaper, she digested the "News of Interest to Women," which summarized local births, wedding announcements, and society events. "News of Local Men Serving in the Armed Forces" featured prominently on the next page. Several Presque Isle County boys had recently been sent to Vietnam. Wondering where in the world that was, she looked at her watch.

"Boys, time to go to school," she called as she gathered her purse and car keys and headed for the door.

SS *Cedarville*—
0745

Eugene Jones, Hughie Wingo, and Reiny Radke filed into engineering from the galley to relieve the midwatch. In the lead, Jones was the old man of the watch. At fifty-nine years of age, the stokerman bore the scars of a life of hard work. Nicks and cuts marked his arms from years of driving timber horses as a teen. His hands were gashed from his work as a line worker at the newly opened Port Calcite plant. A boiler explosion aboard *B. H. Taylor* in 1940 sent him to the hospital for a month with severe burns to his neck and chest, and his deeply lined face and shock of gray hair spoke of decades of service on the lakes. But through it all, his wife, Marion, was there to tend his wounds and nurse him back to health. Somehow, they had even found time to raise five children.

Oiler Hughie Wingo also had several kids, but Reinhold Radke had them all beat. He and his wife, Rita, had been producing babies steadily for twenty years. Their odyssey began as an affair between a young seaman and the wife of a soldier serving in Europe during World War II. When she became pregnant, she obtained a long-distance divorce and settled down with the Bradley Fleet sailor. Over the years, Reiny and Rita had given birth to Rena, Ruth, Reinhold Jr., Richard, Roslyn, Rodney, and Rhonda; Radke was never quite sure when his wife would greet him at the door with more "good news."

As Third Assistant Engineer Radke assumed the watch from Bey, a long and a short ring clattered from the chadburn. The signal indicated the passage of a key navigational point, and Radke would call forward for more information before recording the event in the engineering log. The record would be a tattered collection of grimy pages by the time it was full of entries. Opening the log, Radke dismissed Bey with a wave of his hand and turned to call the pilothouse.

Forward, the bridge team was also turning over. Gabrysiak arrived on deck to find Charlie Cook getting the rundown from Harry

Piechan. Grumbling, he tapped Bill Asam on the shoulder. "Morning, Bill. Tell me where we are."

"Hi, Len. Sorry to hear about Cook being back aboard," he whispered. "Tough break."

Gabrysiak only nodded.

"OK. We are about to go into the Straits. Cordwood Point is coming up on the left, and I just rang engineering."

Gabrysiak strained through the fog to see the green light of the channel marker flash once every four seconds off of the port bow. "Yep, that's Cordwood Point," he said, recognizing the familiar sequence. "Are we on course?"

"Yeah. It's still three-zero-five. We should round the marker in a minute or two. That's about it."

"Alright, Bill. Go get some chow. It's not too bad this morning."

"Thanks. I'll see you later. Lenny has the helm," he said loudly as he walked from the bridge. Cook and Piechan both acknowledged the statement and went back to their conference.

Piechan had finished briefing Cook on the position, course, and speed of all known vessels in the vicinity as the captain continued to brood, peering silently into the gray morning fog. On the port bridge wing, Ivan Trafelet relieved Jungman from the cold, wet vigil, and together the off-going bridge team made their way down and aft to the galley for a good solid breakfast.

Cook was considering Joppich, still reposed in his chair, when the phone rang from engineering. He quickly relayed the ship's position to Radke before hanging up. Eyeing the radar, he awaited the passage of the buoy to swing around into the channel that led to the Mackinac Bridge.

At the helm, Gabrysiak held the compass steady at three-zero-five. With several years' experience, he knew that the *Cedarville* wheel always required two or three spokes of correction due to engine pull. Despite the inherent drift, the seasoned helmsman had no trouble keeping the massive vessel on track.

ROGERS CITY, MICHIGAN—

The Haske family was running late. School started in just a few minutes, and Betty was losing her patience. Sitting in the crowded car, she honked the horn as little Steven tried to climb over the seat. A moment later, Greg bounded down the front steps. He had hidden the little white card and was ready for school.

Pat Gabrysiak tugged at the sheets as the fog-muted light filtered through the curtain. She had a lot to do this morning, but Len would be away for four days. "That's plenty of time," she reasoned, pulling a pillow over her head to block the light.

SS *Cedarville*—
0748

Cedarville was out of the channel by a thousand yards. This was not Len's fault. The course he steered was straight and true. Rather, because the self-unloader had been steaming four degrees north of the designated shipping lane for two hours, she was well north of the channel when Cordwood Point Buoy rolled by.

Coming into the turn, Joppich was concerned. The Poe Reef shallows loomed ahead, and Joppich wanted to steer well clear. "Hey, Charlie, bring us wide around the reef."

Cook took a look at the chart. The Coast Guard–recommended course was two-seven-zero. Taking his bearings from the Poe Reef Light radio beacon and a shoreside radar reflector, Cook confirmed the ship's position on the blue and tan chart, charted a wider course through the Straits, and gave the order.

"Helm, left standard rudder. Come left to two-six-one."

"Aye, sir," Gabrysiak replied, "coming left to two-six-one."

The new third mate reached overhead and keyed the radio. Placing a security call on channels 16 and 51, he announced the course change. Steaming eight miles ahead at ten knots, *Steinbrenner* heard the call and responded. No other ships were in the immediate area.

Behind the propeller, the heavy rudder swung left, routing the water flow to port and kicking *Cedarville*'s stern in the opposite direction. With her fantail swinging to starboard, *Cedarville* gently turned into the Straits of Mackinac.

0759

Sloping gently upward toward the narrows, the gravel bottom above which *Cedarville* navigated shallowed. As the ship motored on, it relentlessly pushed aside a volume of water equal to its own weight. Trapped in the shallows, the displaced water increased pressure on the hull and propeller minutely, which in turn slowed the propeller slightly.

Making his rounds on the maneuvering platform, Radke noted the decrease from eighty-four to eighty-three revolutions per minute. He raised his clipboard and penciled in the changes on the attached scratch sheet. At the end of his watch, he would transfer the observation, along with any speed changes ordered from the bridge, to the bell book.

Unconcerned with the fluctuation, Radke continued his rounds.

PORT CALCITE, MICHIGAN—
0801

Joe Hassett was late for his eight-hour shift. Still rehearsing for his part in *Red Mill,* he fumbled with the spring-loaded door, balancing a 1948 Wilcox-Gay Recordio seven-and-a-half-inch tape recorder he intended to use for rehearsal during slack periods. With nothing said, he took his position before the WLC control panel and scanned the log.

Bradley Fleet vessels were required to check in each day at 0800 and 1900 to report location and local weather conditions. *Calcite II* and *Munson* had already called in, reporting heavy fog throughout the western Great Lakes.

As he reviewed the call sheets, channel 51 crackled to life.

"WLC, this is *Cedarville* with the 0800 position report, over."

Because the call was anticipated, the speaker had been left plugged in. "Go ahead, *Cedarville,*" Hassett replied.

"WLC, we are passing Cordwood Point at the mouth of the Straits as we speak. We are making about twelve knots and ought to pass the bridge by ten. It's real foggy out here, over."

"Roger that. *Munson* reports fog in Lake Michigan, too. Looks like it might be with you for a while. Take care. WLC out."

SS *Cedarville*—

"*Cedarville* out," Cook said, replacing the handset. His eyes met the captain's. They had just been promised zero visibility all the way to Chicago. Despite the danger, Cook resigned himself to the fact that Joppich would steam the ship at full speed the whole way. No anchoring and no slowing down. That was the company policy.

M/V *Topdalsfjord*—

The automatic fog signal echoed across the water once every two minutes as *Topdalsfjord* cleared Gray's Reef Passage behind the German freighter she was overtaking. Karl Fagerli had returned from a quick breakfast to assist with radar navigation.

Briefly switching the unit to the maximum setting of forty-eight nautical miles, Fagerli allowed the relentless sweep to paint the convergence of the Upper and Lower Peninsulas, with the Mackinac Bridge reflecting a distinct line where it spanned the channel. Reducing the range setting to twenty-four miles, he took bearings and ranges to St. Helena Island to port and Waugoshance Point to starboard. With the bearings to these known points, he could triangulate the ship's position to within one hundred yards. In this manner, *Topdalsfjord* could walk right up the channel, her position never in doubt.

SS *Cedarville*—
0812

As Bey, Piechan, Asam, and Friedhoff finished their breakfast overhead, Walter Tulgetske was making his rounds through the depths of engineering. First Assistant Engineer Tulgetske was responsible for overall maintenance, and on a ship this size there was always repair work to be done.

This morning he was accompanied by Jim Lietzow, a new wiper who had just signed aboard. Retrieving his maintenance and repair log from Lamp's desk, Tulgetske called Lietzow to the boilers to show him how to blow the flues. In coal-fired boilers, the burning fuel deposits layer upon layer of soot on the small water tubes, insulating and corroding the pipes. Frequent cleaning is necessary to ensure boiler efficiency and safe operation.

With Lietzow in tow, Tulgetske opened the steam valve that led directly to the boiler. High-pressure steam blasted from perforated tubing, scalding the caked-on soot from the surrounding pipes. With a tremendous hiss, the particulate-laden saturated steam rushed upward through the stack, raining a shower of soot over the passing ship, to drift down into her churning wake.

With that done, Tulgetske closed the valve and put his new assistant to work chipping and painting in lower engineering before turning to his own tasks. A creature of habit, Tulgetske returned to the fantail to start his daily machinery check. Working his way down, he passed through the fantail, steerage spaces, and main engineering. Staying out of the stoker's way, he stopped to speak briefly with Radke before continuing his inspection. In the sweltering lower engine room Lietzow was hard at work chipping a stubborn rust spot, and Hughie Wingo was sweating profusely as he tended the boiler. Heading forward around the firebox, Tulgetske crawled through the scuttle into the tunnel. Separated from the blaze of the furnace by a watertight bulkhead, the tunnel was sixty degrees cooler, and the temperature difference made him shiver.

From the tunnel, Tulgetske would climb its gentle rise, checking that each of the cargo traps was chocked and that the conveyor and switchboard rooms were in good order. He would then continue topside and inspect the boom before returning to engineering. But for the moment, he enjoyed the cool dark at the bottom of the ship as he took time to catch his breath.

On the bridge, the captain was tracking the approach of Poe Reef Light, half a mile to starboard. He wanted to make up some time. Crossing the pilothouse, Joppich studied the flattened chart spread before him. Entitled "De Tour Passage to Waugoshance Point," the well-penciled chart covered the 1,750 square miles of land and water that composed the Straits and its approaches. Prominently crossing the chart lengthwise, the four-mile-wide channel opened at either end to connect Lake Huron and Lake Michigan. Joppich traced the ship's path through the Straits and beyond for the shortest route. The designated shipping lane was oriented on a compass heading of two-eight-five, true. The captain intended to take a shorter path to the bridge.

Seeing that his ship had cleared the reef, it was time to cut some corners. "Len, bring her right to two-eight-one."

With the command, Charlie Cook broadcast another security call. As *Cedarville*'s bow shifted to starboard, the freighter crossed out of the shipping lane on a more direct course to the bridge.

ROGERS CITY, MICHIGAN—

With a groan, Stokerman Jones's daughter, Gena, plopped down for breakfast. In her third trimester, she didn't have much room left for food. But she had to eat something, or so her doctor said. Fine. She could handle Cheerios for just a few more months.

M/V *Topdalsfjord*—
0818

Twenty miles west of the Mackinac Bridge, Karl Fagerli took another radar fix. White Shoal Light, more than three miles distant, was approaching from dead ahead. Fagerli looked up through the window, seeing nothing but the slate gray blanket that enveloped the ship.

Keeping just to the north of Lake Survey track number 093, Conning Officer Gronstol brought the vessel right by three degrees to bear directly up to the Mackinac Bridge.

Forty miles apart, *Topdalsfjord* and *Cedarville* were closing at a combined speed of twenty-three knots.

SS *Cedarville*—

Harry Bey and Bill Friedhoff left the galley pleasantly full. Beyond the fantail, the cottony mist swirled in the huge ship's wake. Retiring from a long night's watch, Friedhoff followed Bey into the engineer's berth. Fishing his keys from his pocket, Bey stopped at his door as Friedhoff continued on. "See you on watch," he said.

"Yeah, g'night," Friedhoff answered without turning.

Inside his room, Bey stripped to his skivvies. He considered taking a shower but decided to wait until he got up. Reclining on his bunk, he switched on the overhead reading lamp, opened his latest novel, and drifted to sleep.

M/V *George M. Steinbrenner*—
0833

Owned by Kinsman Transit Company, the bulk freighter *George M. Steinbrenner* was upbound for Green Bay with a load of coal. Piercing the fog, *Steinbrenner*'s radar painted a vivid return from an eastbound vessel four thousand yards ahead. Having tracked the oncoming vessel for several minutes, Captain Gilbert checked that his guard frequency was channel 16 and keyed the transmitter. "Eastbound vessel south of Zela Shoal in the Straits of Mackinac, this is the freighter *George M. Steinbrenner,* westbound in the South Channel below Bois Blanc Island. Come in, over."

Peering fruitlessly forward, Gilbert waited. At fifty-two, he had sailed the lakes as a licensed officer for almost three decades. A twelve-year captain, Gilbert was intimately familiar with the Straits of Mackinac in all weather conditions but remained cautious despite his experience.

Under the inland rules of the road, vessels meeting in a narrow channel were required to reach an agreement by radio or signal horn as to passing arrangements. In the event of failure to communicate, both ships were to sound a five-blast emergency signal and come to a halt. However, prompt radio contact in this case would ensure a smooth passage.

The reply came quickly. "*Steinbrenner,* this is *Benson Ford,* eastbound at Zela Shoal. How do you want to pass?"

"*Benson Ford,* I'll stay to the north for a port-to-port passage."

"OK, *Steinbrenner,* I'll take the south side of the channel. Have a good one. *Benson Ford* out."

Five hundred yards distant, deckhands on both vessels heard the engines and fog signals of the other as they passed unseen in the fog.

SS *Cedarville*—
0847

Tracing *Steinbrenner*'s wake, *Cedarville* rounded the Cheboygan Bell Buoy close aboard to port and corrected her course to three-zero-two as she too passed *Benson Ford*. A few minutes later, realizing that he had forgotten to record the recent course change, Cook rifled through the chart table for the ship's log. Finding it, he flipped through the sparsely annotated pages until he came to the last entry. Clicking his ball point pen, he made the simple entry "0842 C/C 302, Cheboygan Bell Buoy. Spd 11.7. Wx: Fog." Completing the entry, he returned the volume to the chart table, where it would remain untouched for the rest of the watch.

PORT CALCITE, MICHIGAN—

"Could you get me a cup of coffee?" Buehrens called to his secretary as he settled in behind his desk. "Cream and sugar," he added unnecessarily. Buehrens was "large and in charge"—at least until Parilla got back. "OK, what do we have today?" he wondered under his breath. Quickly scanning his fleet's schedule, he was pleased. "*Cedarville* left before sunrise. *Munson* won't be back until late this afternoon. The boss is away. Looks like a quiet day," he mused, sipping delicately at the steaming cup of coffee.

M/V *Topdalsfjord*—
0850

Pushing east, *Topdalsfjord* was overtaking the German freighter. Though *Weissenburg* was slowed by the fog, *Topdalsfjord* had maintained her speed. During the course of the morning, the ships had been in frequent contact, and the bridge officers had become vaguely familiar. The ships were passing the western edge of St. Helena Island when Rasmus Hoagland made his move. The Norwegian skipper increased the gain on his receiver, cleared his throat, and called his counterpart.

"*Weissenburg, Weissenburg,* this is *Topdalsfjord.* We are one thousand yards astern and gaining. Request clearance to pass to your starboard."

M/V *Weissenburg*—

Having departed Muskegon, Michigan, the day before, *Weissenburg* was steaming eastward to wrap up her fifty-sixth transatlantic voyage. Hailing from Hamburg, the German crew would stop in Cleveland before escaping the Great Lakes and their restrictive, fog-shrouded shipping lanes. Capable of fourteen knots at sea, the twelve-year-old vessel had slowed to little more than nine knots for safety.

Chief Officer Hans Kamberg, Third Officer Walter Voight, and Helmsman Peter Lochman manned the bridge under the watchful eye of Captain Werner Otto May. Captain May had earlier set a fog watch, which was relieved forward by lookout Michael Huss. Perched on the bow, Huss reported the periodic wail of *Topdalsfjord*'s fog signal aft but was blinded by the swirling mist.

Cadet Rolf Glanert, an apprentice officer in training under Kamberg, was serving the captain tea when the call came through. May checked the radar picture before responding. *Weissenburg* was closing on the Mackinac Bridge, but with no other ships in the area, May saw no danger, provided that the passing was executed promptly. Responding, the captain agreed to a starboard passage but advised a speedy maneuver due to the proximity of the bridge.

As the stand-on vessel, *Weissenburg* held her course and speed as *Topdalsfjord* accelerated to thirteen knots, bore off to the right, and slipped past the slower German ship.

Despite the closing range of the two freighters, Huss saw no more than a fleeting shadow cast by the passing Norwegian vessel.

M/V *Steinbrenner*—
0903

Plotting a course through the bridge on radar, Captain Gilbert watched as the two contacts exchanged position on the other side. Glancing up, he strained to find the approaching bridge spanning the channel. Seeing nothing in the obscuring fog, he returned to the radar screen as he reached for the radio.

"Calling eastbound vessel approaching Mackinac Bridge, this is *Steinbrenner*. Come in." No response.

Sounding a single blast to propose a port-to-port passage, he rebroadcast his query as the horn signal echoed between the spans unanswered. Two more times the attempt was made, and twice more silence followed. Finally, *Steinbrenner*'s radio crackled to life. It was *Benson Ford*, whom Gilbert had passed moments before.

"Captain, please be advised that the eastbound ship is the Norwegian vessel *Topdalsfjord*. She has been following me for hours and apparently just passed a German freighter who wasn't going fast enough. Be careful. Her communications have been sporadic."

"Thank you," Gilbert replied before trying again. "Norwegian vessel *Topdalsfjord* eastbound at the bridge, please come in." Again and again, no response.

United States Steel Headquarters
PITTSBURGH, PENNSYLVANIA—

Parilla was shown to a conference room in the headquarters building adjacent to Admiral Khoury's office. A fine hardwood table occupied the length of the room opposite a plate-glass window with an expansive view of the city of Pittsburgh. Facing east, the room was flooded with sunlight, and Parilla found the glare painful. Sitting at the head of the table, Charles Khoury listened as his subordinates reported on their areas of responsibility.

Taking a seat at the far end of the table, Parilla scanned the room, recognizing the faces of several in attendance. Next to Khoury, Vice President Bob Lucas sipped his coffee. Opposite Lucas, a fellow named Leubke and his assistants from the engineering division were flipping through folders containing a status report provided by the Isthmian Line.

Turning his attention to Parilla, Admiral Khoury welcomed him sarcastically to the meeting. He had not yet seen Joe's report and asked that he grace them with its presentation.

Ignoring the barbs, Parilla calmly opened his briefcase. "Of course, Admiral," he said as he passed copies of the Bradley Fleet operational and maintenance summary around the table.

Khoury opened his copy, reclined, and read in silence as Parilla considered the yellow-tinged blanket of industrial pollution resting over the city.

Admiral Khoury received monthly reports from Parilla, and the contents of the material he now read were of no surprise. Reading on, he turned to a table that delineated the vessels of the fleet, the number of runs made, and the corresponding net tonnage of limestone cargo hauled to date. The vice president of lake shipping studied the list with approval. Deliveries were up, and downtime was kept to a minimum. He did not dwell on the implications.

Admiral Khoury was an experienced seaman. Well aware of the distances between Port Calcite and U.S. Steel facilities around the foggy and storm-swept Great Lakes, Khoury had to know that impressive frequency of calcite deliveries could not be maintained at moderate speeds. Despite the fact that frequently adverse weather conditions often called for more prudent seamanship, it was obvious from the record that Parilla's ships did not slow for any reason.

Concluding that the pressure he had focused on Parilla earlier in the year had paid off, he licked his index finger and turned the page.

M/V *Steinbrenner*—
0920

In the blinding fog, the north tower, looming overhead, was completely obscured. Gilbert had been calling *Topdalsfjord* fruitlessly for several minutes. Concluding that his ship might be in danger, he opted to err on the side of caution. Gilbert would give the oncoming vessel a wide berth to avoid collision. "Helm, all stop. Right standard rudder. Let's take her out of the channel to let this guy pass."

Almost seven miles ahead of *Cedarville, Steinbrenner* slowed and drifted north out of the lane of traffic.

M/V *Topdalsfjord*—
0927

As the vessel passed beneath the bridge, Aage Bergkvist heard footsteps on the metal decking. Hoping for a relief, he found that he was being joined by Stale Gule, who had been sent forward as an additional bow lookout. Without warning, *Topdalsfjord*'s fog signal blew, and Gule jumped. "Get used to it," Bergkvist chuckled as he turned to survey the hundred-foot horizon. Overhead, the rumble and whine of passing engines and car tires echoed down to the vessel below.

For several minutes Bergkvist had been following the periodic blast of another ship's fog horn just on the other side of the bridge. He had reported the signal on the pilothouse loudspeaker and was told that the ship was on radar and instructed to keep an eye out for it. Suddenly, a shrieking blast pierced the fog to port. Just then, the fog cleared to two hundred feet. At the edge of the clearing, *Steinbrenner* sat motionless in the water as *Topdalsfjord* clipped swiftly by. Gule nearly jumped out of his skin. Keying the pilothouse monitor, an excited Bergkvist reported the contact much too loudly. Calming his lookout, Hoagland responded on the deck speaker, "Thank you, Mr. Bergkvist. We have the contact. Good job."

As quickly as it had emerged, *Steinbrenner* was wrapped in the ever-changing shroud and disappeared from view.

SS *Cedarville*—

Four miles to the east, Cook was tracking the oncoming traffic, with Trafelet occasionally calling in from the port wing with word of fog signals in every direction. Following *Steinbrenner, Cedarville* was closing on two unidentified eastbound vessels. Despite repeated radio calls, Cook had yet to make contact with either one.

ROGERS CITY, MICHIGAN—

Lou Brege stumbled into the kitchen with a bag of groceries in each arm. "Why did the stockman have to bag them so heavy?" she wondered. Resting the load on the counter, she closed the front door and returned to put away her purchases. Eggs, milk, bread, flour. With the overcast, she wouldn't be doing laundry. Better leave these out for baking, she decided.

Lou always spent more than she intended to at the grocery, and this day was no exception. Well, at least she could put on a big dinner this evening. After all, maybe Dick hadn't forgotten her birthday. Maybe he was planning a surprise. As she finished the groceries and took out her pans and rolling pin, Bradley Fleet radio traffic drifted up from the basement.

M/V *Topdalsfjord*—
0935

As *Topdalsfjord* left *Steinbrenner* behind, her destination lay northeast beyond the Sault Ste. Marie. The most direct course was up past Round Island into the North Channel. Cruising above Round, Mackinac, and Bois Blanc Islands, the restrictive passage would have ensured a much faster passage to Lake Superior. Nevertheless, opting for safety, Captain Hoagland ordered a course change to take his ship down the much wider South Channel. With *Topdalsfjord*'s radar set at only one and a half miles, Hoagland turned the ship to match the recommended course for the southern passage.

Second Officer Gronstol placed security calls on channels 16 and 51, with no reply. Though he thought nothing of the silence, Fagerli was becoming increasingly concerned. As the one-and-a-half-mile radar sweep completed the eastern portion of its circuit, a blip appeared. With the next sweep, it was obvious that the contact was closing fast.

At the bow, Bergkvist and Gule were getting confused. Shaken by the abrupt appearance of an American bulk carrier freighter within spitting distance, they were quickly losing the big picture. Signals came, seemingly, from every direction. Yet none could be placed with certainty. Finding the task impossible, the watchmen shrugged at each other in the dim morning light as *Topdalsfjord*'s whistle sounded overhead.

SS *Cedarville*—

Gabrysiak glanced from the compass as the port hatch opened. Apparently nervous, Trafalet was leaning half inside the opening. "Captain, I'm hearing fog signals dead ahead. Just thought you'd like to know."

"Thanks," Joppich said as he reached for the radio. "We've been tracking him."

Watching to see that Trafelet returned to his post, he waited before transmitting. "Eastbound vessel in the vicinity of Mackinac Bridge, this is *Cedarville*, come in."

Weissenburg responded. "*Cedarville*, this is *Weissenburg*," the German voice crackled. "I intend to take the South Channel and propose a port-to-port passage."

"Very well," Joppich responded. "Port to port. We'll see you in a few minutes."

Sensing a misunderstanding, Captain May added, "*Cedarville*, please be advised that we are preceded by another vessel, a Norwegian freighter. She should be bearing down on you in short order."

Shifting to look at the radar screen, there were indeed two vessels approaching his. "Thanks, *Weissenburg*. Norwegian vessel eastbound in the South Channel, please respond." He repeated the call. After a few seconds of silence, Captain Gilbert's familiar voice broke through.

"*Cedarville*, this is *Steinbrenner*. The ship you are approaching is the *Topdalsfjord*. She nearly ran us down a few minutes ago. Be careful."

"Did you talk to her?"

"Negative. She wouldn't answer me either. *Weissenburg* filled us in."

"Well, if foreign vessels used pilots who knew the Great Lakes rules, there would be less trouble," Joppich quipped.

"You got that right. Just be very careful."

"Roger that. Thanks for the heads up. *Cedarville* out." Next he turned to his third mate. "Keep an eye on that guy, Charlie."

Without moving from the scope, Cook muttered his agreement.

With the ship still steaming at full speed, Joppich strode back across the pilothouse. "I think we will come right and get out of her way."

"Can't do that, Cap," Cook answered. "Majors Shoal is right off of our starboard beam. If we leave the channel, we could have our bottom ripped out."

"Yeah, well, I need to give this Norwegian some room. Lenny, come right to three-two-five and bring her down to half speed."

Making the changes, Gabrysiak glanced at the radar. The new course would take *Cedarville* just north of the channel, but the Norwegian was still closing.

Assuming the other ship had no radio, Joppich sounded a single blast to propose a port passage, repeating with no response. "OK, Len. This guy is bothering me. Let's take some more speed off. Ahead slow."

"Ahead slow, aye," Gabrysiak said as he entered the change in the engine order telegraph. The clang of the response soon echoed through the pilothouse, and the ship began to slow.

The general rules of pilotage require a captain who is unsure of the intentions of an oncoming vessel to sound several short and rapid blasts of his ship's whistle, reduce speed to bare steerageway, and, if necessary, stop and reverse course. Though concerned about the oncoming freighter, Joppich failed to do either. He did not sound the emergency signal or halt the progress of his massively overburdened bulk carrier. Rather, he altered course slightly, reduced speed to six knots, and forged ahead.

On the port side, the closing vessel's fog signal was getting louder and stronger as Trafelet searched in vain for the source. A few steps away, Charlie Cook tracked the contact on radar. "Captain, this guy's angle of approach seems to be widening out, but you might want to come right a little more."

The captain glanced at the radar scope. The return of the oncoming ship was on *Cedarville*'s port bow. "Looks alright to me. We are going to pass to port."

Together, Cook and Joppich made a critical mistake. Lying unused at the bottom of a chart table drawer was a tablet of maneuvering boards, provided to assist in the determination of courses and speeds of other vessels from radar returns. Had either officer plotted the course of the oncoming vessel, *Cedarville* would not have pushed on. *Cedarville* and *Topdalsfjord* were bound for a collision.

M/V *Topdalsfjord*—
0940

Captain Hoagland and Chief Officer Fagerli watched as the other vessel's relative bearing shifted slowly right into their path. With the other ship only half a mile distant, her erratic captain was making Hoagland nervous. "Maintain course and bring her down to dead slow," he ordered.

"Dead slow, aye," Helmsman Oskarsen replied. Beneath the ship, the propeller wound down to forty rotations per minute, but the momentum of the massive freighter pushed her forward through the mist.

M/V *Weissenburg*—

Captain May could not believe his eyes. On the scope before him, the approaching radar contacts merged into one. *Was machts du?* he thought in his native language. *What are you doing?*

SS *Cedarville*—

The tension on the bridge was mounting. This situation was getting out of hand. As Joppich urgently called out to *Topdalsfjord* on the radio, Gabrysiak glanced down at the radar to find the ship's widening return closing on his own.

On the bridge wing, *Topdalsfjord*'s fog signals grew louder and stronger.

Having completed his daily walk-through, Walter Tulgetske was busy stowing supplies on the fantail deck. Although he had grown accustomed to the periodic squeal of *Cedarville*'s fog horn, he was startled to hear another vessel close to port as he stepped through a watertight hatch. Must be a narrow channel, he thought as he went back to work.

M/V *Topdalsfjord*—
0943

"The contact is too close to get an accurate bearing," Fagerli reported, the color draining from his face. Before the captain could respond, Bergkvist, clearly excited, shouted another contact report over the loudspeaker.

"All stop," Hoagland immediately ordered.

The bridge crew were silent as the vessel drifted on. Outside, visibility improved to six hundred feet as the approaching vessel's whistle wailed into the fog.

SS *Cedarville*—

Beneath the pilothouse, Ron Piechan was loading the washer. During the shipping season he was never at home long enough to bother taking his laundry ashore. Unceremoniously dumping in his unsorted clothes, he was pouring an unmeasured dose of detergent when he glanced at the porthole. As if from a dream, the towering bow of an oncoming vessel pierced the fog. Sensing that a collision was imminent, Piechan dropped the detergent and ran for the safety of the weather decks.

Aft, Dave Erickson was busy in the galley. With his head in the potato locker, he was gathering an armful for the coming lunch and dinner. Erickson had long ago discovered that boiled potatoes could be sliced, diced, fried, mashed, and otherwise manipulated into nearly any side dish he wished to make. Maybe he would make au gratin tonight, he thought, as he stood, lifting the basket. Washing dishes at the port side sink, fellow porter Jerry Kierzek suddenly yelled, "Hey, Dave, come and look at this." Erickson rushed to one of the galley portholes. The messmen were stunned to see a freighter emerging from the mist and bearing down on their vessel.

On the port bridge wing, Trafelet saw it too. Less than six hundred feet away, *Topdalsfjord*'s bow was angled directly toward *Cedarville.* She continued to close as *Cedarville* swept forward. Pointing, he shouted, "There it is." Captain Joppich said nothing but, jumping to his feet, yanked the whistle cord with all of his might. Overhead, *Cedarville*'s horn screamed as the ships collided.

11

Collision

May 7, 1965
M/V *Topdalsfjord*—
0945

All the way forward, Gule and Bergkvist leaned over the forepeak to find the source of the whistle blast. Suddenly the other ship loomed out of the fog less than three hundred feet away. White water churned at the other vessel's bow as she passed from right to left across *Topdalsfjord*'s track. Bergkvist shouted into his microphone, "Contact crossing dead ahead. Speed six to eight knots."

Looking up from the cluttered radar scope, Fagerli reached for the bridge handset. "Get the hell off the foc's'le," he screamed, as the two men fled their post.

A few meters aft, the deck crew was working in an open hatch. "Come on," Gule ordered. "We're going to hit."

Standing beside the wheelhouse door on the starboard bridge wing, Captain Hoagland peered beyond the tangle of booms and rigging suspended above *Topdalsfjord*'s deck as he watched the collision unfold. Turning to face the helm, he shouted, "Hard astern!"

Assistant Engineer Roald Strand was unaware of the events unfolding above. He was enjoying an easy watch as his ship crept through the foggy straits when the engine order telegraph unexpectedly sounded twice. Emergency full astern! Cursing as he jumped into action, Strand threw the gear into reverse and cranked the throttle as the ship's diesel engines roared.

Beneath the ship, the propeller backed without effect at more than a hundred revolutions per minute as the *Topdalsfjord*'s momentum carried her forward.

Powerless to avert the catastrophe, Captain Hoagland saw *Topdalsfjord*'s prop wash advance up her starboard side. "Too little, too late," he thought as the passing ship drew nearer.

SS *Cedarville*—

Still holding the whistle cord, time stood still for Joppich. As the steam whistle overhead continued to shriek, Charlie Cook implored the captain, "We're going to hit!" Outside, Trafelet stood silent, pointing to the oncoming vessel, forty-five degrees off the port bow.

Waking from his trance, Joppich thought to push ahead and kick his stern over to turn his bow away from the collision. "Ahead full. Hard right rudder."

As he swung the wheel, Gabrysiak kept an eye on the Norwegian freighter, emerging from the fog bank ahead.

All the way aft, a variable-stroke hydraulic pump extended the port piston, rotating the rudder to starboard. Increased water flow over the starboard surface of the rudder exerted a force in the opposite direction, pushing *Cedarville*'s stern toward *Topdalsfjord*. Though her bow angled away, the laws of physics demanded that she draw nearer still.

Most ships "slide" into turns. Once a course change is given and the rudder shifted, a vessel underway will continue on its original heading as the ship crabs sideways into the turn. Given enough power, the ship will eventually straighten up on the new bearing, having advanced a considerable distance in the original direction of travel. Unfortunately, as *Cedarville* continued to advance toward

Topdalsfjord, her bow swung to the right, presenting a wider target to the Norwegian freighter.

Steaming at right angles sixty-six hundred feet from the south tower of the Mackinac Bridge, *Cedarville* and *Topdalsfjord* collided.

Lifted by a swell, *Topdalsfjord*'s elevated bow fell on *Cedarville*'s deck like a cleaver. Just aft of the number seven port side hatch, the sharply angled metal groaned as it rent downward, easily parting the brittle hull below. Continuing well past the waterline, *Topdalsfjord* pierced the number two cargo hold, grinding metal and stone as it sliced through to the number four ballast tank. White pebbles trickled out and fluttered to the lake bed as the icy lake rushed in to fill the four-foot breach.

Embedded in the newly created void, *Topdalsfjord* was not undamaged. Though *Cedarville*'s brittle plating gave easily, the beams and structural members contained therein managed to pierce *Topdalsfjord*'s ice-reinforced bow. Her once crisp stem was mangled eleven feet aft. Piled with the vestiges of *Cedarville*'s limestone cargo, several of *Topdalsfjord*'s forward compartments flooded, but as the collision bulkhead was not breached, the water was confined to the forepeak.

SS *Cedarville*—

Ron Piechan arrived topside in time to see *Topdalsfjord*'s angled bow ride up and over *Cedarville*'s flat cargo deck near the one hundredth frame. With the crunch of metal, the deck shook lightly beneath his feet. The fog was so thick that he could not see *Cedarville*'s stern, five hundred feet aft. Stunned, he placed his hands on his hairless head as the bow of the other vessel came to rest upon the deck of his own.

Still stowing supplies, Tulgetske was increasingly bothered by the unending whistle blast that, after several seconds, seemed to reverberate in his skull. As the shrill tone ceased, he smiled briefly before, to his surprise, a deep-seated thud echoed throughout the length of *Cedarville*'s metal frame. Curious as to the source of the vibration, Tulgetske started forward.

Overhead, in their separate rooms, Bey and Friedhoff were startled awake by the collision. Unsure of what had happened, Bey got up and dressed to take a look. Friedhoff tugged at his blanket, rolled over, and went back to sleep.

M/V *Topdalsfjord*—

Standing outside, Hoagland cringed as *Topdalsfjord* lurched and shuddered to a halt broadside to the passing bulk carrier. Aft, her engines still churned in reverse as the captain shifted into the damage control mode. "Ready the lifeboats for launching," he ordered, his first thought to ensure the safety of his crew.

At the point of impact, *Topdalsfjord* embedded in *Cedarville*'s side. With considerable momentum, the overloaded *Cedarville* continued on, sweeping *Topdalsfjord*'s pinioned bow to the northeast until she broke free.

With a shriek, the tangled hull plating separated as the Norwegian freighter backed off. Still in reverse, she accelerated aft and disappeared into the fog as *Cedarville* continued on.

12

Miscalculation

SS *Cedarville*
STRAITS OF MACKINAC—
0946

Marty Joppich gripped the handrail in stunned silence. In the still-ness following the collision an odd chill had settled into the pit of his stomach.

"All stop," he shouted over his shoulder. Behind him, Gabrysiak echoed the order, shifting the brass handle on the engine order tele-graph.

As *Cedarville* drifted on through the fog, Joppich surveyed the damage. Below, the roiling water that slipped aft along the port side abruptly turned to flood the gaping hole. Grasping the weight of his predicament, he turned back to the helmsman. "Sound the general alarm," he roared.

Gabrysiak reached for the alarm. Located to the right of the for-ward pilothouse window, the alarm switch was just beyond Gabrysiak's grasp. Releasing the wheel, he lunged forward, quickly depressing the switch seven times. On the bridge, the alarm bell mim-icked his motions, its staccato ring blaring through the open door, past the captain, and over the side to dissipate in the fog.

As old as the hull, the miles of wiring that laced the ship were badly deteriorating. Just beyond the confines of the pilothouse, the alarm signal, routing through the circuitry at the speed of light, encountered a frayed wire. Cleared of its insulation by gnawing rats, the wire was only partially intact and failed to transmit the entire signal. Elsewhere on the ship, the bell sounded only twice.

In his stateroom beneath the pilothouse, Harry Piechan was awakened by the alarm. Confused by the truncated signal, he left his room on the starboard side and followed the passageway to the port ladder. Clad in boxers and a T-shirt, the first mate stepped to the grated platform, one deck below the captain.

Shivering against the cold, Piechan's gaze followed the movement of the deck crew, but he could not find the cause of their alarm. "Enough guessing," he thought, as he hurried back to his room.

Trembling from the stress, Joppich turned to channel 16 and keyed the transmitter. "Mayday, Mayday, Mayday. This is the steamship *Cedarville*. We have collided with an unidentified freighter. Our position is . . ." Joppich paused to look at the radar return. Adjusting the bearing and range indicators, he placed the cursor on a fixed object. Illuminated numbers shifted rapidly in the display windows beside the scope. "Our position is one mile south-southeast of the north tower of the Mackinac Bridge. We are taking on water and need immediate assistance. This is a Mayday, over."

M/V *Weissenburg*—

Having tracked the collision on radar, May was not surprised to hear *Cedarville*'s distress call. He lifted his handset to reply but was interrupted by the United States Coast Guard.

"Steamship *Cedarville,* this is Coast Guard Group Sault Ste. Marie. Please confirm your distress signal and status, over."

"Roger, Coast Guard," Joppich's voice crackled over *Weissenburg*'s receiver. "We have collided with another ship and are taking on water one mile south-southeast of the north tower. The extent of the damage is unknown, but we will report as soon as possible."

"Understood, Captain. Do you have any injuries? Over."

"Not to my knowledge, but we are still assessing damage."

"Understood. Please be advised that units will be underway momentarily. They should reach you within an hour, over."

Interrupting, May entered the conversation. "Coast Guard, this is the motor vessel *Weissenburg*," he said, his accent heavy under the stress. "We are less than a mile from *Cedarville*, approaching from the west. We will come alongside to provide assistance."

"Thank you, *Weissenburg*," the petty officer of the watch in Sault Ste. Marie replied. "Your assistance is appreciated. Do you know the name of the other vessel?"

"*Topdalsfjord*," May replied, scanning the fog before him for a glimpse of the injured American freighter.

SS *Cedarville*—

Piechan was still tucking his shirt in as he stepped into the pilot-house. "What's going on, Cap?" he inquired nonchalantly.

"We just got hit. That's what's going on. I need you to go aft to assess the damage and install the collision mat."

Speechless, Piechan stood in the doorway, staring at Joppich.

"Now!" the captain added.

Joppich turned back to the radio as the first officer rushed from the bridge.

Piechan arrived on the spar deck out of breath, his massive frame heaving as he expelled steamy gulps of air. Before him, a four-foot wedge had been carved from *Cedarville*'s deck. Peering into the void, Piechan saw water from the lake entering the hold and churning against the white cargo below.

As thousands of gallons per minute poured into hold number two, the icy water sifted through the porous cargo to collect at its base. As the hold quickly reached capacity, water pressure mounted on the cargo trap at the bottom until, with the crack of its latch, it sprung open, showering the conveyor and tunnel below.

With the failure of the cargo latch, the ship could not be saved. Though gradually, the rushing lake water would eventually fill the tunnel. Unable to contain the water, the tunnel would necessarily conduct the flood to each of the ship's cargo holds, filling them one by one until *Cedarville* became unstable and capsized.

On deck, Piechan, unaware of his ship's fate, remembered the collision tarp. Grabbing a couple of deckhands, he raced back to the boom. "Come on, fellas. We have to stop that flow."

As the trio struggled to pull the damage control tarp from its storage space at the base of the boom, the ship listed to port.

Tulgetske's first thought was to wake the chief engineer. Leaving his inventory on the fantail, he rushed past the galley and upward to Lamp's starboard-side cabin. Raising his hand to knock, he held back when the door swung open, Lamp stepping out fully dressed.

"What happened?" Lamp asked.

"I don't know," the first assistant responded as the two trotted to port. When they reached the rail, the fog cleared briefly, allowing a full view of the port side damage and the foreign vessel backing in the distance. Without a word, they sprinted toward the engine room.

M/V *Topdalsfjord*—

With his ship still backing, Captain Hoagland felt the rearward acceleration. "All stop," he quietly commanded. With the instant reduction in aft thrust, *Topdalsfjord* settled into a lazy drift, rocked occasionally by the remnants of *Cedarville*'s wake.

"Call the authorities, Mr. Millberg," the captain mumbled to the radio officer.

"Aye, sir," Millberg responded as he dialed the proper channel. "United States Coast Guard, this is *Topdalsfjord*, over."

"Go ahead, *Topdalsfjord*."

"Please stand by for the captain," Millberg said, handing the transmitter to Hoagland.

"Coast Guard, this is *Topdalsfjord*," Hoagland sighed. "We have been involved in a collision just east of the Mackinac Bridge."

"Roger. We just received a report from the other vessel. Do you have any injuries, captain? Over."

"No, I don't think so," Hoagland replied, nervously running his fingers through his hair. "It looks like we have some minor damage on the bow, but the ship is otherwise undamaged."

"Understood, Captain. If you need any assistance, please contact us immediately. Otherwise, please stand by in the area until our units arrive. The investigating officer should be there within the hour. Group Sault Ste. Marie, out."

SS *Cedarville*—

Jim Lietzow was in lower engineering painting a stanchion when he felt the jar. Dumping the brush unceremoniously into the bucket, he wiped his hands on a rag and climbed the ladder to the control room. Finding Radke at the controls, he shouted above the roar of the furnace and engine, "What was that?"

"I don't know. I haven't heard anything from the bridge," Radke replied, wiping the sweat from his brow. "Why don't you go topside and take a look. Let me know what you find out."

With a nod, Lietzow turned down the catwalk and climbed to the fantail. Opening the fantail hatch, he was blasted with cool, fresh air. Before he could enjoy the moment, the chief engineer bustled past, with Tulgetske in tow.

"Son, you'd better get your life jacket on," Lamp said before disappearing below.

Passing the control panel, Tulgetske stopped to check the trim. Mounted amidships above the throttle controls, an inclinometer measured *Cedarville*'s degree of list. Tulgetske was stunned. *Cedarville* was three feet down to port. "Hey, Don, it looks like we're taking on water."

"Yeah, I can feel the list. You'd better go sound the wells."

Each ballast tank in the ship had a sensor that fed a display in the engine room to show the water level in the tank. Even so, the most accurate measure was to physically sound each of the tanks. Though time-consuming, manual sounding was prudent in light of the obvious danger.

"I'm on it," said Tulgetske, gathering a clipboard and pen.

WLC Headquarters
PORT CALCITE, MICHIGAN—

Joe Hassett looked up as the panel loudspeaker crackled to life. "WLC Rogers City, this is the steamship *Cedarville,* calling on channel 51. Mayday, over."

Stunned, Hassett leaned over the control board, removed the plug for channel 52 from the loudspeaker, and plugged in the headphones. Realizing his mistake, he switched out with the channel 51 plug, then keyed the transmitter. "*Cedarville* from Rogers City, did you say Mayday? Over."

"Yes, Mayday," Joppich replied impatiently. "We have been hit amidships on the port side and are taking on water. Get Captain Parilla on the line."

Checking his personnel roster, Hassett found that the fleet supervisor was in Pittsburgh. "Captain Parilla is out of the area, but I will call Mr. Buehrens. Over."

"Fine, just do it fast."

ROGERS CITY, MICHIGAN—

Lou Brege was transfixed. She was greasing a bread pan when the call echoed up from the basement. Hearing the word "Mayday," she dropped the pan and hurried down the nearby steps.

As the ship waited for Buehrens to respond, she found the silence unbearable. Turning up the volume, she returned to the kitchen to keep busy as the situation unfolded.

PORT CALCITE, MICHIGAN—

Hassett's first call was not to Buehrens but to Hassett's supervisor, Russ Smart, in the office next door. "Hey, Russ, it looks like we have an emergency developing in here. *Cedarville* has had an accident."

Without responding, Smart hung up and appeared in the studio doorway. "Let me sit down," he said, as Hassett removed his earphones and stepped aside. Smart took the chair and scanned the control panel. The WLC panel board integrated AM and FM communications circuitry with an emergency power source. Built into the system was a phone patch, allowing the operator to route local calls or to contact the marine operator for long-distance communications.

Lifting the telephone, the WLC traffic manager dialed the familiar number. "Mr. Buehrens, please . . ."

M/V *Weissenburg*—

Captain May supervised the preparation of *Weissenburg*'s lifeboats from the bridge. He had ordered them manned when he heard *Cedarville*'s Mayday and intended to launch as soon as his ship was within range.

Through the increasing radio traffic, his ship was hailed. "*Weissenburg*, this is *Cedarville*, come in, over."

Stepping across the pilothouse to answer, he kept an eye on the deckhands working below. "This is *Weissenburg*, go ahead."

"Yes, I would just like to confirm the name of the ship that hit me. Can you help me out?"

"Captain, we are preparing to launch our lifeboats. Do you require assistance?" May inquired.

"No. At the moment I am fine, but I'd like to have the name of that ship."

"To the best of my knowledge, you collided with the Norwegian freighter *Topdalsfjord*."

"Thank you, Captain," Joppich replied. "*Cedarville* out."

Shrugging, May replaced the transmitter on its hook and turned to his watch officer. "Let's hold off on launching the boats. This guy sounds like he doesn't need our assistance."

SS *Cedarville*—

With his hands in his pockets, Ron Piechan stood idly on deck, watching his brother deploy the crash tarp. Suddenly he remembered Jarvis. Piechan had assigned his helper to the tunnel to inspect the conveyor for cracks.

Reaching the forward hatch, he quickly descended the three unlit levels to emerge beside the control booth. Overhead and underfoot, crisscrossing conveyors lay dormant. Piechan shouted into the conveyor well, his voice echoing back without response.

Continuing aft, he entered the tunnel, sloping downward into the darkness. Running along the conveyor belt, Piechan heard the flow of water from the number two hold just before he splashed into the flood. With water up to his knees, Piechan cried out for his assistant once again. No response.

Erickson quickly shed his apron and burst from the galley. Ducking aft, he turned into the crew's passageway and started banging on doors. Jolted awake, Oiler Raphael Przybyla, Third Assistant Engineer Mike Idalski, and Stokerman Billy Holley emerged into the passageway to find the cook systematically sounding the alarm from room to room. Friedhoff was the last to be roused from his off-duty slumber.

"What's going on?" Friedhoff asked, yawning and scratching the back of his head as he opened the door.

"Come on, get up. We have been hit," a wide-eyed Erickson exclaimed. Not saying a word, Friedhoff jumped back into his room, pulled on his pants and shirt, and quickly laced his shoes. Scanning the emergency instructions mounted at the foot of his bed, he grabbed a life jacket from the closet and strapped it on as he raced for his lifeboat station.

Friedhoff turned the corner on deck to find the port lifeboat station empty. Idalski, Holley, and Przybyla had reported to starboard, and Friedhoff was alone. Grumbling, he untied and stripped off the tarp cover. As he struggled with the bulky tarp, several more crewmen joined him. Motivated by fear, the men gathered at the station worked hastily to prepare the lifeboat for launching.

Friedhoff took a moment to consider the configuration of the block-and-tackle launch assembly. The wooden lifeboat swung gently, suspended by rotating davits several feet above the deck. "OK, fellas, let's swing her outboard."

Together, the seamen pushed against the rusty davits until, with a creak, the boat was shifted up and over the lifeline. Turning aft,

Friedhoff removed all but one turn of the frapping line from the deck cleat and loosed the hand brake. Satisfied that the forward line was similarly prepared, he called out, "Lower away together." Loosening the final turn, Friedhoff instantly felt the weight of the boat on the line in his hand. As the crewmen payed out line hand over hand, the boat came to rest just out of sight below the deck. With the boat still high enough to allow safe boarding, the frapping lines were secured and the brake set.

"Now what do we do?" Friedhoff asked. No one had an answer.

0949

Seeing the damage to port, Third Mate Cook spoke to the captain. "We need to drop the hook, Marty."

"Yeah, go take care of it," Joppich responded, leaning against the rail, seemingly disinterested.

Leaving Joppich, Cook passed quickly through the pilothouse, summoning Gabrysiak along the way. Together, they disappeared down the ladder well, weaving forward to the windlass room.

Cedarville's anchor dangled securely from its indented housing high upon the bow. Opposite the massive flukes, designed to dig into the muddy lake bottom, its shank was connected to a section of chain that fed upward through the hawse pipe into the windlass room.

Gabrysiak's eyes adjusted quickly to the darkness of the room as he set out to release the chain. Emerging from the deck-level hawse pipe, the two-foot links draped across the space to a sprocketed windlass, known as a wildcat. Wrapping around the windlass gears, the chain made a turn before falling off and disappearing into the chain locker below. The anchor itself was held in place by a series of chain stoppers that fastened the anchor chain to the deck, thereby relieving the strain from the windlass.

"Stand by to release the stoppers," Cook said as he took his position on the gear's friction brake. As he pressed a large, red button, the electric windlass whined to life, slowly pulling in on the anchor chain. The effect was just enough to allow Gabrysiak to loosen and remove the stoppers. With the stoppers clear and the helmsman safely out of the way, Cook released the hand brake. With a clatter, the anchor fell, paying out chain from the locker below.

Beneath the ship, the double-fluked anchor raced downward for more than a hundred feet before striking the gravelly bottom in a blur of muddy debris. The anchor fell on its side as the ship overhead drifted away. After a few minutes, the flow of chain was halted, and the ship's momentum put a strain on the anchor, forcing the flukes to bite deeply into the muddy gravel.

With the anchor set, the men replaced the stoppers and returned to the bridge.

Breathless from the climb, Gabrysiak paused at the wheel, noting that the engines had stopped. Remembering the collision, he started scanning the bridge for a life jacket. Finding none, he muttered, "Geez, what's going on here?"

"What's that?" Joppich asked, closing the port bridge wing hatch.

"We don't have no life jackets up here, Captain. Request permission to leave the pilothouse and get a few."

"Go ahead," Joppich waved dismissively.

Cook barely noticed the helmsman's absence when Gabrysiak reappeared in the pilothouse, life jackets draped over his arms.

Back at his post, Gabrysiak wasted no time in donning the bulky white vest. Joppich and Cook thought he was overreacting and casually dropped theirs to the deck.

M/V *Weissenburg*—

Aboard the German freighter, the port and starboard life rafts were made ready and swung outboard. With his crew standing by, Captain May paced the bridge as his ship neared the anchored vessel.

SS *Cedarville*—

The incoming water was quickly robbing the ship of its buoyancy. Unnoticed by the captain or crew, *Cedarville* had lost twelve inches of freeboard in only three minutes, her hull gradually sinking into the frigid waters.

0950

Though concerned for his missing assistant, Ron Piechan was afraid. He gave up the search in the tunnel and went back to his room to find a life jacket. Approaching the door, he was surprised when it swung inward, with Jarvis on the other side, struggling into his flotation gear. "Ha!" Piechan exclaimed in relief and amusement. "I thought you were dead, boy."

"Not yet," Jarvis smirked as Piechan ducked into the room for his life vest.

A few seconds later the pair rushed back to the main deck to find the first officer still struggling with the crash tarp.

Supported by men on either side of the gash, the semi-flexible tarp was repeatedly lowered over the side, sucked into void, and retrieved for another attempt.

"It's not working," Harry Piechan boomed. "The hole's too big."

"Maybe it will hold if we can place it below the waterline," Ed Brewster suggested.

"Not a chance. This tarp was designed to be placed over small holes and cracks, not something this big." As he spoke, the crash tarp was torn from their hands and swept back into the filling cargo hold. "We're wasting our time with this," the first mate announced as he pulled the tarp dripping from the torn deck. "You men go to your lifeboat stations. I need to talk to the captain."

With that, the deck crew dispersed, each man to his assigned emergency post.

Tulgetske worked his way aft along the main deck, sounding each of the wells on the port side. Stepping over and around the abandoned crevice, he came to well number four. Adeptly unscrewing the cover, he lowered a long bamboo pole into the darkened void below. When he pulled it out again, the situation was clear. Number four ballast tank was almost completely flooded. The foreign ship's bow must have sliced into the tank well below the waterline.

Closing the hatch, Tulgetske continued on to the next well. He was tempted to race back with the information, but incomplete data could do more harm than good. "Better to be thorough," he thought as he opened number six.

M/V *Weissenburg*—

Easing to within a quarter mile of the stricken vessel, Captain May again offered his assistance. "*Cedarville,* this is *Weissenburg.* We are standing by to help remove your crew, over."

"Thank you, but that won't be necessary," the radio crackled.

The German captain stared at the radio in disbelief. "But Captain, you have declared an emergency. We are standing by to assist."

"Thank you, *Weissenburg.* We appreciate that, but we are fine for now. I will let you know if we need help, but I expect the Coast Guard here soon enough. *Cedarville* out."

Replacing the handset, May shook his head. "Foolish American," he thought out loud.

SS *Cedarville*—

With one of the port ballast tanks flooding, *Cedarville* listed noticeably. Even so, no one aboard recognized that the ship was down by fifteen inches.

COAST GUARD STATION MACKINAC ISLAND—
0955

Clad in dungarees and blue utility jackets, the boat crew trotted along the pier, their steel-toed boondockers clomping out of rhythm on the wooden planks. The boat captain, a first-class boatswain's mate, was already in position at the helm, his finger on the ignition. Seeing his crew aboard, he turned the switch, the diesel engine roaring to life.

Identified in the Coast Guard inventory as *CG-40527*, the forty-four-foot motor lifeboat surged against its mooring lines as the cold clear water of the harbor churned around its hull.

"Cast off," the senior petty officer shouted above the din. Forward and aft, nonrated seamen loosed the one-inch lines, lifting the bites from the deck cleats before heaving across to the pier.

Freed from its ties, the boat drifted sideways in the slip. Keeping an eye on the pilings approaching to port, the boat captain scanned the adjacent channel as he nudged the throttle into reverse. Backing through the boat's own diesel exhaust, the crew collectively held their breath as the blue-gray cloud wafted across the deck.

With the boat finally clear of the sporadic pilings, the petty officer shifted gear, slammed the throttle, and spun the wheel. With the bow rising high in the air, the powerful engine cut deeply into the icy water as the motor lifeboat turned sharply through the fog for the crippled freighter, anchored five miles distant.

CHEBOYGAN, MICHIGAN—

Across the channel, the icebreaker *Mackinaw* was tied securely to the city pier, crewmen high aloft painting the superstructure in preparation for the upcoming Armed Forces Festival. In the radio shack below, the duty radioman took the message and quickly alerted the captain.

Rushing in from his stateroom with the executive officer, Captain Chiswell reviewed the message and turned for the bridge. "Get Mr. Stewart in here," he barked to the yeoman, trailing a few paces behind.

"Aye, sir," came the response.

Stepping onto the spacious bridge, the captain took his place in the elevated chair as the 1MC boomed, "Lieutenant Stewart, your presence is requested on the bridge."

Frank Stewart appeared a moment later, his blue coveralls splattered with red and white paint. "Did you need me, Skipper?"

"Yes. Do you still have men aloft?"

"Yes, sir. We should finish the mast and the stacks before lunch," the junior officer replied.

"Well, bring them in. A ship has been holed in the Straits, and we need to get out there in case they go down. We're getting underway in half an hour."

"Aye, sir. We'll get it wrapped up immediately." Coming briefly to attention, Stewart departed the bridge.

Heading aft, the officer rounded the superstructure to find his division chief barking at the seamen working aloft. Equally splattered, Chief Boatswain's Mate Charles Melanson smiled at the first lieutenant. "What did the old man want?"

"There's been a collision in the Straits. Bring the men down. We're getting underway in half an hour, and they will be needed for sea and anchor detail," he said, referring to the line-handling duties his division routinely performed with each new voyage.

"Consider it done, El-tee," the salty old chief assured.

Back on the bridge, Chiswell and Commander Rojeski were preparing to get underway.

"Let's get the engines fired up and get all hands back aboard if anyone is working on the pier."

"What about emergency medical personnel?" Rojeski asked.

"Good idea. Have the OOD call ashore and get a couple of docs on board. See if they can send us a chaplain and a coroner too. No telling what's going on out there."

SS *Cedarville*—

Following World War II, the United States Navy instituted an educational program designed to train junior officers on improved damage control techniques. The Navy establishment had found—through great loss—that in the event of an emergency a ship must first consider whether to evacuate all hands and, if not, to determine what steps to take to save the ship. In the face of serious damage, a captain must maintain buoyancy and stability if he is to save his ship. *Cedarville* was rapidly losing both.

Rushing along the canted deck, the first assistant engineer had found that the holds, tunnel, and port ballast tanks were flooding. With the loss of buoyancy, the ship was settling unevenly into the water. More troubling, however, was that, with each slosh of the uncontrolled flow, *Cedarville*'s center of gravity was creeping upward and to the left. Unchecked, the flooding would soon cause the self-unloader to roll over.

Pausing at the junction between the aft crew quarters and engineering, Tulgetske diverted to his room for a life jacket before continuing down.

In main engineering, Tulgetske brought Lamp up to speed on the progression of flooding and the deck crew's failure to deploy the crash tarp. Based on his observations, the chief engineer ordered the number four port side and bottom tank pumped. Soon thereafter the main ballast pump was coaxed into operation, ejecting 5,250 gallons per minute from the flooded voids. Even so, the volume of incoming water far exceeded the pump's capacity, and *Cedarville*'s list worsened.

"Negative, Coast Guard, the flooding cannot be controlled." Having returned to the pilothouse, Harry Piechan briefed the captain on his damage control efforts and placed a call to the Coast Guard station on Mackinac Island. Shifting the radio-telephone receiver to his other ear, he continued. "We are taking a tremendous amount of water in the number two hold. It is pouring over the limestone cargo. We tried to deploy a crash tarp, but the hole was just too big. We are going to need assistance very soon."

"Understood, *Cedarville*," the voice crackled in his ear. "Units are on the way. Just hang in there, and let us know if your skipper decides to abandon ship."

"Will do," Piechan confirmed before signing off. Replacing the handset, he eyed Marty Joppich for a moment—sitting dejected and uncertain in his swivel chair—before returning to the deck.

PORT CALCITE, MICHIGAN—

Waiting for Buehrens to arrive, Hassett set up his tape recorder. Quickly removing the molded cover, he plugged into the power panel beneath the radio console and slapped a new five-inch reel on the left spindle. With the loose end threaded through the recorder and wound around the empty reel on the other side, he turned the switch, setting the take-up reel in motion as Buehrens burst into the control room.

"Get Captain Parilla on the line," he commanded.

Under most circumstances, WLC calls out of area were routed through a marine operator in Alpena, Michigan. However, U.S. Steel had recently purchased a series of tie lines that provided direct land-line communications between company facilities. Smart dialed the Pittsburgh headquarters.

"It's ringing, sir," he said, handing the phone to Buehrens.

U.S. Steel Headquarters
PITTSBURGH, PENNSYLVANIA—

Parilla was speechless. He could not believe his ears. He had been summarizing fleet statistics for Admiral Khoury when a soft knock on the door broke his train of thought. Khoury's secretary stepped halfway into the conference room. "Captain Parilla," she said, "Mr. Buehrens is on the line from Rogers City. He says it's an emergency." Excusing himself, Parilla set his notes aside to take the call as Lucas launched into a commentary comparing the Atlantic and Great Lakes fleets.

In the outer office he held the receiver in both hands as he responded in measured tones. "Alright, I'm going to brief Khoury. Keep this line open and set up a patch to the ship. I want to talk to Joppich as soon as possible." Gently placing the receiver on the desk next to the phone, Parilla quietly rejoined the meeting.

Blustering over Pittsburgh Steamship's quotas, Khoury caught sight of Parilla as he slipped into his chair. His ashen appearance stopped Khoury in mid-sentence. "What's wrong, Joe?"

Parilla spoke softly, without emotion. "*Cedarville* was holed amidships by a foreign freighter in the Straits of Mackinac. She is in serious trouble. There is uncontrolled flooding in the fully loaded number two hold and no way to stop it. If we don't do something, she is going to sink like a brick."

"What do you want to do?" Khoury asked.

Sweating beneath his collar, Parilla felt trapped. Thirty-five souls sailed aboard *Cedarville,* but Parilla knew what Khoury wanted.

Without *Cedarville*, the Bradley Fleet could not possibly keep up with scheduled limestone shipments, and steel production would soon falter. Khoury could not let that happen—and neither could Parilla.

"A fellow named Marty Joppich is in command," he replied. "I'm going to tell him to beach the ship if he can."

Khoury closed his eyes and nodded almost imperceptibly. Understanding the silent command, Parilla stood. "If you will excuse me, Admiral, I have a few calls to make."

SS *Cedarville*—

Much of the crew shuffled aimlessly around the aft lifeboat stations. They had come to assist but were idled in the absence of guidance from the bridge. Wearing rain gear, hard hats, and life jackets, the twenty men were evenly divided between the port and starboard boats as they nervously discussed what had happened.

Ron Piechan was the first to notice that the waterline seemed much closer than before. *Cedarville* was down by thirty inches.

1002

With the primary bilge pump chugging along satisfactorily, Lamp took muster of the personnel present. Two were missing—Bey and Idalski. "Go find those two and bring them down here," he said to Tulgetske. "We need all the hands we can get."

The first assistant engineer was getting tired. He had been racing up and down the engineering ladder well for fifteen minutes, and now he faced another climb.

Passing through the fantail, Tulgetske was winded as he emerged on the port side. There, standing at the railing, were Bey and Idalski, watching and pointing at the lifeboat crew below as if the whole episode were nothing more than an interesting diversion.

"What do you think you are doing?" Tulgetske barked, startling the pair. "We are trying to keep this ship from sinking and could really use some help below."

Still out of breath, he leaned against the rail. Bey and Idalski stood motionless, staring at the first assistant. "Let's go, guys," he ordered, as the two jumped into action and scurried below.

Chuckling, Tulgetske turned to follow. Idalski was obviously the smarter of the two—he was wearing a life jacket.

When the first assistant returned to main engineering, Lamp was on the phone with the captain.

". . . No, Marty. You have to listen to me. We are listing thirty-five degrees. The incoming water is too much for the pumps to handle. I recommend that we start ballasting to starboard and even out the trim. OK, thanks." The chief engineer hung up the phone.

"Start ballasting?" Tulgetske asked.

"Yeah. Go take care of it."

Tulgetske disappeared down the ladder to lower engineering. With Bey and Idalski in tow, the damage control team stopped the main ballast pump, adjusted manifold valves to route the discharge into one of the starboard ballast tanks, and powered it up again. Thereafter, Tulgetske rigged the 3,600-gallon-per-minute centrifugal steam pump to assist in the transfer from port to starboard. Bey and Idalski each configured a 2,000-gallon horizontal steam drag auxiliary ballast pump to clear the tunnel space sump well, and with all pumps functioning properly, the ship evened out as water poured into all seven starboard ballast tanks.

Third Mate Cook answered the call from WLC. Surprised, he turned to Joppich. "Hey, Cap, WLC has Captain Parilla on the line. He wants to talk to you."

Joppich wrenched the receiver from Cook. "Joe, Marty here."

ROGERS CITY, MICHIGAN—

Louella Jane Brege nearly spilled her coffee as she leaned to adjust the volume. She had called her father with news of the collision but was now glued to the radio. Just as Joppich took the phone, a nearby hospital activated its X-ray machine, producing an annoying chirp that made her jump. Aggravated, Brege adjusted the reception and moved closer to the speaker as Joppich's voice cut through the light static.

SS *Cedarville*—

Still at the helm, Gabrysiak leaned against the pedestal, listening to the captain describe the damage.

"What do you think I should do?" Joppich shouted into the mouthpiece, with his index finger in his left ear. Gabrysiak watched his expression during the pause—Joppich's brow furrowed behind his thick glasses.

"No. We are at anchor. It will take a few minutes to get underway."

Another pause.

"Alright. I'll take care of it. I'll call back when she's beached."

Replacing the receiver on the hook, Joppich turned to the waiting bridge crew. "We're getting underway. Charlie, bring up the anchor. Take Trafelet with you. I need Lenny at the helm."

Calling Trafelet in from the cold, Cook departed once again for the anchor windlass.

In the following silence, Gabrysiak averted his gaze from the captain, shuffling aimlessly across the bridge. What about the men? Joppich didn't say a word about evacuating the crew, and Parilla apparently didn't ask. The ship was obviously sinking, and no one seemed to care. Adjacent to the helm, Harry Piechan studied the radar scope, seeming not to notice the disoriented captain. "Am I the only one who sees the danger?" Lenny wondered.

Tightening the straps of his life vest, Gabrysiak stared into the milky fog that still enveloped his ship as he pondered the safety of his shipmates working below.

Releasing the brake, Cook engaged the anchor windlass. An electric motor hummed below as the sprocketed drum rotated slowly. Dripping, the pitted links were hauled through the hawse pipe, over the deck, around the winch, and into the waiting chain locker.

Cedarville inched toward the submerged anchor as the chain shortened. Most large vessels are held in place not by the gripping power of the anchor but by the massive weight of the chain payed out to the bottom. As the tug of the windlass begins to exceed that diminishing weight, the anchor breaks free to rise into position on the vessel's bow. However, with *Cedarville* hovering directly over the taut chain, the anchor held fast. Fouled on the rocky bottom, the ship's ground tackle showed no sign of loosening its grip.

Electrical smoke wafted from the laboring motor. Disengaging the winch, Cook allowed the ship to back off and slacken the anchor chain. With sufficient dip in the cable, he reset the brake. "Ivan, get up to the pilothouse and tell the captain that we are stuck. The anchor won't come up."

Joppich responded to the news with a command to the helm. "Reverse engines. Give her all she has."

"Full astern, aye, sir," Gabrysiak sang out.

Satisfied with the response, Joppich called the engine room to repeat the order as the engine order telegraph rang out the instructions from the helm.

Cook stepped clear of the straining chain as it groaned against its metal housings. Suddenly, the ship lurched backward and the chain fell silent. *Cedarville* was free. A change in deck vibration soon told him that the engines had reversed. With the vessel moving forward, he repeated the procedure, this time raising the anchor into the proper position.

Joppich was losing the ability to command. Without checking his position, direction, or distance to nearest land, or the *Cedarville*'s rate of sinkage or time needed to beach the vessel, the captain ordered full speed as the ship swung wildly in its unguided path.

As *Cedarville* curved through the water toward an unknown heading, Joppich tried to think. He was on the verge of making a decision as to the proper heading when the radio interrupted his thoughts.

"*Cedarville,* this is *Weissenburg.* We are standing by close at hand with two lifeboats. Please let me come alongside to remove your crew. Which side do you prefer that I approach?"

Joppich was losing patience with foreign captains in general and this one in particular. "Get out of my way," he barked. "I'm going to try to beach her."

Water continued to pour into the gaping wound in the ship's side unabated. As the water rushed through into the ballast tank and tunnel beneath and combined with the ballast flow into the starboard tanks, *Cedarville* was settling quickly. With a loss of fifty-one inches of freeboard, the ship would soon capsize.

M/V *Weissenburg*—
1005

"He doesn't seem to understand that his ship is going to sink," Captain May thought as he scanned the foggy surface for the crippled vessel. Without warning, *Cedarville* emerged from a fog bank, cutting directly across *Weissenburg*'s bow. "All stop," May shouted. "I believe this captain is a madman."

As the German freighter drifted to a stop, *Cedarville* turned down its port side, circled its stern, and passed back up to starboard before it steadied up on a new course.

Stepping from the window, Captain May activated the intercom. "All hands, this is the captain. Stand down from rescue stations. The captain of the damaged ship intends to beach her. That is all."

Securing the intercom, May eyed his conning officer questioningly. Third Mate Voigt merely shrugged.

SS *Cedarville*—

Cook returned to the pilothouse as *Cedarville* completed its turn around *Weissenburg*. "We're going to beach her. Give me a heading," Joppich said in Cook's direction.

Jumping to the chart table, Cook plotted a hasty course to land. "Captain, Nipigon Point is one-four-zero, six miles."

"Do it," Joppich said to Gabrysiak, not checking the chart. "Keep us at full speed."

The helmsman kept the turn as the compass passed 180 . . . 170 . . . 160. As the spinning display approached 150, he steadied up, allowing the vessel's bow to line up with 141. A few more spokes of correction and she was on course.

As the sinking vessel labored southeast at three knots, no one noticed that Graham Shoal and Mackinac Point were each only two miles distant. Had the vessel been steered to either point, she might have been saved.

Idalski fidgeted nervously as the crew monitored the pumps. "What's wrong with you?" Tulgetske asked.

"I don't like it down here," he said. "I want to go topside. This ship is going down, and I want to get out of here."

"Hold fast until we get the order," Tulgetske replied calmly as he checked the flow rate on the screaming pumps.

Friedhoff leaned against the handrail. The wooden whaleboat swung gently outboard with the rocking vessel, tapping the rusting steel hull lightly as the list shifted back to starboard. The water surging less than five feet below the swaying lifeboat silently declared that *Cedarville* had already lost more than half of her freeboard.

M/V *Weissenburg*—
1010

As *Cedarville* passed lighted gong buoy number two close aboard to starboard, *Weissenburg* fell into her wake, slowly tracking the crippled vessel. From the bridge wing, Captain May listened to the strain of steam engines laboring to push the submerged bulk to the shore, six miles distant.

Less than three thousand yards to the east, *Topdalsfjord* lay motionless. She did not follow.

SS *Cedarville*—

From the bridge wing, Captain Joppich surveyed the crewmen clad in survival gear and huddled around the after lifeboats. It did not occur to him that his decks were nearly awash. Nor did he consider the men manning their posts below, oblivious to the imminent danger. His only thought was to beach the ship.

Judges and boards of inquiry would later determine that at this moment it became clear that Joppich did not really know his vessel. He had never educated himself on *Cedarville*'s trim and stability characteristics. He had never seen the hydrostatic curves of his ship. He did not know the metacentric height of his vessel. In short, Captain Joppich had ignored the master's edict: "Know thy vessel."

As Friedhoff considered the possibility that he may have to get wet, he remembered the *Bradley*. When she went down in 1958, the two crewmen who survived wore extra clothing to keep warm. "I"ll be back," he announced suddenly.

"Where ya going?" It was Stan Mulka. He had always struck Friedhoff as out of place on the ship. An aspiring seminarian, the deckhand was on his first sailing trip, and he did not quite fit in with the rest of the crew. This occasion was no exception. Wearing only thin pants and a light shirt, he was already shivering against the cold.

"I'm going to get some more clothes. Why don't you come with me. You aren't going to make it if we have to swim."

"Yeah, well . . . I won't make it if this ship rolls over and takes me with it," Mulka nervously replied to Friedhoff's back.

"OK. I'll grab you something too," Friedhoff called over his shoulder as he disappeared around a corner.

With the ship down seventy-five inches, lake water was starting to lap up on deck, creating slick spots where the water drained through scuppers back into the Straits.

ROGERS CITY, MICHIGAN—

A call from its sister station in Cheboygan alerted the WHAK station manager to the collision. Rushing the news snippet to the morning DJ, he cued the microphone.

Barbara Fuhrman was in mid-sentence, singing a duet with Elvis in her kitchen, when the two were rudely interrupted by the announcer. "This just in," the sing-song baritone voice chimed.

Instinctively, she scanned the room for James Arthur. Playing contentedly in the corner, the toddler had not gone far. Six-month-old June Ann was sleeping peacefully in the crib, and Barbara had been enjoying the break.

"The United States Coast Guard has reported that the Bradley Fleet steamer *Cedarville* has been involved in a collision in the Straits of Mackinac this morning. Preliminary reports are incomplete, but it appears as though *Cedarville* is damaged and has issued a distress call. Stay tuned to WHAK, Rogers City, as this story develops."

"What? What do you mean 'stay tuned'?" Barbara cried as she reached for her son.

SS *Cedarville*
1017

Forward, Ivan Trafalet had slipped away from the bow and gone to his room for a life jacket. Tightening the straps on the white vest, he made his way down the starboard ladder to the main deck. Amidships he crossed over to the port side to take a closer look at the hole. With the water levels equalizing within and without, the flow through the void had slackened to an oily current. White pebbles continued to swirl like slow-motion popcorn, spilling out of the gash into the depths of the Straits.

Nervous laughter cut through the now sporadic fog, reminding him of the danger. Hurrying aft, he caught a glimpse of the starboard lifeboat and smiled. Bob Bingle and Bill Asam huddled in the swinging boat. To port, the crew were once again considering the launch mechanism. A quick test of the release gear proved that the release brake had malfunctioned. The port lifeboat was stuck.

U.S. Steel Headquarters
PITTSBURGH, PENNSYLVANIA—

Parilla checked his watch for the hundredth time. Alone in a small conference room, he worried that Joppich might not be able to beach the ship. Picking up the landline, he asked Buehrens which other Bradley Fleet vessels were available to render assistance at the scene (and keep the incident as low-key as possible).

Checking his notes, Buehrens confirmed that *Munson* was inbound, only about two hours away.

"Good. Patch me through."

More waiting as Parilla tolerated the alternating hum, buzz, and squeal of the radio link. Finally, the grainy voice of *Munson*'s captain crackled through. "Ursom here. We've been monitoring the situation. How can we help?"

Parilla smiled. This was what he wanted to hear. "Proceed to the scene at full speed and render whatever assistance you can. . . . And keep in touch!"

ROGERS CITY, MICHIGAN—

Lou Brege perked up at the mention of her husband's ship. Dick Brege was coming to the rescue, but she still had work to do. Turning up the radio's volume, she returned to the kitchen.

PORT CALCITE, MICHIGAN—

Hassett looked up from the console. A faint tap, tap, tap echoed through the room as the magnetic tape at the end of the first reel spun around the spindle.

Reaching into his bag, Hassett rooted around his lunch to find a blank tape. Without thinking, he continued to listen to the radio traffic as he removed the black stoppers, shifted the take-up reel to the opposite spindle, and threaded the tape through the magnetic reader. Satisfied that it was wound properly, he twisted the switch to "record" and resumed his position next to Buehrens at the console.

SS *Cedarville*—

Beneath the laboring triple expansion reciprocating steam engine, lower engineering was filled with the sound of ballast pumps transferring water into the starboard tanks at a frantic pace. The captain had ordered water pumped into the starboard ballast tanks, but this act was soon forgotten. With the slackening flow topside, water was filling the starboard tanks faster than the flooding to port. *Cedarville*'s center of gravity was rapidly shifting to starboard.

Just forward of the pumps, the tunnel hatch kept engineering dry. On the other side of the iron scuttle, the tunnel was completely submerged. Debris and silt clouded the darkened space as the dirty lake water seeped into each of the holds, quickly saturating the porous cargo and inundating nearly every open space forward of engineering.

Cedarville was down by ninety-six inches, but no water entered the engine room to give warning, and nothing was heard from the bridge.

1023

Climbing halfway down into lower engineering, the chief engineer called Tulgetske. "There is nothing more we can do down here without further orders. Bring the men up."

Glancing from face to face, the first assistant replied, "Someone needs to man the pumps."

"I'll stay." It was Hughie Wingo. "Just don't leave me down here too long," he smirked. Tulgetske nodded and, with Idalski and Bey, turned toward main engineering.

Lamp met Tulgetske at the top of the ladder. Holding his arm, he shouted over the din. "Take a few of these guys topside and see what's going on."

Without answer, Tulgetske pointed at the two seamen emerging from the ladder well and darted up the starboard ladder through main engineering and up to the fantail deck. As he ascended the ladder, Bey surveyed the space. Radke had returned to his desk and, with his life vest in place, was writing in the bell book.

On the fantail deck, water was spraying from around one of the large gangway doors through which supplies and equipment were normally loaded. As Tulgetske stopped to tighten the lugs with a wrench, Idalski considered the porthole above Tulgetske's head. The glass glowed with a dim greenish hue. The ship was almost completely underwater. Idalski bolted for the ladder, leaving an astonished Tulgetske and Bey in the flooding space.

Topside, *Cedarville* was down by 120 inches. The main deck was awash.

M/V *Weissenburg*—

Shivering at his perch on the bow, Seaman Huss keyed the bridge microphone. "Captain, I see a white boat on the port bow. It looks like the American Coast Guard."

On the bridge, the captain had no time to reply before his radio crackled to life. "Merchant vessel to port, this is Coast Guard unit four-zero-five-two-seven. Please identify yourself."

"Coast Guard, this is the German vessel *Weissenburg*. We are following the damaged vessel *Cedarville*," May answered.

"Thank you, *Weissenburg*, but can you tell us where the Norwegian vessel is anchored?"

"*Topdalsfjord*? She is about a mile astern, one mile south-southeast of the north tower."

"Roger that, *Weissenburg*. We will have a look. Coast Guard out." With that, the small boat accelerated and turned with a plume of white water in its wake.

"Curious," May thought. "They don't seem to care about *Cedarville*."

SS *Cedarville*—
1024

Stability is the measure of a ship's tendency to return to the upright after taking a roll. Evenly supported by the force of buoyancy, an undamaged ship will right itself from minor inclinations, but that force may be overcome by uncontrolled flooding. As the center of buoyancy edges downward, a sinking vessel will lose equilibrium. With each new list, the floodwaters will shift to the low side, causing the angle of heel to increase. Eventually, such a vessel will continue to incline and capsize as equilibrium becomes an impossibility.

Such was the case as *Cedarville*'s starboard ballast tanks and cargo holds reached capacity, inducing her final roll.

Having broadcast another Mayday call, Joppich had just secured the telegraph when his ship went down at the bow, lurching to starboard.

At the port lifeboat station, Harry Piechan took charge. "Get in the boats, boys," he boomed.

As the starboard side submerged, there was a mad rush to port. Climbing the steep deck, Holley jumped over the rail and into the boat. Turning, he shouted, "You better get in here," and pulled Idalski in by the collar. Off-balance in the confusion, Idalski lost his footing and fell into the water with a splash.

Friedhoff was watching the water advance up the deck when he realized that he needed to trip the boat falls. Leaning over the seat, he struggled to release the mechanism as his shipmates continued to pile in. It was no use. The gear was still stuck.

Trafelet did not make it into the boat. With the increasing list, he slipped on the wet deck, wrapping his arm around a lifeline. He would dangle from the line until *Cedarville* completed her roll.

By the time the first assistant engineer rounded the cabin to starboard, water had covered the forward chocks and a wave was advancing up the deck. Without stopping, he dove for the lifeboat, still attached to the davits. Most of the occupants sat quietly as Tulgetske picked himself from the deck. "Where's Bey?" he wondered, sitting next to Przybyla, who was crossing himself and muttering, "I'm not ready to die. I'm not ready to die."

Struggling against the list, Third Mate Cook braced himself against the helm as he fought to untangle his life preserver.

Ignoring Cook, Captain Joppich shouted, "It doesn't look like she's going to make it," grabbed his vest, and climbed to the port bridge wing. Wasting no time, Len Gabrysiak abandoned the wheel and followed.

Looking back, he briefly locked eyes with Cook. The deck was too steep. The third mate would never get out. Turning, Gabrysiak caught a glimpse of the captain, life jacket in hand, climbing the rail. Joppich jumped without a sound, leaving his third mate on duty in the pilothouse and the engineering team trapped below.

The men in the engine room knew nothing of the conditions above. As the lights flickered, Lamp, Radke, and Wingo braced themselves against the ship's lumbering roll to starboard.

For these men, their darkened world turned upside down.

13

Capsize

SS *Cedarville*—

1025

Clutching a life ring, Gabrysiak turned back to see a wall of water sweep through the pilothouse, overtaking Charlie Cook. As the ship continued her roll, the helmsman stepped from the tilting deck to the pilothouse wall, now level with the surface of the water. Below, Cook's life jacket popped to the surface of the surging water.

"When the water hits, I'll take a deep breath and let go," Len thought as *Cedarville* lurched suddenly, throwing him into the submerged cables that had supported the massive boom.

Tangled in the rigging, he struggled against the lines. "Hail Mary, full of grace, the Lord is with thee," he prayed, pulling through the cables. "*Which way is up?*" his mind interjected. Shivering with the cold, he tried to focus. "B-Blessed art thou amo-mongst women. . . . *P-please God . . . I need air!*" Kicking against the cables for what seemed an eternity, he finally broke free. Still praying, he passed out as his life vest buoyed him quickly to the choppy surface.

With the bow submerged, the starboard lifeboat crew worked desperately to launch the swaying boat. Aft, a frantic thrashing broke the stillness as the four-bladed propeller broke the surface of the water. The engines were still running.

The confused crew leaned against the increasing deck angle. Erickson climbed the rail to step into the aft seat, but seeing the massive deck rising up and over his small boat, he jumped into the icy water to swim to safety. Ivan Trafelet followed suit, hitting his head on some debris that had rolled into the water. With the blood warming his face, he floated, dazed in the thirty-seven-degree water.

Harry Piechan stepped to the boat, but as the ship rolled, it swayed outboard. Losing his footing, Piechan plunged between the two hulls, banging against the rolling steel plate in his descent.

Forward, a large green wave broke over the side and rushed, unobstructed, down the length of the deck. Lifted by the swell, the starboard lifeboat catapulted its passengers into the water. Falling opposite his crewmates, Asam tumbled inboard. He held his breath as he shot down the deck, grasping for a handhold. Washing up against the galley door, he lost his bearings. Orientation on the sinking ship was impossible. Remembering that bubbles always rise, he let out some air. Smiling at the bubble's path, Asam lunged for the surface, but went nowhere. He struggled against an unseen force, which held him in place as he slowly lost consciousness. The newly wed helmsman would drown, fastened to the galley doorknob by a loose strap on his own life vest.

Tulgetske surfaced and swam away to avoid the suction of the sinking ship. Finally, out of breath, he turned to watch. Still underway, *Cedarville* was moving forward under its own momentum as she continued her roll.

The starboard lifeboat did not come back up.

Harry Bey was the last of the engineering crew to escape from below. As he emerged from the starboard passageway, the wave knocked him to the deck, dragging him into the flooding galley. With the entrance submerged and the room quickly filling, he scrambled to the rising port side and onto a table bolted to the deck. Gripping the dusty pipes running overhead, he kicked the second porthole with all of his strength. On the fourth kick, the glass shattered and his leg turned and fractured under the force. Picking away the glass, he scrambled through and into the rising water just a few feet below.

"Good thing I didn't have a life jacket on," he thought, grimacing through the pain as he kicked slowly away from the moving ship. The ship passed, and he read the name on the stern. "CEDARVILLE, Rogers City, MI." Below the caption, the wheel spun effortlessly before the rudder, now well out of the water.

On his escape, Bey swam past Art Fuhrman. He was running to the port lifeboat station when the deck tilted, dropping him into the overhead. Buoyed by the rushing water, his life vest trapped him in the flooding alcove, where he would struggle for air pockets as *Cedarville* pulled him mercilessly to the lake bottom.

As the swell advanced on the port lifeboat, Stokerman Billy Holley helped Brewster aboard. Jarvis jumped for safety but fell between the boat and the ship. Brewster and Holley searched in vain for Jarvis, agreeing that he would probably get sucked into the screw, when a shout caught their attention. Casey Jones had rounded the passageway from aft berthing and was staggering against the list for the boat. "Hey, wait for me!" he cried.

"Here, I'll help you," Brewster said, reaching for his friend. As their fingers touched, Jones looked away in fear and was swallowed by the wave, swept away to be crushed in the after rigging.

In the boat, Friedhoff was struggling to release the launch pin when the boat heaved up and over, discharging most of the crew. Thrown into the air, he saw the stack splash to the side just before his immersion into the painfully cold water.

Galleyman Jerry Kierzek fell into the water as Brewster and Ron Piechan were thrown against the after cabins, adjacent to the galley. Brewster was knocked out, but Piechan, finding himself trapped beneath the davit arm, took a quick inventory. His glasses and cap were missing, but he was otherwise unharmed as the ship continued its roll.

Overhead, the lifeboat swung like a pendulum on its davits. Holley stayed dry as he rode up and over the rolling vessel.

With a splash, the lifeboat settled into the water, an amazed Holley sitting warm and dry. Tumbling from the rotating bulkhead, Piechan was bobbing a few feet away. "Hey, Billy, give me a hand here," he called.

Holley leaned over to grasp Piechan's belt. With Piechan simultaneously pulling up and kicking against the water, Holley hauled him dripping from the straits. From the deck, Piechan could see that his lifeboat was still attached to the ship sinking beneath it when he felt a distinct bump from below.

Scrambling to the side, Holley and a shivering Piechan found Kierzek clawing his way up around the hull of the lifeboat. Holley and Piechan helped him aboard.

Once aboard, Kierzek considered the davit hoists, connected to the sinking ship. Afraid of being sucked below or blown apart by a boiler explosion, he panicked, walked to the stern, and jumped back into the water.

Holley looked up at the sound of the splash but quickly went back to work. He was consumed with removing the cotter pin from the block to get away from the davits and didn't have time to waste. *Cedarville* was sinking beneath the boat and would soon pull it under. The boat was equipped with a hatchet to cut the painter in just such an emergency, but it was lost when the boat was jolted by the swell.

More desperate crew gathered about the tethered boat. Piechan helped Deckhand Elmer Emke and Stokerman Tony Romys out of the water as Holley concentrated on the block. Another crewman surfaced to starboard, face down. Glancing aside, Holley called out, "Hey, guys, look over here. Someone's in trouble."

Reaching together, Piechan, Emke, and Romys grabbed their shipmate by the arms and belt. Limp, he offered no assistance as they hauled him aboard. As he cleared the rail, Piechan stumbled backward, falling to the deck. The body they were holding flopped unceremoniously into the boat, pinning Piechan to the deck. It was Jungman. His eyes were opened, and his mouth was wide in a silent scream, pouring water onto Piechan's face. It was clear that he was dead. Repulsed, Piechan squirmed beneath the heavy body but could not help but think, "*There but for the grace of God . . .*"

With Piechan trapped beneath his dead shipmate, the others helped to free the boat. Holley loosened the pin, and the block came free.

"Get him off of me!" Piechan screamed.

With the boat drifting safely, Holley and Emke pulled Jungman away. Shaken, Piechan sat upright and stared at the body as the others rowed to safety. Behind the retreating boat, the water sizzled as the remaining air was forced from the sinking hull.

When Brewster came to, he was underwater. Semiconscious, he sensed that his feet were tangled. Something was pulling him down. Struggling briefly, he pulled loose, and his life vest carried him to the surface. Turning, he found the ship. With its wheel slowly turning, air bubbled up from around the railings as *Cedarville* slipped beneath the surface.

Without warning, the engine room turned upside down. Lamp, Radke, and Wingo were slammed into the overhead as tons of coal, tools, bilge pumps, chairs, and boiling hot water from ruptured steam lines pummeled and scalded the stricken engineering team. Dazed and broken, they would probably have had no real cognizance of their fate as it unfolded over the next few minutes.

M/V *Weissenburg*—

The *Weissenburg* crew tracked the incident. "The sinking vessel is straight ahead," the third mate reported, his face against the radar hood.

"Full astern," the captain ordered. Stepping to the bridge wing, May saw the shadow of the submerged ship and heard the hiss of escaping air as *Weissenburg* slowed. Just beyond her bow, a bubbling geyser marked the spot where the self-unloader had slipped beneath the surface.

"All stop," he commanded as he crossed the bridge to the aft bulkhead. Depressing the switch, May spoke into a mounted microphone. "Man the lifeboats. The ship has sunk."

SS *Cedarville*—

Rushing water filled the inverted engineering spaces as Lamp, Radke, and Wingo drifted semi-conscious amid the oily debris. As the boiler submerged, the hinged door warped, allowing water ingress. The resulting explosion flashed throughout the spaces, churning air and water into an unbreathable mixture of steam, soot, and noxious gasses. If any of the engineering crew had survived the initial roll or subsequent explosion, they would quickly succumb as their lungs were seared by the poisonous, burning mixture.

Beneath the rising flood, a single piece of paper drifted through the railing of the maneuvering platform. On it, every speed change ordered by the bridge was recorded as executed by the engineering watch team. At the end of the watch the rough notes on the scratch sheet were to have been transferred to the bell book. Lamp never had the opportunity. Investigators would later search for the sheet in an attempt to solve the mystery of the sinking.

Cedarville had traveled more than two miles from the point of collision when she came to rest in 102 feet of water, 17,000 feet southeast of the Mackinac Bridge. Broken at the number seven hatch, the ship settled in pieces on her starboard side, eight of her crew already lost.

News reports kept the community informed in the days following the collision, as concerns turned from the crew and their families to understanding why it happened. Newspaper clippings courtesy of Len and Pat Gabrysiak.

Vessels Crash In Thick Fog

Norwegian Freighter, Limestone Carrier Hit

BY JOHN MUELLER AND JAMES TRELOAR
Free Press Staff Writers

The Great Lakes limestone carrier Cedarville collided with a Norwegian merchant vessel and sank in the fog-shrouded Straits of Mackinac Friday. Two men were killed. Eight others were missing and presumed dead. All were from the Cedarville.

Twenty-five of the Cedarville's 35-man crew were rescued from the frigid water about two miles east of the Mackinac Bridge which connects Michigan's Upper and Lower Peninsulas.

The dead are:

Stanley Haske, of Rogers City, wheelsman.
Edmund H. Jungman, of Frederick, deck watchman.

Listed as missing and presumed dead were:

Charles H. Cook, third mate.
William B. Asam, wheelsman.
Arthur J. Fuhrman, deck watchman.
F. Donald Lamp, chief engineer.
Reinhold F. Radtke, third assistant engineer.
Hugh Wingo, oiler.
Eugene F. Jones, stokerman.
Wilbert W. Bredow, stewart.

All eight reportedly lived in Rogers City.

Dr. Nicholas Lentini, chief of surgery at Cheboygan Hospital, said all were "undoubtedly dead."

"No one could survive the cold this long," he said.

Injured and admitted to Cheboygan Community Memorial Hospital were:

Angus E. Domke, Rogers City, watchman.
Ivan Trafelet, Millersburg, watchman.
Harry H. Bey, Rogers City, second assistant engineer.
William J. Friedhoff, Rogers City, oiler.

All from Cedarville

All the victims were from the crew of the 588-foot Cedarville, which sank within 21 minutes after colliding with the 420-foot Topdalsfjord, of Oslo.

Survivors said the Cedarville was hit "toward the bow" and took on water fast through a gaping hole in her hull.

The Cedarville, of the U.S. Steel Corp.'s Bradley Transportation Co. fleet, was loaded with limestone and was en route from Calcite, Mich., to Gary, Ind.

(Calcite is just south of Rogers City along the Lake Huron shoreline.)

The Topdalsfjord was headed for Port Arthur, Ont., for a load of grain.

E. C. Dagwell, of Mackinaw City, a former marine radio operator, said radio reports indicated the Norwegian vessel struck the Cedarville, which sank in about 100 feet of water.

Dagwell said the last word from the laker was: "The Cedarville is sinking."

Failed to Beach

He said the ship's captain, Martin E. Joppich, tried to beach the ship but was unsuccessful.

The Norwegian vessel was reported heading for port

Turn to Page 7A, Column 2

2 Die, 8 Missing In Ship Sinking

● Continued from Page One ●

for repairs. There was no immediate word on the extent of damage.

A Coast Guardsman said some of the missing men may have been trapped inside the shattered hull of the Cedarville.

Area residents said visibility when the ships crashed at 9:50 a.m. was less than 50 feet.

James G. Lietzow, 18, of Rogers City, a repairman helper who has been sailing less than two weeks, said:

"I was in the engine room when the jolt came. It wasn't bad, but I knew right away we had collided with something.

"I ran up on deck and the captain told us to get our life preservers on. We got the life boats ready to go and stood by, while the captain had her on full ahead, trying to beach her, trying to reach shore.

"She tilted a little but we stood by. Then, all of a sudden, she started going over. She turned right over. I tried to get into a life boat but missed and fell into the water."

Lietzow said he swam to a raft about 50 yards away and was rescued. He said "Everyone was hollering for help."

"But I thought we did pretty well," he said. "There was no panic."

Picked Up Quickly

Some of the Cedarville's survivors were picked up by the Topdalsfjord before she headed for port.

Others were picked up by the passing German vessel Weissenburg. A doctor aboard the Weissenburg cared for the injured.

Michigan State Police launched small rescue boats and asked private boat owners in the area to help in the search for survivors.

The Coast Guard icebreaker Mackinaw and cutters Sundew and Mesquite were sent to the scene, as were two smaller Coast Guard boats from nearby Mackinac Island.

Helicopters and planes from the Coast Guard station at Traverse City also were sent.

The Coast Guard said the search for survivors would continue until nightfall, but that the temperature of the water made it unlikely anyone could survive long.

Capt. Robert Waldron, a Coast Guard official in Cleveland, said a Board of Inquiry started an investigation immediately after word of the disaster was received.

Waldron said the Cedarville "must have really taken a wallop to go down that fast."

Shrouded by Fog and Grief, Rogers City Tries to Smile

BY WILLIAM SUDOMIER
Free Press Staff Writer

ROGERS CITY — At the foot of Ontario Street, Lake Huron laps at the shore of Rogers City.

On Saturday—the morning after the town's latest ship tragedy—it was foggy; the same kind of grayness that must have obscured the limestone carrier Cedarville from the Norwegian freighter Topdalsfjord until it was too late.

On Saturday morning, it looked like the world ended where the sloping beach dropped off into the nothingness that was lake and sky and fog.

* * *

AND, FOR MANY, the world had ended — for the numbed wives and the staring children of those the lake had taken.

No one was unaffected.

The sun burned down and on occasion, the beacon light on rocks at the end of the marina showed mysteriously, then faded.

Debby Jachcik, 11, a chubby blond girl in shorts, rode her bike down to the park and played on the swings.

Sometimes Debby played there with the older Haske boys, but the boys weren't there Saturday. Their father, Stanley, was dead, and they were home with their mother.

The foghorn at the nearby port of Calcite, the home of the limestone fleet, moaned.

Debby's dad, Stan Jachcik, was on the boats before he got married. He runs a gas station-garage now.

* * *

BEYOND DEBBY, kids sailed Dixie Cup boats in a storm drain that led to the lake and pretended they were limestone ships.

Debby stopped swinging and answered a question. "I think that Norwegian ship caused all the blame."

A block and a half away, a gray-haired woman named Esther Joppich answered the door at a white-shingled house.

She didn't open the door, saying:

"My husband's asleep. He's not talking to the newspapers. He gets shook up. He gets too upset. I'm just glad he's saved."

Martin E. Joppich, 54, was master of the Cedarville.

A block and half away, a blond woman in stretch pants showed up at the office of the weekly Presque Ile County Advance, and asked if she could help.

The blond was Gretchen, the burgomeister's daughter in the Kiwanis Club-sponsored Victor Herbert operetta "Red Mill," at the high school Friday night, but now she was back to being Mrs. Betty Claus, 34, again. She said the show went on—shakily—despite the tragedy. She said:

* * *

"FATHER (Robert G.) Smith — he's our director and a real professional — gave us a pep talk. He said we'd have to forget what happened, forget our personal feelings until the job was done.

"When that first laugh came through, it was a real good feeling. If it hadn't come, I think we — the cast, I mean — would have cried."

Outside the Advance offices, a tousle-haired man in a beige sport coat with "Lions Club" written on the back was hawking white canes to aid the blind.

Elmer Radka, 44, is prosecutor of Presque Isle County. He said that every time he stepped into Third Street to sell a cane someone would

Turn to Page 15A, Column 8

Rogers City Tries Hard To Smile

● Continued from Page One ●

approach him and remark: "Wasn't it terrible?" or "To think it could happen twice."

Soon cars, which had shunned Third Street most of the morning, began to glide slowly by.

No one drives fast in Rogers City. You have to allow time for approaching drivers to pause for middle-of-the-street chats.

* * *

THE SURVIVORS came downtown to talk, to have a drink, to feel the sun.

Half a block from the Advance, Bill Zinke, 35, a mild man with glasses, served a drink at the Servicemen's Club, which is in the Veterans Memorial Building.

Zinke went out Saturday morning and raised the American flag over the club. He figured the mourning wouldn't start until Monday. But for Rogers City, it seems the mourning never begins or ends.

Zinke heard on the radio that Mayor Karl Vogelheim had proclaimed a 30-day period of mourning.

Zinke went out and slowly lowered the flag to half-staff.

Rescue Captain Describes
Sinking of the Cedarville

SAULT STE. MARIE AP — been possible.

"I saw the shadow of the ship ~~under~~ and heard ~~the~~ hiss-

Jan A. Gronstol, second officer of the Norwegian vessel,

the helmsman repeat the orde[r] for a starboard turn, to tur[n] the wheel completely to th[e] right. Together, the two ma[n] uld turn the shi[p]

Saturday, May 8, 1965

2 DEAD, 8 MISSING AS SHIP SINKS IN MACKINAC STRAITS

Veteran of Seas Laid to Rest

BY E. J. DENO

ROGERS CITY — This Presque Isle County port city of 5,000 today began the grim task of burying its dead.

Stanley F. Haske, a 19-year

their sailors. They filled the church to capacity.

The Rev. Adalbert Narloch, pastor, was celebrant at the Reqieum High Mass. Pallbearers included Donald White, [Ja]mes Den[o]

dow, steward.

The news spread quickly but quietly across the Mt. Calvary Cemetery hillside as Rev. Narlo[ch] latin, "Requies-" "Rest in Peace."

Helmsman, Captain Don't Jibe on Stories

By WOODIE and JANE JARVIS
Times Special Writers

ST. IGNACE — The helmsman who steered the ill-starred freighter Cedar[ville] ~~from at his~~

the time he left Calcite with 14,000 tons of stone at 5 a.m. last Friday until only a few minutes before the collision with the Norwegian ship in heavy fog in the Straits of Mackinac.

Capt. Joppich said in his testimony Wednesday that he had ~~gone~~ half speed in the traffic

on the new course and was in danger of running aground on Major Shoals, a reef about three miles east of the Mackinac Bridge and one and one half miles east of the collision spot.

When advised by Cook that the ship was in danger of running aground on the reef the captain ordered a new course that would clear the reef to the ~~safe~~ testified.

turn until he sighted the Topdalsfjord visually at a distance of 900 feet, and that he did so then only in an attempt to escape the collision.

At some point while on the hard right turn, Gabrysiak said, the captain reduced the speed of his ship to half speed ahead. This would bring the ship's speed through the water to about five miles an hour compared to full speed of 12 miles an hour.

Gabrysiak contradicted ~~sa~~

Lost Ship's Captain Takes 5th Amendment at Inquiry

By STODDARD WHITE
Detroit News Marine Writer

ST. IGNACE, Mich., May 13. —The American captain whose lake freighter sank last Friday in the Straits of Mackinac refused to submit to cross-examination yesterday after telling a

District merchant marine safety officer, said all parties have the right to cross-examine and call witnesses and instructed the captain to answer Keig's first question.

MORE BODIES FOUND

Keenan in

terday in the engine room after divers cut open an outside door with a torch. They were the bodies of F. Donald Lamp, the chief engineer; and Reinhold F. Radtke, the third assistant ~~engi~~

house at the time of the collision.

Other highlights at the inquiry yesterday:

● Joppich said he never was able to get the Norwegian ship to answer him on the radiotelephone, and that other vessels had made the same complaint.

RADAR REPAIRED

Joppich said the Cedarville's radar equipment and its two radiophones both had t

was servic[e] it failed it had app[eared] satisfactor[y] ● He said ship neve[r] except th[at] blasts mea[nt] ing with c[?] he said he[?] matic fog long blas[ts] which he

Tuesday, Aug. 24, 1965 —THE DETROIT NEWS

Coast Guard Probes Role of Captain in Loss of Ship

ST. IGNACE, Mich., Aug. 24. —The Coast Guard opened a hearing here today to decide whether Capt. Martin Joppich, skipper of the freighter Cedarville, which went down last May

7 with 10 crewmen, should be allowed to keep his license to command ships.

The Cedarville rolled over and sank in the Straits of Mackinac after colliding with the Nor-

wegian motor vessel Topdalsfjord in thick fog.

The hearing opened amid charges that the captain, acting on orders from his employers, the Bradley Transportation Lines, a U.S. Steel Corp. subsidiary, was more concerned with attempting to save his ship than in protecting the lives of his crewmen.

Coast Guard on four charges of faulty seamanship. Testimony from four Topdalsfjord crew members was heard July 16 in Chicago.

Four crew members of the Cedarville are scheduled to testify today plus a fifth witness, Capt. Joseph Parrilla, fleet captain of the Bradley line. Scheduled witnesses at today's

● Wheelman Leonard T. Gabrysiak, who was in the pilot house steering the ill-starred vessel at the time of the crash.

● Watchman Ivan Trafelet, who was on lookout duty in the bow of the ship at collision time. Joppich is not expected to testify.

LAWYER ACCUSES

against U.S. Steel r $175,000 to $900,000.

In the damage su charged that: "Afte lision, the owner of through its agents, the captain of the tempted to save the proceeding to shore, allowing the crew to leave the vessel."

Coast Gd. Opens Probe In Collision Today at the Soo

MACKINAW CITY, AP — Boats and planes continued today to look for more survivors of Friday's freighter collision, but rescue workers believed that the seven seamen still missing had perished in the frigid waters of the Straits of Mackinac.

Two men were known dead as a result of the mishap in the fog-shrouded Straits, the narrow stretch of water which separates Michigan's two peninsulas.

"No one could survive the cold water this long," said Dr. Nicholas Lentini, chief of surgery at Cheboygan Community Hospital where five injured men were treated.

All the victims were members of the 35-man crew of the U.S. Steel Corp.'s Cedarville, a limestone carrier.

An immediate Coast Guard inquiry was ordered. It was called for today at Sault Ste. Marie.

The Cedarville and the 424-foot Norwegian freighter Topvalsfjord collided in thick fog four miles east of here.

Ripped in her port side, the Cedarville tried to make a dash for shallow water beaching but sank within 24 minutes.

Survivors told of clinging to life rafts in ice-cold water.

"I'm incredibly lucky," said Anthony W. Romys, 49, a Great Lakes seaman for nearly 20 years.

Romys said he was asleep on an upper deck of the Cedarville and, awakened by an alarm bell, leaped into a lifeboat.

The water temperature was reported in the low 40s.

The collision brought tragedy for a second time within seven years to the Lake Huron port town of Rogers City, Mich.

The freighter Carl D. Bradley, a sister ship of the Cedarville, broke in half in a furious Lake Michigan storm and lost all but two of her 35-man crew Nov. 19, 1958. Most were Rogers City men.

The Cedarville's three dead were wheelsman Stanley Haske, 36, father of five children; Edmund H. Jungman, 51, deck watchman, father of three, and Reinhold S. Radtke, 48, third engineer, father of seven.

Both Haske and Radtke lived in Rogers City. Jungman lived in the inland town of Frederic.

All the missing men lived in Rogers City.

The Bradley Transportation Co. of Rogers City operated both the Cedarville and the Bradley for U.S. Steel.

The Cedarville, bound for Gary, Ind., with a limestone cargo, and the Topvalsfjord, heading for Port Arthur, Ont. for a grain shipment, smashed together at 9:55 a.m.

Fog was so thick that visibility was reported at barely 50 feet. The straits were reported calm at the time.

The Cedarville's plunge to the bottom of 80 or 90 feet of water came quickly.

A spokesman for the Mackinac Bridge Authority said the Cedarville sent a radio "May Day" distress call at 10:10 a.m. and she sank at 10:19.

The Topvalsfjord, with her bow reported smashed, anchored for examination and then proceeded to Sault Ste. Marie.

The Coast Guard searched the straits all night. Planes were ordered to join the hunt with the first daylight today.

Witnesses said the Cedarville was hit on the port side

Continued on page 8

Coast Guard

Continued from page 1

approximately amidships by the Norwegian vessel's bow.

The Cedarville was reported approaching the Norwegian ship and was about to make its turn into the channel proper when the collision took place.

Woodrow Jarvis, free lance writer and photographer of DeTour, Mich., quoted an unidentified Cedarville survivor as saying his ship "gave a shudder" after the collision and then "went straight down like a stone."

Say Ship Running at Full Speed

ST. IGNACE (UPI) — The wheelsman of the limestone carrier Cedarville continued running his ship at full speed in dense fog despite a radar picture showing another ship coming at him on collision course, testimony at a Coast Guard inquiry revealed Thursday.

On the stand was Leonard Gabryziak, a licensed mate who was at the wheel of the Cedarville when she collided with the Norwegian merchantman Topdalsfjord in the Straits of Mackinac last Friday. The Cedarville sank within 21 minutes after the collision and 10 of her 35 crewmen died.

Cuts Speed in Half

Gabryziak, 35, said the two ships were only a few minutes apart when Capt. Martin Joppich ordered the speed cut in half. Joppich testified two days ago that he had slowed and was proceeding carefully long before he was aware of the immediate danger.

Regulations require Great Lakes ships to maintain a "prudent" speed in dense fog, but no speed is specified.

Gabryziak said he was in a position to observe everything in the pilot house. He said he could hear the captain and the third mate conversing and could hear all radio conversations. He said he could watch his compasses, the tachometer and the telegraph signaling the engine room. He could not, however, see the radar screen which was in a corner of the pilot house. The radar scope was being watched by Charles Cook, the third mate and one of the 10 crewmen who went down with the ship.

Gabryziak said evasive efforts were made to avoid a collision with the Topdalsfjord, which was heading east under the Mackinac Bridge while the Cedarville was heading west around the top of the Lower Peninsula toward Lake Michigan. The paths of the two ships had to cross.

Hear Fog Whistles

In a short time, Gabryziak said, the crew on the Cedarville began hearing the fog whistles of the approaching Topdalsfjord. He said Joppich made repeated efforts to contact the ship on the radio, but failed. The Cedarville began blowing its whistle.

Cook looked up from the radar and said, "She's pretty close." Tension mounted in the pilot house. Then a lookout on the port wing outside shouted, "There she is!"

Gabryziak said he looked out the window and saw the bow of the Topdalsfjord about 100 feet away. Joppich immediately ordered the engine room to "show."

Then Cook shouted, "Captain, we're going to be hit."

Joppich then signaled the engine room for full ahead and hard left.

First Mate Harry H. Piechan testified that Joppich never gave the order to abandon ship, although he did say, "get ready." The Cedarville was hit by the Topdalsfjord, was badly damaged and made a run for the beach. But she never made it and went down.

The St. Ignace phase of the inquiry was to end today. Topdalsfjord officers and crewmen gave testimony at Sault Ste. Marie earlier in the week and testimony was taken in Cleveland Sunday from the crew of a German merchantman that picked up the survivors.

The hearing will reopen in Grand Rapids next Friday. At that time a Federal Court judge will determine whether Joppich had the right to refuse to be cross-examined by attorneys for the Norwegian ship. Joppich's attorney had cited the 5th Amendment Wednesday in refusing to let the captain be cross examined.

Captain of Sunken Ship to Be Charged

ST. IGNACE, Mich., July 10. —The captain of the sunken lake freighter Cedarville will be charged with negligence by the U.S. Coast Guard at a hearing in Chicago Friday.

Martin E. Joppich, of Rogers City, was master of the 588-foot Bradley Thansportation Line limestone carrier when it collided with a Norwegian motor vessel during a heavy fog May 7 in the Straits of Mackinac.

While the second vessel, the Topdalsfjord, suffered no casualties and was able to proceed under her own power, the Cedarville sank, carrying 10 of her crew to their deaths.

CHARGES PLANNED

Lt. Cmdr. Arthur W. Gove, a member of the three-man Coast Guard of inquiry that held hearings into the sinking, said he will make the charges against Joppich.

Gove said the charges are only against Joppich's master's license, which could be revoked, suspended or otherwise restricted. Joppich faces no personal penalties as a result of the hearing, said Gove.

Even if it desired, the Coast Guard could not bring charges against the other captain, Rasmus Haaland, because it has no jurisdiction over his license.

'EXCESSIVE SPEED'

Specifically, Gove said, the charges against Joppich involve his alleged excessive speed while proceeding through the fog and his failure to take proper precautions when he encountered the Topdalsfjord.

The first charge is that "while under way on May 7 under conditions of fog and restricted vision he failed to navigate his vessel at a moderate speed . . ."

The second charge, containing three counts, states that once he heard the fog signal of another ship not far off his bow, he failed to immediately reduce his speed.

Also, that he failed to sound a danger signal when there was no reply from the approaching vessel to the Cedarville's one-blast passing signal, and that he failed to reduce his vessel to bare steerageway or to have stopped and reversed "within one half mile" of another vessel "whose intentions were not known."

All of these things, the Coast Guard charges, "contributed to the collision with the Topdalsfjord."

The Chicago hearing, where Joppich will be represented by Roman Keenan, an attorney for the U.S. Steel Corp., which is parent company of the Bradley Fleet, was scheduled to coincide with the arrival there of the Norwegian motor vessel.

FIRST TRIP BACK

The Topdalsfjord is making its first trip back into the Great Lakes since the collision. Gove said officers of the Topdalsfjord will be called to substantiate the Coast Guard's claims.

A second session of the same hearing, which is being held by Charles Carroll, hearing examiner for the 9th Coast Guard District in Cleveland, will be held Aug. 24, probably in St. Ignace, so that testimony may be taken from the Cedarville's surviving crew members.

MILLIONS IN CLAIMS

Meanwhile, 11 claims totaling $3,750,000 will be filed in Chicago's Federal District Court Monday against the Topdalsfjord by three widows of Cedarville crewmen and eight injured survivors.

Victor G. Hanson, a Detroit maritime attorney who heads a trial committee representing the claimants, said similar suits are pending against the Cedarville's owners, but will not be filed until photographs have been taken of the sunken ship by divers later this month.

Lake Tragedy Clouded by Contradiction

66th Year - No. 255   ALPENA, MICHIGAN, SATURDAY MORNING, MAY 29, 1965   12 PAGES   10 CENTS

The last fateful voyage of the ill-fated freighter Cedarville

and into the predawn grayness the Cedarville was tied up to the dock in Rogers City, into the Great Lakes.

huge quarry and stone crushing Calcite operation.
Th loading tower was pouring her hatches full of steel chunks of lime-

self-unloader in the ship-building and repair yards of the Defoe Shipbuilding Co. in Bay City.
The Cedarville's tragic story opens with First Mate Harry H. Piechan, a huge man weighing

went to his cabin, cleaned up, and finished out his watch on call there.
Now the scene shifts to the bridge of the ship, where the navigators and the helmsman took over their responsibilities

Third Mate Charles H. Cook, 51, of Rogers City, who was operating the radar screen, charting the course, and keeping the log in the chartroom about 20 feet from his main position at their radarscope.
Cook's first entry in the log

Waiting Continues for 3 Rogers City Widows

BY IRENE BEYST

It is a period of waiting and mate; Hugo Wingo, oiler, and Eugone F. Jones, stokerman, all of Rogers City.

Ship Searched

Both scuba and hard-hat divers have been through every part of the ship, which is sunk in 106 feet of water on the east side of the Mackinac Bridge, and have proceeded to search the ruins

Cheboygan in the Lower Peninsula, and along the Upper Peninsula from four miles west of the bridge east and north seven miles. They also have walked around Round Island completely and 21 miles of the Bois Blanc Island beach.
It is likely the search will be called off in a few days

It is a time of waiting for findings of the Coast Guard Board of inquiry which completed hearing for the time being at least—a week ago in Grand Rapids after Cedarville Capt. Martin Joppich answered questions by attorneys of the Norwegian ship operators. At the advice of his counsel

laws to answer questions dealing with the collision. His attorney objected that cross examination by counsel for a foreign flag was contrary to regulations.
Going at Full Speed
Testimony revealed that the Cedarville was going full

was heavy static making communication difficult.
There were three ships headed downbound toward the Cedarville, the Benson Ford, the German Weissenberg and the Norwegian Topdalsfjord and the Upper

The Cedarville took a hard right turn and reduced to half speed to avoid a ship coming straight at it, but Major Shoals reef, was ahead and the ville's course. And

May 10

Board Quizzes Norwegian Seamen

Norse Ship's Efforts to Avoid Crash Told

Lost Ship Ran at Full Speed in Fog, Wheelsman Testifies

By STODDARD WHITE
Detroit News Marine Writer

ST. IGNACE, Mich., May 14.—Though radar was showing a suspicious ship approaching him headon in dense fog, the captain of the steamer Cedarville maintained full speed ahead until minutes before the collision that sank it, the ship's wheelsman testified here yester-

when she collided last Friday with the Norwegian freighter Topdalsfjord and sank in 102 feet of water in the Straits of Mackinac, with the loss of 10 lives.
At one point Gabryziak seemed to confirm previous testimony by the Norwegian captain that the Cedarville sud-

sion—that he had slowed and was proceeding carefully long before he became aware the danger ahead was becoming acute.
But Gabryziak said the ships were only a few minutes apart when Joppich finally ordered the speed cut in half—still not

ship." he maintained stoutly, frequently exhibiting pride as he told how he kept the ship on the changing courses as ordered.
The Cedarville was curving west around the top of the Lower Peninsula, bound for

pich and the missing third mate, Charles Cook, conversing. He could hear all radio conversations.
He could watch not only his two compasses but the clock, the tachometer and the

order "Hard right!" in fort to get out of the ship's path.
This headed the ship erly, perhaps across the of the Norwe-
"hard eelsman ble dur long

Cedarville's Skipper Due to Face Negligence Count

Coast Guard Set to Take Action in Ship Sinking

Home Port of The Coast Guard Cutter MACKINAW   **CHEBOYGAN DAILY TRIBUNE**   Be A Booster Talk Up Your Own Home Town

7TH YEAR NO. 192   TUESDAY AUGUST 24, 1965 CHEBOYGAN, MICHIGAN   Serving Cheboygan County and the Mackinac Straits Bridge Area   SEVEN CENTS

CAPT. JOPPICH OF CEDARVILLE GIVES GUILTY PLEA IN SINKING

☆ ☆   ☆ ☆   ☆ ☆

Washington
Merry - Go - Round
By
DREW PEARSON

Washington — It has now been seven months and twenty

58 GI's Perish In Plane Crash

HONG KONG AP — Fire believed there were at least 20

☆ ☆ ☆ ☆ ☆ ☆ ☆ ☆

At His Desk In the City Hall   **Army Jeep** Takes Blame

Accepts Blame on All Counts

Capt. Joppich Faces Loss or Suspension of Master's License

By WOODIE JARVIS
Times Special Writer

ST. IGNACE — Capt. Martin Joppich, master of the sunken freighter Cedarville, through his attorney, pleaded guilty today to all charges of negligence the Coast Guard has brought against his Master's License.

In a hearing that lasted only 15 minutes, U.S. Steel attorney Roman Keenan opened the hearing by pleading the captain guilty in absence, to the four charges.

Keenan said the captain is now confined to a hospital under medical treatment as a result of the sinking. He declined to name the hospital.

By pleading guilty, none of five scheduled witnesses were called to the stand. Four of these were Cedarville seamen who were to testify against their captain.

* * *

The Coast Guard charges against Joppich were:

—That while under way in the Straits of Mackinac May 7, under conditions of fog and restricted vision, he failed to navigate his vessel at a moderate speed, and that this failure contributed to the collision with the Topdalsfjord;

—That Capt. Joppich violated Coast Guard statutes for safe navigation on three specific counts.

1—He failed to reduce at once the vessel's speed to bare steerageway upon hearing approximately not more than four points from the right ahead the fog signal of another vessel, thus contributing to the collision with the Topdalsfjord. 2— That he failed to sound the danger signal when there was no reply from the approaching ship to the Cedarville's one blast signal. 3— That he failed to reduce the speed of his vessel to bare steerageway, or to have stopped and reversed after having been approached within one half mile by another vessel, the intentions of which were not known.

* * *

The hearing was held before Charles Carroll, civilian hearing examiner for the U.S. Coast Guard Ninth District.

Carroll accepted the plea of guilty to all charges, and said he would issue a determination in the case within the next few weeks.

Carroll asked both Keenan and Lt. Cmdr. Arthur W. Gove who presented the Coast Guard case whether or not they wished to make any recommendations concerning possible sanctions that might be brought against the captain's license.

Commander Gove said "He

See TESTIMONY—Page 2

14

Rescue

May 7, 1965
M/V *Weissenburg*—
1030

The cries of surviving seamen echoed across the choppy surface. As *Weissenburg* drifted closer to the struggling crew, the forward lookout heard their shouts dead ahead. This he reported to the captain.

"Stand by to launch the lifeboats," May ordered. The command was passed, and on the forward deck fourteen German sailors scrambled into their boats.

STRAITS OF MACKINAC—

Tossed into the frigid waters, deckhand Bob Bingle surfaced no more than six feet from the forward life raft, which bobbed placidly over the gentle swells. Despite the drag of his boots and trousers, Bingle swam to the raft and hoisted himself aboard. As he climbed in, the second mate appeared on the opposite side and steadied the raft. Seconds later, the two huddled together against the chill, wet and shivering, searching the fog for signs of their shipmates.

In the port lifeboat, Holley and Ron Piechan listened for signs of struggle. They had already pulled ten men to safety when they spotted Kierzek in apparent distress. Maneuvering the lifeboat to his aid, they dragged him aboard as he clutched his abdomen in pain.

Fifty yards distant, Stan Haske was drifting away from the pack. Stunned by the thirty-seven-degree water, his body went into shock with the sudden drop in skin temperature, which left him gasping for breath as hypothermia set in.

With his head barely above the surface, Haske's teeth gently chattered and his chalky skin rippled with goose bumps as he pulled through the water in search of his comrades.

Len was cold and confused. Shouts from every direction through the fog only disoriented him more. "Am I going to die?" he wondered haltingly with the cold. As he struggled to stay warm, he saw his brothers' faces. Clarence, Gene, and Martin had each sailed for a few years and now wore suits and ties to the office each day. Stanley had survived the boiler explosion aboard the *White* but had been severely burned. Frank, of course, had been lost at sea. "And now," Len thought, "I'm going to . . ."

Unable to complete the thought, he reverted to his prayer. "Hail Mary, mother of God . . . ," he continued as he drifted above the sunken vessel.

M/V *Weissenburg*—

Alone in the wheelhouse, Captain May steadied his ship as his lifeboats were lowered away. As the ship inched forward, it sliced through the eddying whirlpool and bubbles that marked *Cedarville*'s grave.

Suddenly, a Coast Guard workboat emerged from the mist to starboard. May reached for the tranceiver as a voice crackled on the loudspeaker. "German merchant vessel located one mile east of the Mackinac Bridge, this is Coast Guard four-zero-five-two-seven, responding to a Mayday. Please state your condition, over."

"This is Captain May of the motor vessel *Weissenburg*," he replied. "We are also responding to the Mayday. The American vessel *Cedarville* has capsized and sunk. I have boats in the water looking for survivors. We have heard shouts throughout the area. We are standing by for your direction."

"Understood, *Weissenburg*. Keep up the search. We will contact you with further instructions as the situation develops. Coast Guard out."

May sighed as he hung up. This would be a very long day. So much for meeting his delivery schedule, he thought.

ROGERS CITY, MICHIGAN—

Jean Brewster frantically paced her living room, not knowing what to do. She had just turned on her marine radio when a report issued that *Cedarville* was lost. Her mind racing, she finally decided to call Ed's family. She broke into tears as his grandmother answered the telephone.

"Hello? Jean, is that you, dear? What's wrong?"

Between sobs Jean managed only a few words. Ed's ship had sunk.

Across town, Elaine Przybyla was in a better frame of mind. She too had received word of the sinking but refused to worry. She had lost her brother, Alva, when the *Bradley* sank, but her cousin was one of the two survivors. Anything could happen, and she would not panic until she had a reason to do so.

Beth Haske prepared lunch for her five sons. The three oldest would be coming home from school soon, and she had much to do. As she sliced sandwich meat, she had no idea that her husband was struggling for his life.

STRAITS OF MACKINAC—
1033

Survival in cold water depends on several factors, including water temperature, body size, and activity. Haske was a tall, slender man, and the temperature of the Straits was barely above freezing. As

Haske thrashed about, his arms and legs stirred through the water, increasing the cold circulation over his skin.

Haske's core body temperature had slipped below ninety-seven degrees Fahrenheit. Although the metabolic processes of his body were sufficient to generate enough heat each hour to warm two liters of ice-cold water to body temperature, heat transfer through the skin and lungs was robbing him of precious energy. Sensing the drop in his core temperature, his hypothalamus triggered waves of shivering to increase surface heat production by more than 500 percent in a desperate attempt to stem the heat loss.

Haske tried to tighten his jacket but found the effort futile. He thought it curious that his fingers would no longer respond to his command.

WLC Control
PORT CALCITE, MICHIGAN—

The sound of screeching celluloid filled the small space as the tape wound ever tighter around the small rubber gears through which it ran. Lunging for the machine, Hassett turned it off, cursing to himself as he struggled to free the jammed tape without breaking it. With a miniature screwdriver in hand, he removed the faceplate and slowly reversed the gears. Eying the damaged tape, Hassett opted to change the reel. Better safe than sorry.

M/V *Topdalsfjord*—

Having tended to his own vessel's damage, Captain Hoagland ordered *Topdalsfjord*'s lifeboats launched. He had drifted southeast from the point of collision, and the cries of desperate seamen cut through the fog like a knife. "What has happened here?" he mumbled aloud as he watched the lifeboat crews scramble into position.

STRAITS OF MACKINAC—

Clinging to a bumper block, Mike Idalski started when a shrill whistle pierced the fog. Thirty-five yards distant, Gabrysiak was whistling with his fingers as he kicked against the cold waters. The signal worked, and Gabrysiak was soon relieved when the remaining lifeboat appeared to his left. Pulling alongside him, Holley and another crewman leaned over to reach him as he grabbed for the gunwale. His last thought as they pulled him aboard was that he would live.

Passed out, he was laid on deck and wrapped in a blanket.

"Hey, what about me?" Idalski called as the raft drifted on.

CHEBOYGAN, MICHIGAN—
1042

Eighteen miles from the point of collision, the Coast Guard cutter *Mackinaw* cast off her lines and got under way. Clearing the harbor, she opened up, reaching for the site of the collision as quickly as possible.

STRAITS OF MACKINAC—

Counting the minutes he had been in the water to distract himself, Przybyla was jolted back to the present when a raft emerged from the mist. Shivering uncontrollably, Przybyla slowly swam through the choppy waters to the raft. He discovered two men huddled aboard when he reached the side. They helped him up, and together they struggled on to find more survivors.

Three hundred feet distant, Przybyla could hear his friend Jarvis and assistant cook Arthur Martin crying for help. But with only one oar they were unable to paddle against the swells to rescue their shipmates.

Haske shivered violently as his core body temperature dropped below ninety-two degrees. Sluggish and confused, and with his abdominal incision aching dully, he bobbed in the choppy swells, supported only by the buoyancy of his life vest. His last thoughts were of his wife and children as he struggled against the cold.

PITTSBURGH, PENNSYLVANIA—
1046

Within an hour of the reported collision a company plane roared to life, bound for Cheboygan with Vice President James Gray, Chuck Khoury, and Joe Parilla. Their mission: damage control. Before take-off, Parilla telephoned Buehrens with instructions to set up a communications command post and to employ local divers to get control of the site. Implementing preplanned damage control measures, Khoury and Parilla were expected to present U.S. Steel as responsive to the needs of the local community while maintaining exacting control over the investigation and the flow of information therefrom.

Along the way, the team would stop in Cleveland to pick up Thomas Harbottle and his engineering support staff before turning northward toward the Straits. Meanwhile, in Port Calcite, a weary Buehrens shouted through his open door to his secretary, "Put me through to Durocher and Van Antwerp in Cheboygan."

Przybyla helped Idalski, Erickson, Stan Rygwelski, and Harry Piechan into the raft. Piechan proved the most challenging as it drifted on. Weighing in at 350 pounds, he could not pull himself aboard. After a few minutes, Ed Brewster considered the coil of rope upon which he had been sitting. Together, he and Przybyla fashioned a loop that they secured around the first mate's leg. Heaving together, the six men balanced along the opposite side of the raft to roll Piechan aboard the raft, which sagged under the weight.

M/V *Weissenburg*—

May received word that a survivor had been found near the ship. Floating in his life vest, he had been taken into tow and brought alongside to the gangway. Leaving the wheel, May darted to the bridge wing to see Harry Bey struggling up the ladder with an obviously broken leg. Aghast, the captain shouted to the chief engineer on the forecastle. "Eric! Help that man aboard. And swing the derrick over to assist the others."

"Aye, sir," Chief Engineer Rhodes replied, energizing the crane and lowering a personnel basket for the injured seaman.

STRAITS OF MACKINAC—

Having come upon a seaman flailing in the water, the men of *Weissenburg*'s port lifeboat stopped to bring him aboard. After pulling the delirious man from the water, however, it was all they could do to restrain him from jumping from the boat. As they struggled to keep him safe, Wilbert Bredow appeared in the distance, waving and calling for help. Sadly, before they could bring their boat around, he grew silent and slipped beneath the icy surface.

As Haske's core temperature dropped below ninety degrees, his hypothalamus shut down all peripheral blood flow and reduced pulse and respiration to conserve energy. Violent waves of shivering continued to rack his body, but they were becoming less frequent as fatigue and carbon dioxide buildup caused muscle rigidity.

Instinctively curled into a fetal position, Haske panted slowly as the heat-bearing vapor escaped his mouth, swirled across his puffy blue skin, and faded into the foggy air.

1055

Tulgetske had been treading water for nearly half an hour when *Cedarville*'s lifeboat pulled alongside. Ron Piechan and Holley grinned over the side. "Need a lift?" Holley joked.

"Very funny. Just get me out of the water," Tulgetske replied. Stiff, numb, and cold, he offered little assistance as the two hoisted him in. He was badly bruised as his arms and ribs scraped over the gunwale, but he was glad to be aboard.

With Tulgetske safely aboard, the lifeboat continued on. Martin and Jarvis were found clinging to a propane tank. Trafelet drifted separately and was too stiff to help himself aboard. Together, the growing boat crew dragged him to safety.

Scanning for shipmates, Tulgetske shouted as the large gray bow of the *Weissenburg* cut through the fog. Beside it, a smaller whaleboat motored along, veering in their direction upon contact. Back-paddling to clear the massive hull, the lifeboat crew stopped as the whaleboat pulled alongside. *Cedarville*'s lifeboat was trailing a painter in the water from the bow. With boat hook in hand, one of the rescuers lifted the painter and tied off, towing the stricken lifeboat to the larger ship. The tethered vessels maneuvered alongside, where the lifeboat was brought parallel with the gangway. Secured to the shifting platform, the lifeboat crew started the long, hard climb to the *Weissenburg*'s weather deck.

Topside, First Officer Kamberg counted heads. Thirteen saved, one dead. Unable to bring him aboard, the weakened lifeboat crew left Jungman behind. With the ship's steward herding the survivors below, Kamberg ordered the rescue platform shifted to the lifeboat. Jungman was solemnly lifted by the rescuers to the platform and hoisted to the deck to be discretely carried below.

Stan Haske was now beyond caring. Unconscious and drifting, supported only by his life vest, he was coming perilously close to death as his body temperature plummeted through the eighties. His pulse no longer palpable, his body was entering a state of metabolic hibernation in a desperate bid for survival.

ROGERS CITY, MICHIGAN—

Jones's family doctor stood over the bed of Eugene's daughter, Gena. In her seventh month of pregnancy, Gena heard news of the sinking on the radio. Panicked and grief stricken, she began to bleed badly. The family physician was called immediately.

The doctor had checked the baby's heartbeat, and it sounded fine, but he stood frowning at his patient. "I want you to take one of these this afternoon and again tonight if you feel anxious. They will help you rest." The doctor handed a bottle of sedatives across the bed to her mother.

Marion assured the doctor that Gena would take them as prescribed.

Gena protested, insisting that she would be alright, but the doctor was firm. She was to take her medicine and stay in bed for at least one day.

Frightened by the near-miscarriage, Gena agreed, took her medicine, and promptly went to sleep as the doctor left her family to gather by the radio in the living room.

M/V *Weissenburg*—
1101

The ship's medic examined each of the men in turn. Though cold and bruised, most were none the worse for wear.

Holley had to be cut from his life vest. He had tied several knots in the strapping to prevent the cork vest from coming loose and breaking his neck if he was thrown into the water. Visibly shaken, he was unable to hold the warm drinks offered by the crew. An assistant helped Holley drink from a cup as the medic applied warm compresses to his face and neck.

STRAITS OF MACKINAC—

The *Cedarville* raft bobbed gently in *Weissenburg*'s bow wave as the freighter slipped alongside. With a shout, the seven shivering seamen, huddling in the swamped raft, strained for the line tossed from above. Though they first feared that the oncoming ship would run them down, they were awestruck as one of the German crewmen slid down the line to secure the raft.

"I've never seen such seamanship," said Brewster, steadying *Weissenburg*'s Jacob's ladder as Erickson, Przybyla, Bingle, Idalski, and Harry Piechan scrambled topside. Once aboard, they were all shown to empty passenger cabins scattered amidships, stripped, wrapped in blankets, and given dry clothes. Soon the ship's steward appeared with rum and steaming pots of tea, coffee, and hot chocolate.

Still shivering, most of the frightened raft crew were then tucked away into warm bunks, where they tossed fitfully until overtaken by exhaustion.

Drifting alone, Haske panted softly. Shallow puffs of steam escaped his blue lips as his core temperature dipped below seventy-eight. Unable to sustain its normal pace, his chilled heart faltered. Even so, as he went into ventricular fibrillation the stalwart muscle struggled on until, no longer capable of sustained activity, it stopped.

With a hiss, his lungs deflated, and his face pitched forward into the water. Though unconscious and apparently lifeless, brain activity continued. With the proper medical attention, Haske could still be saved.

1110

Still searching, one of the *Weissenburg* boats spotted a balding man waving and calling hoarsely for help. Within a minute, Captain Joppich was aboard, shivering beneath a wool blanket at the bottom of the boat.

Returning to their ship, which had drifted on, the rescuers found five more men struggling in the frigid waters. A sixth they found floating facedown in the water. "Oh no, Haske didn't make it," a dejected Joppich thought as the German crew hauled him aboard.

Though apparently dead, two of the *Weissenburg* seamen began artificial respiration on the man as the coxswain opened the throttle to hurry back to the ship.

Detecting a faint pulse, the rescuers smiled as they rolled him onto the lift platform for transport topside.

M/V *Weissenburg*—

Kamberg called up to the captain to report the incoming casualty.

"Understood," May replied as he keyed the radio. "Coast Guard, this is *Weissenburg*. Please be advised that we have taken twenty-seven men aboard, including one dead, several wounded, and one who appears to be hypothermic and not breathing. We could use a doctor out here."

"Roger, *Weissenburg*," the radio crackled. "The icebreaker *Mack-*

inaw is approaching your position with a doctor aboard. Should be there in an hour or so. Do what you can to keep the hypothermic man alive. Contact us with any new developments."

"Will do, Coast Guard. *Weissenburg* out."

Stepping from the bridge, May called to the first officer across the deck. "Medical help is about an hour away. Get that man below and see to it that he is warmed up."

"Aye, sir," Kamberg replied as he directed the two men who carried Haske to the waiting hatch.

ROGERS CITY, MICHIGAN—

Lou Brege glanced nervously at the clock. The boys would be waiting for her to bring them home for lunch, but she found it difficult to pull herself away from the radio. *Weissenburg*'s account of survivor rescue and body recovery was riveting. Transfixed, she waited until the last minute before finally breaking away, rushing up the stairs and out to her car to speed down Third Street to the nearby school.

Pat Gabrysiak had heard about the collision on the radio, then turned on the television. Nothing. The two staticky channels carried nothing but mindless soap operas. She had called the plant twice in the last half hour, but they would tell her nothing. Now, holding Lenny Jr., she listened to the radio, waiting for news.

MACKINAW CITY, MICHIGAN—

Dick Ireland turned his vehicle into the parking lot at the William Shepler Marina. At the far end, a police officer waved at him through the haze. Beckoned forward, the ambulance passed the narrow gate onto the nearly abandoned pier to join two other emergency vehicles called in from Indian River to help deal with the expected casualties.

Backed into position, the three converted station wagons effectively blocked the pier, forming a barricade beyond which the local authorities could keep the curious and the media from encroaching as the survivors started to arrive.

CG-40527—
1115

Skirting the area, the senior petty officer turned toward the Norwegian vessel hove-to near the point of collision. "Foreign vessel, this is Coast Guard four-zero-five-two-seven. Please identify yourself."

"This is the *Topdalsfjord,*" Captain Hoagland responded. "We have sustained minor bow damage but are otherwise seaworthy. We are standing by for your instructions."

"Understood, *Topdalsfjord,*" the young enlisted man replied as he jotted the name on a notepad beside the helm. "If you are not declaring an emergency, please proceed to . . ." Silence ensued as he consulted his chart and radar for a clear anchorage. "Please proceed to anchorage off of Mackinaw City and stand by for further instructions."

With that, the small boat turned from the freighter, arcing past the collision site. Several minutes later, the forward lookout shouted over the noise of the Norwegian vessel's engines. "Debris, dead ahead." *Cedarville*'s forward life raft floated empty through the oil slick that marked the vessel's grave. Indeed, as all of the survivors had been rescued by *Weissenburg,* the efforts of the Coast Guard would prove fruitless hereafter.

M/V Weissenburg—

Gabrysiak was amazed. Huddled beneath his blanket, he shared a room with Holley, who appeared shaken but none the worse for wear. Holley drew from a pack of dry cigarettes in his shirt pocket, handing one to the helmsman.

"How come you look so dry?" Gabrysiak demanded, a wry look on his face.

"Well, it's like this," Holley responded. "I was sitting in the port lifeboat when the ship rolled to starboard. Most everyone else was throwed out, but I held on. The ship swung me over and set me down in the lifeboat, pretty as you please."

Gabrysiak pulled aside the blanket to examine his bluish legs.

"Lucky you," he mumbled. He was told that the German crew had cut his pants from around his swollen legs as they placed him in a hot shower, but he remembered little of the episode. Now, leaning toward the offered light, he puffed deeply, trying to forget the dull throb in his lower extremities before returning to the warmth of his bunk

Forward, Captain May ducked as he stepped onto the mess decks. Those who were not bed-ridden sat together in stunned silence sipping their coffee and tea. A few murmured, mourning their lost friends and blaming Captain Joppich for not releasing the crew, but most sat quietly, enjoying the warmth of the room. As one of the survivors poured a glass of rum from the bottle in the middle of the table, May approached, laying a hand upon his shoulder. "No, son," he said with a heavy German accent, "take the whole bottle."

James Lietzow smiled back at him, nodded, and upended the bottle. He needed it.

CHEBOYGAN, MICHIGAN—
1132

Joseph Van Antwerp Sr. turned onto the company pier, making a line directly for the tug *Joe Van*. Having spoken with Buehrens, he was anxious to get the vessel on-site. Shifting the car into neutral, he left the key in the ignition and slammed the door before jogging across the pier and up the gangplank. Stepping through the red-rimmed hatch, he swung upward onto the ladder and climbed to the pilothouse. Dive foreman Chuck Marsh was waiting in the pilot's chair.

"What's up, boss?" Marsh asked.

Van Antwerp did not reply. Instead, he lifted the microphone, keying the energized transmitter. "Coast Guard, this is the tug *Joe Van*. Do you require assistance with the search and rescue in the Straits, over?"

"That's affirmative, *Joe Van*. Check in with the on-scene coordinator. We can use the help."

Van Antwerp smiled. As expected, the Coast Guard needed more search vessels. "Prepare to get under way," he said as he left the bridge.

M/V *Weissenburg*—
1148

Stanley Haske was not responding. Although he was receiving constant attention in the ship's sick bay, his pulse never exceeded a murmur and he had yet to take a breath on his own. Exhausted, the medic finally gave up. "Call the captain," he said to his assistant. "We've lost this one."

Haske's body was cold and blue, and his brain function dwindled to silence as the German sailor respectfully drew a sheet over his lifeless face and made an appropriate entry in the infirmary log.

M/V *Joe Van*—
1205

Joe Van departed the Cheboygan yard with five men aboard. In charge, Marsh was the most anxious. He had sailed with five of the *Cedarville* crew aboard *Clymer* in 1953. As the tug passed the breakwater, he whispered a prayer for his friends.

CLEVELAND, OHIO—
1248

The company plane touched down briefly to embark Pittsburgh Steamship technical advisors as well as a few communications technicians to augment the WLC crew and to establish a mobile command post in Cheboygan. Captain Harbottle shook hands with Gray, Khoury, and Parilla before finding his seat. Leaning across the narrow aisle, Khoury brought him up to speed. Fully laden, *Cedarville* had been holed amidships and sank in about a hundred feet of water attempting a run to the shore. The search and rescue was ongoing, and it was entirely possible that men were trapped below. The Coast Guard was already on the scene, and it was imperative that company representatives get the wreckage site under control.

"Do we have anyone in the area?" Harbottle asked.

"*Munson* is steaming in from the west, and we have retained

Durocher and Van Antwerp to coordinate the salvage," Parilla interjected from the seat behind.

Harbottle nodded, glancing over his shoulder. "OK. As soon as we land, I'll hook up with Durocher and monitor the salvage and search for bodies, uh, survivors."

With that, Khoury leaned back in his seat. The officers passed the remainder of the flight in silence, considering the potential for loss of life and damage to the company that the situation presented.

M/V *Weissenburg*—

Captain May had ordered his boats retrieved to shift his freighter from the debris field when his radio crackled to life.

"Merchant vessel located two miles east of Mackinac Point, this is the Coast Guard icebreaker *Mackinaw*. Please identify yourself."

"Roger, *Mackinaw*, I am Captain Otto May of the German freighter *Weissenburg*. We have been on scene since the collision and have taken on survivors. We also have two dead. Please advise the availability of medical assistance, over."

A few seconds later, a different voice answered. "Captain May, this is Captain Chiswell. We have a doctor and several medical assistants aboard. We have you on radar, but please sound your horn as we approach. I intend to round up to come alongside to starboard. Can you have your crew standing by?"

"Yes. I am retrieving my boat and will have my deck crew in place when you arrive."

Still holding the microphone, May reached with his left hand to pull the well-worn cord. Overhead, *Weissenburg*'s whistle pierced the fog as the icebreaker adjusted to maintain an intercept course.

Even as the rescuers converged, formal search and rescue operations were well under way. Adjacent to the runway at the nearby Coast Guard Air Station in Traverse City, a pair of Sikorsky S-62 Seaguard helicopters, their rotors whipping through the fog, were cleared to take off despite the limited visibility blanketing the region. Surface units of varying size and shape from both sides of the Straits were also dispatched to the scene. No platform was spared the grim task as even the aging buoy tender *Sundew* and harbor tug *Naugatuck* labored through the fog-laden expanse in a race with small craft launched by the state police to be the first to join the Coast Guard units already on-site.

Throughout the day, merchant vessel and private craft alike would be pressed into service in a vain search for more survivors. In fact, all who had survived the tragedy were now safely aboard *Weissenburg*.

William Shepler Marina
MACKINAW CITY, MICHIGAN—

Filling the tiny office, the state police, the county sheriff, and several reporters from local newspapers gathered around the harbormaster's marine radio, listening intently as *Weissenburg* guided *Mackinaw* into position to transfer the survivors. During the course of the evolution, the shortwave radio crackled with news of the sinking and the body count.

Hospitals in St. Ignace, Mackinaw City, Cheboygan, and Petoskey had been alerted to the situation and had long since prepared their emergency staff for the expected influx of casualties. Ambulance stretchers were rolled out onto the narrow pier, just beyond knots of anxious bystanders and family, just beginning to arrive from Rogers City.

USCGC *Mackinaw*—

At the terminus of the bow, an unrated seaman squinted through the fog, searching for the ship apparently sounding a signal dead ahead. Clad in dungarees, a thin blue utility jacket, and a woolen watch cap, the teenaged Coastie shivered against the cold, damp air. As his ship inched forward, he finally caught sight of the other vessel. Atop his head, sound-powered phones were plugged into the microphone unit attached to a harness about his neck. Depressing the button on the microphone, he put his mouth against the rubber mouthpiece and spoke.

Powered only by the sound of his voice, the signal routed through the ship's internal communications links to a similarly clad watchman on the bridge. Having received the message, the bridge talker notified the captain. "Sir, merchant vessel dead ahead. Aspect is starboard quarter-to."

"Very well," the skipper replied as he keyed the transmitter. "*Weissenburg*, we are coming alongside to starboard. Please have line handlers standing by to make fast for transfer."

"Understood, Captain. Will comply," May answered succinctly.

Taking the conn, Chiswell expertly maneuvered *Mackinaw* until she lay motionless, parallel to *Weissenburg* with only a few feet of separation.

A few minutes later, the vessels were lashed together and survivors were herded across the gangway, down a ladder, through the maze of the unfamiliar vessel, and into the enlisted galley, where they were served hot coffee and sandwiches. With the survivors below, four of the *Mackinaw* crew were sent with stretchers to retrieve the dead.

Before casting off and coming about, the bodies of Haske and Jungman were placed side by side, just forward of *Mackinaw*'s superstructure. Father Linus Schrems administered the last rites under the watchful gaze of coroners Harry Ireland and Tony Schneider. Satisfied that the victims were properly blessed, they turned to the inventory and identification of the deceased as civilian medics busied themselves below, examining each of the survivors and tending to the five most seriously injured.

STRAITS OF MACKINAC—

Far below the keel of the departing vessel, Charlie Cook drifted with the icy current, past bulkhead and porthole, east toward the depths of Lake Huron. Elsewhere, tangled in rigging or trapped below, the remnant of the crew, the unfortunate and the stalwart, kept watch over their vessel with glassy eyes, as silt settled on the upturned hull.

M/V *Joe Van*—
1330

Chuck Marsh peered through his binoculars, useless in the fog, as the tug patrolled its assigned search area. His crew had retrieved

Cedarville's aluminum work skiff and a few odd pieces of debris, but they had yet to see any sign of either survivor or deceased. Marsh knew that the crew could not last this long in the frigid waters, but no one was willing to give up hope as long as any of the crew were unaccounted for.

Turning back through the fog, *Joe Van* began another pass through its assigned sector in a search that, though futile, would last for several more hours.

MACKINAW CITY, MICHIGAN—
1355

Anxious relatives, police, and nearly two score reporters crowded the marina's lesser pier as rumor of *Mackinaw*'s imminent arrival spread.

At the foot of the pier, Sergeant Andy Palik of the state police and Sheriff Stan McKervey chatted about the proper placement of police support. Neither knew if the rickety structure could accommodate the *Mackinaw*. Calling the officer assigned to the marina office, Sergeant Palik raised his concerns with the harbormaster.

Stunned, the harbormaster placed an immediate call. "Coast Guard cutter *Mackinaw*, this is Mackinaw City Harbor Control. Come in, over."

The reply was immediate. "Go ahead, Harbor Control."

"Yeah, *Mackinaw*, what is your draft?" he asked, referring to the depth to which the vessel's keel extended below the waterline.

"Nineteen feet, two inches," he replied without hesitation.

The harbormaster swore silently under his breath. "OK, *Mackinaw*, please be advised that the clearance at the municipal pier is insufficient for your draft. Please proceed to the state dock, and we will make arrangements for the ambulances to meet you there."

"Understood, Harbor Control. Will comply. *Mackinaw* out."

"Get Sergeant Palik on the radio," he said, turning to the state police officer. "We have to move the show over to the state dock."

1403

The growing crowd followed the ambulances and police cars to the other pier, a few hundred yards distant. By the time the stretchers were laid out, news of the tragedy had spread beyond the marina, drawing the attention of tourists. Clad for warmer weather, they swelled the ranks of the watchful, uncomfortable in the cold, moist air rolling in from the Straits.

Press reports would describe the atmosphere as festive, as if the crowd, now including schoolchildren, awaited the docking of a cruise ship. But the faces of friends and relatives of the *Cedarville* crew who had driven up from Rogers City continued to reflect the gravity of the occasion as *Mackinaw* hove into sight through the fog.

ROGERS CITY, MICHIGAN—

Father Adalbert Narloch, pastor of St. Ignatius Catholic Church, placed the phone gently in the receiver. Struggling into his jacket, he spoke softly to his secretary. "Terrible news. I've been contacted by the plant. Stan Haske has been killed in a shipping accident up in the Straits. They've asked me to go with a few company men to break the news to Mrs. Haske."

Speechless, her eyes welled up, as Father Narloch patted her arm and turned for the door.

A few minutes later Stan's mother answered the door. She had heard the news and told Betty, who sat on the couch, stunned and weeping, as the solemn delegation filed into the living room.

WLC Control
PORT CALCITE, MICHIGAN—

Finally out of tape, Hassett switched off the recorder. With the entire event recorded on five reels, he felt a sense of accomplishment, having done his part to ensure that the Norwegian ship would not get away with murder. It occurred to him that he might even get a raise for his quick thinking. Smiling, he leaned back in his chair as his supervisor walked in to introduce new operators, sent by the company to lend a hand.

MACKINAW CITY, MICHIGAN—
1422

Two flag-draped bodies rested on the black nonskid deck as *Mackinaw* nestled up to the pier to be tied off. With the vessel secured, *Mackinaw* struck the underway colors and the gangway was lowered into place. The dead were off-loaded first, followed by the more seriously injured.

Gabrysiak was the last to be carried ashore. Wrapped in only a blanket, he felt self-conscious as the throng strained for a glimpse of the shipwreck victims. Thankfully, he was carried directly to an awaiting ambulance, loaded in, strapped down, and briskly driven from the crowded pier.

Most of the remaining survivors milled about the pier for several minutes, hugging family, some crying, and others chuckling grimly about the experience until, one by one, they drifted off to be examined at the local hospital. Only Ron and Harry Piechan refused treatment. They didn't intend to whine about a few aches and pains. An old friend who had come to investigate the ruckus gave them a ride back to Rogers City.

Community Memorial Hospital
CHEBOYGAN, MICHIGAN—
1514

Bethalie Thompson blocked the entrance, her hands raised above her head as a stream of reporters and photographers converged on the hospital. City police cars were parked at each end of the drive to keep the ramp clear for emergency vehicles, but the hospital administrator was finally forced to come out to encourage some semblance of order and—more importantly—quiet.

Her tiny voice seemed lost in the din as she called for their attention, but after a few seconds she appeared to gain a modicum of control. "If you will all be quiet and listen," she shouted, "I will read the names of the *Cedarville* survivors who have been admitted." With that, she had their full attention. Only the click and whir of photo and film equipment broke the silence.

"Thank you," she said, finally lowering her arms. Unrolling the sheet held in her left hand, she took a deep breath, suddenly aware that all eyes were on her. "Twenty-one sailors from the *Cedarville* have been seen at Community Memorial Hospital. Five with more serious injuries have been admitted." Beginning with Bey and ending with Gabrysiak, she flew through the list so quickly that several voices rang out for clarification. Smirking, she repeated the list.

"What about the captain?" an anonymous voice called from the group.

"Captain Joppich has sustained a few minor injuries but will likely be released with the rest of the crew as soon as he is fully examined and treated. Now if you will all remain quiet," she said, turning into the lobby, "I will show you to the cafeteria, where you may sit and speak with the men as they are released."

An excited buzz grew as the gaggle of journalists followed the administrator, but a stern glance over her shoulder squelched the noise as they walked the rest of the way in relative silence.

USCGC *Mackinaw*—
1515

The icebreaker was well underway, heading back to the search area. On deck, teams of lookouts peered vainly through binoculars at the choppy surface, their vision fading in the fog only a few hundred yards distant. *Mackinaw* would cut circles in the water all night and well into the next morning, but nothing would be found. Only bits of flotsam marked the spot where *Cedarville* now slept, and further rescue efforts would prove fruitless.

CARP LAKE, MICHIGAN—

Ethel Brewster was ecstatic. Following the saga on the radio like many coastal residents, she heard her grandson's name called as one of the survivors receiving treatment in Cheboygan. Muttering as she fumbled the number on the rotary dial, she hung up and tried again. This time, she heard the gratifying chirp of a ring on the other end of the line.

"Hello?" Jean Brewster answered warily, not knowing what to expect.

"He's alright, Jean," she blurted out, not wasting time with a greeting. An audible sigh, then tears on the other end. They cried together for several minutes as Ethel told her what she had heard. That Ed Brewster had been rescued by the Coast Guard ship, transported to Cheboygan, and was now ready to be released. That he must be OK. That he had better never set foot on another ship as long as he lived.

Highway 23
MANITOU BEACH, MICHIGAN—

Pat Gabrysiak squinted through the fog as her windshield wipers slapped at the mist accumulating on the windshield. Bound for Cheboygan, she had to get to the hospital. Pat Holley had called to tell her that Len was there. He was alive. But in what condition? Could he speak to her, she wondered? Could she even see him? Her mind raced with questions as the LTD skidded around one curve after another up the coastal road.

ROGERS CITY, MICHIGAN—

At 450 East Woodward Avenue, one of the twelve communications specialists assigned to the hotel suite dialed Jean Brewster's number. Busy. Good news merited only a phone call. Bad news required a personal visit. So far, only two of their number had been dispatched with news of a death, but more grim notices were sure to come.

Another group of company employees occupied a suite in Mackinaw City and prepared to pass word of the ongoing search and rescue by telephone back to the home port. Touted as a service to the grieving families, this communications link also served to keep United States Steel officials abreast of the body count for purposes of public relations and mitigation of liability.

STRAITS OF MACKINAC—
1600

Joe Van was released from search duty with nothing more to show for their efforts. The men aboard were anxious. They would be diving on the hulk tomorrow according to Mr. Van Antwerp. Maybe the next day at the latest. He had been in touch with the owners of the sunken ship and seemed to know of their comings and goings. It was all the same to most of the crew. They had a job to do, and they would do it in a professional manner. But for now, they had to get back to prepare the dive barge for the task.

ROGERS CITY, MICHIGAN—
1700

Sitting in the living room of a lakeside bungalow, her hands clasped tightly in her lap, Cecilia Bredow startled at the sound of the knock. Holding a vigil with a friend whose sister had lost her husband on the *Bradley*, she had held out hope long after the rescue workers had lost heart. The first knock sounded just as the clock on her mantle began to chime.

With a knowing glance, Cecilia nodded, and her friend rose to answer the door. Standing on the step, fidgeting with his hat, was a smartly dressed company man. He had bad news. Wilbert Bredow was missing.

A few minutes later, the company man stepped outside. His next stop . . . the Asam residence.

STRAITS OF MACKINAC—
1730

With the search and rescue winding down, Coast Guard Group Sault Ste. Marie ordered *Topdalsfjord* to weigh anchor and proceed via the locks to Port Arthur, Ontario, for repairs. Even so, the captain and crew were instructed to stay in the area and make themselves available for the coming inquiry.

MACKINAC ISLAND—
2325

Shortly before midnight, the Coast Guard detachment received a call. A young expectant mother from St. Ignace had gone to visit her parents on the island. During the course of the evening she began to experience labor pains. Feeling that her time was near, the family summoned a doctor, who immediately recommended that she be taken to medical facilities on the mainland.

Transported in the back of her father's sedan, she was gently helped across the pier and lowered into the Coast Guard whaleboat as the crew made ready on the lines.

With the doctor aboard, the thirty-six-foot lifeboat set out through the heavy fog on the six-mile run to Mackinaw City.

Midway to land, the baby crowned. Assisted by an able-bodied seaman, the young mother delivered a daughter as the boatswain mate kept a steady course through the Straits.

Torn from the warmth she had known to the cold, damp, misty night air, the infant cried—the joyful sound echoing where dying men had given their last cries only a few hours before.

The fog continued unabated on Saturday and then again on Sunday. Lifting briefly before settling back even thicker, it closed the St. Marys River to traffic. Three steamers had already grounded in the fog when the remaining sixty-eight ships were forced to anchor throughout the river. It was the largest traffic jam in the Soo in recent memory.

15

Damage Control

May 8, 1965
STRAITS OF MACKINAC, MICHIGAN—
0829

People turned out early on both sides of the Straits to look for bodies. As the volunteers combed the lonely shoreline, boats blowing fog signals continued their relentless patrol within earshot. The Coast Guard was directing the formal search for the eight missing crewmen as the cutters, utility boats, ferries, yachts, and tugs involved in the effort pierced the persistent fog in ever widening circles. Overhead, military helicopters hovered and fixed-wing aircraft swooped, looking for bodies and debris.

Several miles to the east, *Topdalsfjord* limped into port. Her bow staved in, she would be repaired at the Soo as her officers shuttled to and from the upcoming hearings to explain their actions of the previous day.

SAULT STE. MARIE, MICHIGAN—
0900

The mood was solemn as the Coast Guard officers filed into the room and took their seats.

Opposite the board of inquiry members, Roman Keenen sat calmly, his fingers laced casually atop a blank notepad. A senior associate at the respected Cleveland law firm of McCreary, Hinslea, and Ray, Keenen had been summoned by Khoury to represent the interests of United States Steel at the hastily scheduled hearing.

Keenen's clients were nervous. Considering the gravity of the situation, it was inevitable that the Coast Guard would rush headlong into the inquiry, and this worried Khoury and his superior, Vice President Jim Gray. Diffusing the mounting corporate panic, Keenen urged patience. It was better for the company to stay calm and await the outcome of the hearings. After all, the Norwegian vessel would likely be fully charged with the incident.

Rapping his gavel on the wooden table, Captain Willis Bruso called the hearing to order. Having invited the various parties to introduce themselves, he notified the agents and representatives of the freighters *Cedarville*, *Weissenburg*, and *Topdalsfjord* that their officers could expect to be summoned during the proceedings of the next few weeks.

STRAITS OF MACKINAC, MICHIGAN—
1530

Suspended by a narrow cable, Don Hockin found the soft hiss of bubbles that escaped his brass helmet reassuring. Dangling between the moored barge overhead and the wreck below, the "hard-hat" diver checked his pressure gauge as he focused on the task at hand.

Joe Van and *Crane Barge 507* had been out most of the day. Loaded before sunrise, the tethered pair had arrived early, dropping anchor near the buoy recently placed by the Coast Guard. United States Steel was well represented. Observers included Tom Harbottle, his assistant John Rankin, and Pittsburgh Fleet engineer "Max" Maxiomocwz. Their instructions were succinct. Find the bodies and keep an eye out for evidence. Management was particularly concerned with finding the ship's log, which, they hoped, would prove that the collision was caused solely by *Topdalsfjord*.

The first diver was in the water shortly after lunch. As he

descended, Jim Bush found the ship to be almost completely inverted, lying on her starboard rail and broken in two at the point of collision. With the after section lying forty-five degrees from the horizontal, it would be impossible to gain easy access to the engine room where several of the dead were believed to be.

Bush mounted the dive buoy cable at the break and continued aft. As he balanced on the canted deck, Bush was shocked by the cold spray of water in his face. His helmet had sprung a leak. "Hey guys, I have a problem here," he said into the headset.

Overhead, the Durocher crew tended Bush's umbilical and monitored the flow of air from the reciprocating engine mounted to the deck of the barge. Supervising the operation, Chuck Marsh made the call. "Bring him up," he said to the winch operator before keying his microphone. "OK, Jim. We're going to pull you up. Stand clear of obstructions."

With that, Bush lifted off of the mangled deck like an ungainly bird taking to flight.

A few minutes later, he stood topside with Marsh. He had not been down long enough to require decompression in the portable tank, and he enjoyed the fresh air as his dressings were changed out.

"It's pretty bad down there, Chuck," he reported. "There's no way to get below. The after superstructure is twisted around, and I wouldn't want to take an indirect route into the engineering spaces. We need the torches." Bush referred to the oxyacetylene cutting torches that the crew had stowed aboard the previous evening.

Now, several hours later, Hockin wrestled with the torch as he cut through the external bulkhead into the after berthing section. It was speculated that maybe some of the missing crew had returned to their rooms for personal items, and the salvors would leave no stone unturned. Hockin would keep at it for another hour, at which time he would retire to the decompression chamber topside to gently leach the nitrogen bubbles accumulating in his bloodstream.

The work was exhausting in the thirty-seven-degree water and, with only two hard-hat divers, excruciatingly slow. But they would soon be augmented with scuba divers who would significantly broaden the maneuverability of the team throughout the silting corridors of the twisted hulk.

DETROIT, MICHIGAN—
1600

Public relations officer Bill Ferry vehemently denied the accounts. Standing at the company podium, he addressed local media, who were well familiar with both the conference room and U.S. Steel's tendency to deny the obvious.

Raising both hands to stress the point, he said it again. "There is no foundation for any report that the death toll is more than two. No other bodies have been found, and at this time we cannot confirm any other casualties."

The journalists were not fools, and none expected the missing men to dog-paddle in near-freezing water for hours. Sensing their disbelief, Ferry braced for their questions. He knew that it would be a long night.

PORT OF CLEVELAND, OHIO—
1640

Captain May sounded the ship's whistle as the deck crew cast off the mooring lines. *Weissenburg* had spent the day unloading her cargo. Now, more than a day behind schedule, she would make for the first of her Canadian ports on the return voyage through the St. Lawrence Seaway.

May knew that his officers would be periodically called to testify at the tribunal back in Sault Ste. Marie, but he hoped to keep his ship advancing until he was cleared to depart for Europe.

Community Memorial Hospital
CHEBOYGAN, MICHIGAN—
1910

With dive operations suspended for the night, Marsh checked in with his old shipmates at the local hospital. "Hey, Gaby, whad'ya say?" he beamed, knocking on the partly opened door to Gabrysiak's semiprivate room. Gabrysiak's doctor had allowed his wife only a brief visit, and he had fallen asleep soon after she left.

Opening his weary eyes, Len smiled, his stubbly chin accentuating his underbite. "Chuck, what brings you here?"

"I'm working on the salvage and wanted to come see how you were doing."

"Well, pull up a chair. It's a long story," Gabrysiak warned.

For the next half hour, Gabrysiak relived the nightmare until, with a sigh, he fell asleep.

"Sleep well, old friend," Marsh whispered as he adjusted the blanket and slipped quietly from the room.

Down the hall, Jean Brewster sat beside her husband's bed. Marsh had known Ed as a boy. Having heard the tale a second time, he asked, "Do you think you'll go back out again, Ed?"

"I might," Brewster answered, but his wife's glare said something else entirely.

It was obvious to Marsh that Brewster's sailing days were over.

2100

Outside of the hospital, Jim Gray spoke with reporters.

Answering a journalist from the *Tribune,* he detailed the actions that United States Steel was taking in the wake of the tragedy. "Our job right now is to determine what happened to all of the personnel on our vessel," he explained.

"As you know, only twenty-seven of the thirty-five-man crew have been accounted for. In addition to the Coast Guard air and sea search, we have rescuers combing the beaches and have arranged for divers to attempt to reach the sunken vessel. We are and will continue to make every effort to locate the other crew members. Thank you," he concluded abruptly as he turned and walked into the lobby with Khoury, Parilla, and Keenen.

Moving as a pack, the four executives wandered from room to room, questioning each of the survivors in turn. Keenen took notes. Harry Bey knew nothing of the events leading up to the collision.

Trafelet had the limited perspective of a lookout who saw nothing in the fog until the time of the collision. But Len Gabrysiak was at the wheel.

Opening his eyes, Gabrysiak was surprised to find four men in suits standing at the foot of his bed. "Where's Chuck?" he asked.

"Who?" Gray responded as the men exchanged awkward glances. After a few seconds, he continued. "Mr. Gabrysiak, I am Jim Gray, Administrative Vice President at United States Steel. This is Admiral Khoury, Captain Parilla, and Mr. Keenen."

Each nodded in turn.

Len knew Parilla and smiled. "Evening, Cap. It's been a rough day."

"I know," Parilla replied. "That's why we want to talk with you. How are you feeling?"

"Well, my legs hurt real bad. I think they're swelled up like balloons. The docs have these hot pads on me to bring the swelling down," he said, turning his blanket aside.

"Mr. Gabrysiak," Khoury interjected, "where were you at the time of the collision?"

"I was at the helm."

"Did you hear what Captain Joppich said and did in the moments following the collision?" Parilla asked.

"Every word," Gabrysiak beamed.

With that, Keenen whispered pointedly to Gray and left the room. A few minutes later, he returned with the company doctor. After a short conference with the doctor at the door, Gray stepped back to the bedside.

"We are going to check you out and take you where you'll be more comfortable," Gray said, smiling down at Gabrysiak.

"What?" Len mumbled incredulously as the men filed from the room.

MACKINAW CITY, MICHIGAN—
2130

"Alright, gentlemen, let's not lose our heads."

Keenen's clear voice cut through the debate to quiet the nervous executives. Cliff Buehrens had joined them at the Mackinaw City hotel suite, and for several minutes the tension had mounted as they considered the implications for the company.

Flopping into an overstuffed chair, he mused aloud as he considered the situation. As Keenen saw things, the foreign ship was hauling through the Straits, refusing to communicate with anyone. It was likely that the board of inquiry would find that the collision was caused solely by the foreign skipper's negligence. And even if they didn't, the "limitation of liability" defense was available to keep the company's exposure to injury and death claims relatively low. By this, he was thinking of the statutory defense available to shipowners that limited their liability for accidents to their actual monetary interest in the vessel. In this case—practically nothing.

Then Buehrens dropped the bombshell. A WLC radioman had taped the entire episode after the collision. To say that Parilla was not pleased was an understatement, and Buehrens soon burst from the room—dispatched to retrieve those tapes. In the ensuing silence, Keenen supported his forehead on his fingertips and groaned. Given Parilla's involvement in the incident, this was not good news.

Finally, lifting his head to face Parilla, Keenen made a suggestion. "Let's find out exactly what Gabrysiak heard."

Parilla stood. "I'll get him."

A sharp rap on the door startled Gabrysiak from his slumber. Without waiting for an invitation, Parilla opened the door and stepped in. "Come down to our room," he said. "We need to talk."

Gabrysiak spent the next three and a half hours telling and retelling the story as Keenen hammered on the details. Maybe they were going to try to blame him, Gabrysiak worried, as the interrogation went on into the night.

May 9, 1965
STRAITS OF MACKINAC, MICHIGAN—
0645

Joe Van had loaded an extra anchor to allow a three-point moor. With the three anchors set widely astride the wreckage, the tug could maneuver the work barge over any part of the ship with ease.

On-site with the sunrise, Bush and Hockin went down together to search from the break, aft. They had covered a little more than seventy feet of deck and rigging before coming up. Waiting topside, another pair of hard-hat divers from Bultema Dock and Dredge, Don Olsen and Don Koon, took note of the other team's progress as they suited up. With the search plan confirmed, they were lowered over the side as Bush and Hockin stepped into the portable tank for their hour-long decompression.

ST. IGNACE, MICHIGAN—
0900

The distinctive rap of the gavel announced that Captain Bruso had once again called the hearings to order. The *Weissenburg* crew had been permitted to give their testimony in a separate hearing in Cleveland the previous day, and the *Topdalsfjord* crew would be expected to testify next. Seated at the back of the room in their dress blues, Jan Gronstol, Karl Fagerli, Kjell Oskarsen, and Aage Bergkvist fidgeted, awaiting their turn under the microscope. Conspicuously absent was Captain Hoagland, who was rumored to be hospitalized with a nervous condition.

As the senior officer present, Chief Officer Fagerli was first to take the stand. Under the scrutiny of Captain Bruso, he recounted the events leading to the collision.

"What was the speed of your ship as she passed beneath the bridge and into the eastern Straits?" Bruso asked.

Taking a moment to calculate the distance traveled, he looked up from his position at the table before the Coast Guard officers. "I would estimate that *Topdalsfjord* was traveling at approximately six point five knots," he answered, his Norwegian accent echoing thickly about the room.

"And that is just too damned fast for the heavy fog," Keenen commented from his nearby position.

"Thank you for the commentary, Mr. Keenen. But if you don't mind, I am presiding over this hearing," Bruso sniped.

"Sorry, sir," Keenen allowed, before returning to his notes.

Ignoring Keenen, Fagerli brushed at his graying temples and steeled himself for the next question. It would prove to be a long morning for the Norwegian officer.

CHEBOYGAN, MICHIGAN—

Having been shooed from Len's room the previous afternoon, Pat spent the night with her brother Jerry and his family in Cheboygan. But upon her return, she found an empty bed. Len was missing, and no one seemed to know where he had gone. Distraught, she pleaded with the duty nurse for information on her husband. Finally, in tears and creating a scene, Pat attracted the attention of chief surgeon Nicholas Lentini, who was just completing his rounds.

Supervising the treatment of the *Cedarville* survivors, Lentini had authorized Len's release the previous evening. "Yes, ma'am," he said, trying to calm the hysterical woman as he glanced nervously down the hall. "He was discharged last night into the care of the gentlemen from Pittsburgh. I believe that they told us where he would be staying. Let me just check the discharge summary."

Moments later, Pat was back in her car. She would swing by her brother's house, pack her few belongings, and check into the motel in Mackinaw City to wait anxiously for her husband's return.

STRAITS OF MACKINAC, MICHIGAN—
1200

So far, the efforts of the divers had proved fruitless. Olsen and Koon were back up, but they hadn't found anyone. A team of skin divers from Sturgeon Bay, Wisconsin, had joined the search but were equally unsuccessful. Even so, Marsh was impressed. He had had little regard for scuba divers in general, but these boys seemed to have their act together. They worked from a small boat tethered near the bow of the sunken vessel, augmenting the hard-hat divers working farther aft.

ST. IGNACE, MICHIGAN—
1303

Before the tribunal adjourned for lunch, Keenen was informed that Len Gabrysiak would be next to testify. Len was anxious to tell his story, but as he was being sworn in, with his hand on the Bible, he had second thoughts.

"Mr. Gabrysiak, we need to ask a few questions concerning the events leading up to the loss of the *Cedarville*," Bruso began.

"Excuse me, sir," Len interrupted. "If it's possible, I think that I would like to take the Fifth."

Keenen's glare was lost on the helmsman as Bruso held his rapt attention.

"Why do you think you need to take the Fifth?" he asked.

"Well, sir," Gabrysiak stammered, "if I am going to be charged with anything in this matter, I have a right to not say anything that could hurt my case."

Suppressing a smile, Bruso considered the helmsman. "You have not been accused of any misconduct, Mr. Gabrysiak. It is your constitutional right to invoke Fifth Amendment protections if you so choose. But if you refuse to testify today, you will be subpoenaed and forced to testify tomorrow under penalty of contempt."

Confused, Gabrysiak looked to Keenen, who nodded in return.

"Alright, sir. I guess I'm ready."

With that, Gabrysiak detailed his own ship's actions as the hearing stretched into the evening. Under intense scrutiny, both friendly and otherwise, he told the panel how *Cedarville* had been steered on a course of three-two-five for several minutes prior to the collision, deviating substantially from designated shipping lanes. He spoke of the captain's orders, slowing the speeding vessel's engines only when faced with the emergency. He described how the captain apparently panicked, calling for left full rudder and thereby exposing his ship broadside to the oncoming vessel. How Joppich had conferred with Captain Parilla and had not ordered abandon ship. How Joppich deserted his men and their sinking ship. In all, his testimony was damaging—both to Joppich and to the company.

Tiring, Gabrysiak fidgeted in obvious pain. His legs had long since fallen asleep, and the dull ache that now coursed through his lower extremities was distracting.

"Mr. Gabrysiak," Captain Bruso offered, "would you like to take a break? You can take a few minutes to stretch your legs if you like."

"No, thanks. I want to finish up so I can get some medical attention."

His testimony continued, but Gabrysiak got no relief for his discomfort. He would be kept on the stand into the night.

ROGERS CITY, MICHIGAN—
2015

The children tearfully approached their mother, who was lying on the couch. A small white envelope held in trembling hands, they gave it to her as their father had instructed.

Taking the envelope, Betty Haske tore clumsily at the sealed flap. Frustrated, she unceremoniously ripped it open and removed the card. Then, crying silently, she covered her mouth and read it over and over again.

Framed with hearts and flowers, it read:

May Mother's Day and all year through bring everything that's dear to you. Because my darling wife, you see, You're everything that's dear to me!

Below, her husband had personalized the card.

To my dearest girlfriend and my loving wife. I love you very much. Stan.

MACKINAW CITY, MICHIGAN—
2358

"I just don't understand all of this," Pat fussed as she wrapped Len's legs in hot, wet towels. "You were just on the wheel. What could they possibly want with you?" She had worried the day away in the small hotel room. Len had only just staggered in, and she felt the need to talk.

"I don't know," Gabrysiak replied, wincing as the improved circulation brought renewed sensation. "Some of my shipmates have died. Charlie Cook is dead. Bill Asam and Stan Haske too," he said, his voice cracking. "I guess they just needed a scapegoat."

"I'm sorry, sweetie," Pat said, taking his hand. "I know we are both under a lot of stress. I suppose we just have to be strong, do the right thing, and see this thing through to the end. It's just that I . . ."

Len's soft snoring broke her train of thought. Smiling, she reached over, turned off the bedside lamp, and snuggled up to her husband, thanking God that he was alive.

May 10, 1965
STRAITS OF MACKINAC, MICHIGAN—
1000

"We got one!" the tender shouted. Word spread quickly across the dive barge, and soon several men had gathered to help lift the body aboard and place it in a plastic zippered bag.

Hockin and Bush had been cutting the dogs on the gangway door when they drifted up into the rigging. There, tangled in the smokestack cabling, a body hung motionless in the current.

Startled, they secured the remains and notified the surface. Now, as they were hoisted aboard, the body was already laid out on deck, awaiting identification.

Joe Parilla was aboard to observe for the day and had been sitting in the tug's pilothouse when the call came through. Climbing past the forecastle, he dropped down onto the barge and raced forward. Then, crossing himself, he knelt over the body and said a short prayer. "It's Wilbert Bredow," he finally said, looking up. "He was one of the cooks."

Standing, he turned to Marsh as the body was covered. "Do you know the code?" he asked.

"Yes, I'll take care of it," Marsh responded. A code had been arranged with the Coast Guard to secretly convey the fact that a body had been found. Management had been explicit on this point. They did not want a media circus each time one of the crew was brought to the surface.

As Marsh made ready to transport the body ashore, the scuba divers, still working below, had made another important find. The deck log and ship's clock had been recovered from the bridge. The latter had stopped at 1025, the moment the ship had capsized.

ST. IGNACE, MICHIGAN—
1330

Keenen ceremoniously placed *Cedarville*'s log book, still dripping, before Captain Bruso. A key piece of the puzzle had been found, but Bruso had a full slate of witnesses to question before the log book could be properly considered.

Topdalsfjord's second mate, radio officer, and chief engineer were expected to testify, but the captain was still indisposed, confined to bed for extreme exhaustion caused by overwork and lack of sleep.

ROGERS CITY, MICHIGAN—

Standing on the steps of the municipal building, Mayor Karl Vogelheim declared the month of May as a period of mourning for the city as a couple of reporters from the *Presque Isle Advance* took notes. Flags would be flown at half-mast, and local merchants would close their doors from noon until one o'clock on the following Monday in observance of an hour of mourning.

The Michigan legislature also passed a resolution conveying its deepest sympathies to the families of the deceased. To many, it was inconceivable that it could happen again. First the *Carl D. Bradley* and now the *Cedarville*. How much heartache could one small community bear?

May 11, 1965
ROGERS CITY, MICHIGAN—
0855

"There is always the possibility of disaster," Father Adalbert Narloch commented to reporters on the steps of St. Ignatius Catholic

Church before excusing himself to prepare for the emotionally wrenching service. A few minutes later, he stood at the pulpit as the family tearfully trailed in behind the coffin, oblivious to the ornate beauty of the brick and stained-glass structure. How his heart went out to this widow and her five children.

Gripping the podium, Father Narloch composed himself and, taking a deep breath, spoke directly to Elizabeth. "Stanley was a good man. A loving man. Father of five and faithful husband. He will be sorely missed. . . ."

Parilla was annoyed when Buehrens arrived late to the grave site. "Where have you been?" he whispered heatedly.

"Just got word. Another body has been found," he replied quietly, ignoring Parilla's tone. "They think it's Asam. It looks as though his foul weather gear hung up on the galley door. He couldn't break free and he drowned."

"OK. Keep it to yourself. We'll deal with it after the funeral," Parilla said. With that, the executives watched quietly as the Haske family said their final farewells.

SAULT STE. MARIE, MICHIGAN—
1107

The case for the American skipper seemed to be going well as the hearing shifted to the Soo City-County municipal building. Keenen and his senior partner, Lucien Ray, were pleased. All evidence pointed to the Norwegian freighter as the sole cause of the collision. U.S. Steel might just escape liability altogether.

The inquiry could not have been going better for the company when Captain Hoagland made a surprise appearance. He wanted to take the witness stand.

Under the direct questioning of Captain Bruso, Hoagland testified that, just prior to the collision, *Cedarville* had been traveling at a high rate of speed. He further charged that Captain Joppich, absent and undergoing treatment for a nervous condition, was guilty of poor seamanship. Closing, he leaned toward Keenen and, with tears in his eyes, asked him to extend his deepest sympathies to Captain Joppich.

Charges and countercharges followed Hoagland's testimony. Counsel for Den Norske Amerikalinje demanded that Joppich appear for cross-examination. In the face of the unanticipated onslaught, Keenen invoked the Fifth Amendment for his client.

May 12, 1965
STRAITS OF MACKINAC, MICHIGAN—
0720

The high-pitched whine of the oxyacetylene torch permeated the water for hundreds of feet as the combustion gasses filled the inverted compartment. Squinting against the glare, Olsen adjusted the flow of pressurized oxygen while Koon tended his hoses at the gangway. The diver was cutting a jammed hatch that led to lower engineering. With the molten slag accumulating at his boots, the door finally gave way.

Releasing the trigger, Olsen cut the flow of fuel to the copper cutting tip, and the flame died out. In the ensuing silence, Koon appeared at his side. Together, they forced open the heavy metal hatch, which gave way with a rush of air and water. Caught in the flow, a body swept through the opening and immediately buoyed into the overhead, a life vest fastened securely on the bloating remains.

"Oh jeez," Koon shouted as he stumbled backward. Olsen was already calling topside. Within a few minutes, the lanky body of Don Lamp was secured and gently rising to the surface on the utility tether. Koon and Olsen continued through engineering. There were more bodies to be recovered.

U.S. Coast Guard Ninth District Headquarters
CLEVELAND, OHIO—
1000

Chester Bender stubbed out his cigar as he read the report. Most of the air and surface assets of the region had been diverted to search for survivors and bodies in the Straits. Rescuers had long since given up on finding any crew still alive in the near-freezing water, but since the day of the collision, searchers had found nothing at all. No bodies or debris. And the amount of jet fuel and diesel already consumed by his rescue units was staggering. His decision was clear. Admiral Bender could not afford to continue the fruitless search.

Pressing the intercom, he called to the first-class yeoman who served as his personal secretary. "Step in here for a moment," he said. "I have a message to draft."

STRAITS OF MACKINAC, MICHIGAN— 1830

Marsh was getting tired of the drill. More bodies had been found. Fuhrman under the aft starboard overhang, Lamp and Radke in engineering. All were clad in life jackets. All were trapped by the irresistible flow of the waters that had consumed the ship so suddenly. As *Joe Van* transported the bodies, his divers returned to the task. Rigged with cutting torches, they continued to slice through the fantail and lower engineering in their macabre search for victims.

PORT CALCITE, MICHIGAN—

Back at the office, Parilla considered a stack of letters, each printed on ornately embossed United States Steel letterhead. Drafted by his secretary, in keeping with the well-used company format, the first read:

> *Dear Mrs. Fuhrman,*
>
> *My words cannot adequately express the deep sorrow we all feel for those who have lost their loved ones in the ramming and subsequent sinking of the S/S* Cedarville *on the morning of May 7.*
>
> *Art was well known and highly respected by his neighbors and shipmates, as well as me and my associates in the Corporation family. I can only wish that a lasting comfort will accompany you through the future and that you will bravely carry on.*
>
> *Within a few days contact will be made with you to help you understand some of the items of insurance and other*

benefit programs. We will be of every assistance to you in processing these benefits promptly.

Along these lines, I am enclosing a $500.00 check which is to cover the loss of Art's personal effects.

If I can help you further during this tragic period please let me know.

Sincerely,

J. J. Parilla

Signing across the bottom, Parilla turned to the next identical letter.

Dear Mrs. Radke,

My words cannot adequately express the deep sorrow we all feel . . .

STRAITS OF MACKINAC, MICHIGAN—
2315

Chuck Marsh peered into the dark just beyond the range of the floodlights that bathed the work area. The ominous sound of boiling water was just audible over the drone of the air compressor. "Get some of those lights trained over this way," he shouted.

The Durocher crew instantly obeyed. As the lights were swung into place, it was obvious that large pockets of air were billowing up from a breach in the cargo hold fifty feet forward of the section that the divers were searching.

Marsh immediately saw the danger. The combined gases from the divers' exhalations and use of cutting torches were apparently filling the cavernous hold, making the wreck unstable. With the buoyant forces shifting, *Cedarville* could roll, trapping the divers and shearing their air supply. Turning to the line tenders, he ordered the divers to the surface.

A few minutes later all were safely on deck. Standing with Marsh, they considered the best way to vent the hold. "OK. Hockin will take care of it in the morning," Marsh finally decided. "Let's call it a night."

May 13, 1965
STRAITS OF MACKINAC, MICHIGAN—
0525

With only a few hours of sleep, Hockin dressed and returned to the wreck. As agreed upon the previous night, he carried a cutting torch to vent the port side ballast tanks. Cutting the hull near the upraised edge, he left a trail of air columns that rushed noisily from the newly made vents. Having opened the hold sufficiently, he was making his way aft to continue the search when the breeze topside shifted. Unexpectedly, the wind doubled back from its original course and carried a concentrated parcel of diesel exhaust from the air compressor, past the sign that read "Divers air supply—Do not touch," and through the filtered intake.

Pressurized for its descent to the bottom, the exhaust passed through the compressor, into the feed hose, and over the side. Less than a minute later, Hockin took a deep breath as he struggled with an inverted hatch. With his helmet full of blue smoke, he nearly passed out. Coughing, he made an emergency call to the surface. "I'm getting a lot of exhaust down here. I need to come up." Fighting the nausea, he made his way to the open deck, where he was lifted back aboard the work barge.

Wrenching the traditional brass helmet from his shoulders, Hockin fell to his hands and knees, panting in the cool, clean air. Nearby, Olsen and Koon were already suiting up. They would spend most of the day cutting vents and fruitlessly searching voids under the watchful eye of the ever-present visitors from Pittsburgh. Though they didn't know it yet, they would find no more bodies in the wreck.

May 14, 1965
ST. IGNACE, MICHIGAN—
0945

Properly sworn in, Marty Joppich took the stand before Captain Bruso and the board of inquiry.

On friendly examination by Keenen, the *Cedarville* captain calmly explained that he had held course through the narrows in compliance with Coast Guard regulation; that he had reduced speed to slow long before the collision; and that he had ordered right full rudder to avoid exposing the ship to a broadside collision. Throughout the room, counsel murmured and exchanged incredulous glances. Joppich's testimony was in direct contradiction to Len Gabrysiak's damaging account.

On cross-examination, questions posed by Joseph Keig, counsel for *Topdalsfjord*, were more challenging. Sensing trouble, Keenen called for a break. Several minutes later, on Keenen's advice, Captain Joppich declined to answer any questions. "I wish to invoke my rights under the Fifth Amendment against self incrimination," he read nervously from the crinkled paper in his hand.

"Do you intend to testify in response to any portion of this inquiry?" Captain Bruso asked.

"No, sir," Joppich replied. "I intend to exercise my rights under the Fifth Amendment to the Constitution throughout the course of this hearing."

Rolling his eyes, Bruso informed Keenen that the board would obtain an order compelling Joppich's testimony and adjourned the hearing.

Outside, Joppich climbed into his car as Keenen, Khoury, and Parilla spoke on the steps.

"Do you think Bruso can force him to testify?" Khoury asked.

"It's possible. All depends on what the federal judge says," Keenen replied.

The speculation went back and forth, but in the end they all agreed. Blaming *Topdalsfjord* was not working. It was becoming painfully obvious that Joppich might have to fall on his sword for the company and take the blame himself.

May 15, 1965
United States District Court
CLEVELAND, OHIO—
1630

Keenen was taking no chances. With the body search still underway, a company paralegal had been dispatched to Cleveland with a handful of pleadings designed to short-circuit the anticipated claims of the widows and survivors. Keenen hoped to take advantage of the 1851 Limitation of Liability statute, which drastically limited claims against the owner of a ship to the value of the vessel itself—in this case, scrap value for the twisted hulk and about twenty thousand dollars for the lost cargo.

Management agreed. Realizing that the combined exposure from wrongful death, personal injury, and property damage claims could well exceed $10 million, James Gray authorized Keenen to file the Limitation action, along with a separate demand against *Topdalsfjord* in the amount of $3.5 million for the loss of *Cedarville*.

Unbeknownst to Keenen, counsel for Den Norske Amerikalinje had filed a similar action against U.S. Steel in Chicago, seeking an injunction against all other claims. The various lawsuits would eventually be combined, but early on the parties scrambled to establish their positions in what they perceived to be the more favorable court.

May 21, 1965
ROGERS CITY, MICHIGAN—
1045

Pat was busy in the kitchen, so Len responded to the knock at the front door. Through the window, he could see Lenny Jr. playing in the side yard. On the front porch a young man in a dark brown suit started to knock again as the door swung open.

"Yes?" Gabrysiak asked.

"Mr. Gabrysiak, I am an attorney for Den Norske Amerikalinje. I represent the owners of the *Topdalsfjord*." Len didn't speak, so the young man continued. "Pardon my prying, but I need to ask, are you represented by counsel?

"What?" Len asked, squinting into the mid-morning glare.

"Do you have an attorney, Mr. Gabrysiak?"

"No," he answered cautiously. "Do I need one?"

"Yes, I would advise you to retain an attorney as soon as possible. Good day, sir," the young man concluded abruptly before turning and walking to his car.

"Well, what do you make of that?" Len wondered as he watched the man drive away.

"Who was that?" Pat called from the kitchen.

"You wouldn't believe me if I told you," Len replied, closing the door.

May 22, 1965
ROGERS CITY, MICHIGAN—
0715

The Gabrysiaks would not have to wait long for an explanation. Sitting at the breakfast table, Len read the *Presque Isle Advance* for other news to take his mind off of the tragedy. Having finished an article detailing the escalating presence of U.S. military advisors in Vietnam, he turned to the next page. There, a notice concerning *Cedarville* caught his eye.

"Hey, Pat, take a look at this," he said.

Filling her coffee cup, she crossed the kitchen and took the paper. "Well, I'll be," she muttered, reading the notice. In a small box near the top of the page, the advertisement announced that United States Steel had filed a lawsuit requiring all survivors to make a claim within the next sixty days. Failure to make a timely claim, it warned, could result in the loss of the right to do so in the future. "What does this mean?" she asked, handing the section back to her husband.

"I'll tell you exactly what it means," Gabrysiak snapped. "They're trying to railroad us, and I'm not going to let 'em do it," he swore, slamming his fist on the table and rattling the empty breakfast plates.

DETROIT, MICHIGAN—

Victor Hanson, Esquire, was well known in Rogers City. Having taken a leading role in the *Carl D. Bradley* litigation five years earlier, he had built a reputation in the small lakeside community as a seaman's representative. He was eager to jump into the present controversy, but it was still too early to begin direct solicitations. Instead, he would have to bide his time until, under the Michigan canon of ethics, he would be free to begin networking among the survivors.

Hanson was no novice. Earning his stripes with the *Andrea Doria* and SS *Noronic* disasters decades before, he was well familiar with maritime catastrophe. For years he had also represented the interests of several large mariner's unions, including Seafarers International, Tugman's Union, Dredgeman's Union, Rigger's Union, and Sailors Union of the Pacific. In this capacity, he had spent a good deal of time on Capitol Hill arguing for legislation to advance benefits afforded servicemen to the merchant seamen who had served in equally hazardous conditions during World War II and thereafter. He saw himself as the seaman's representative. And, in fact, he was.

Reviewing newspaper clippings from the past few weeks, Hanson was tallying potential clients when his phone rang. "Mr. Hanson, I have a call you may want to take," his secretary said in an annoying sing-song voice. "It's about that ship that sank." Smiling to himself, he told her to put the call through. Picking it up on the second ring, he answered, "Victor Hanson."

"Yes, Mr. Hanson," came the tinny voice from the other end of the line, "my name is Leonard Gabrysiak. I was aboard *Cedarville* when she sank. There's a notice in the newspaper this morning that says something about U.S. Steel and limitation of liability. I don't know exactly what that means, but I think I need your help."

"I will be glad to help," Hanson replied. "But first, let me get a little background information," he said, taking furious notes on his legal pad.

16

Limitations

Chuck Marsh was relieved. U.S. Steel had terminated his macabre tasking. The Durocher & Van Antwerp divers had covered practically every corner of the ship, including as much of the engine room as was accessible. However, with nothing to show for the last two weeks' labor, the Bradley Fleet decided to declare the last three men missing and to move on.

As the *Joe Van* heaved out of sight, an Army Corps of Engineers survey vessel swept past in its wake, training a sounding bar. Although the ship was lying in 102 feet of water, the survey revealed that *Cedarville*'s twisted frame and rigging extended to within 32 feet of the surface, creating a hazard to navigation. A notice to mariners would be issued within the month, and navigational charts of the Straits would soon bear the innocuous marking "wreck-32" southeast of the Mackinac Bridge.

June 14, 1965
PORT CALCITE, MICHIGAN—

Little more than a month after the collision, Captain Joseph Parilla penned the following letter to Admiral Bender and Colonel Edward Bruce of the U.S. Army Corps of Engineers:

Gentlemen,

Please be advised that effective immediately, United States Steel is abandoning all rights, title and interest in the wreck of the SS Cedarville *currently located in one hundred and two feet of water, two and a half miles southeast of the Mackinac Bridge in the Straits of Mackinac.*

It is the opinion of United States Steel that the wreck constitutes a menace to navigation and an attractive nuisance to the general public. Accordingly, we recommend the demolition of the ship by explosives as soon as possible.

Sincerely,
J. J. Parilla

July 16, 1965
CHICAGO, ILLINOIS—
0958

At a hearing in Grand Rapids on May 21, Judge Wallace Kent considered the Coast Guard's request to compel Joppich's testimony. Also present, Keenen argued that, historically, foreign flagged vessels have had no opportunity to cross-examine American seamen before boards of inquiry and to do so in this case would set a bad precedent.

Rejecting U.S. Steel's position, the district judge ruled that Joppich enjoyed no privilege before a Coast Guard board of inquiry under maritime law and ordered him to submit to questioning.

Thereafter, the Coast Guard set Joppich's hearing to coincide with the return of *Topdalsfjord* to Chicago.

As the parties took their places in room 705 of the U.S. Customs Building, Charles Carroll, a civilian hearing examiner for the Coast Guard's Ninth District, dropped a bombshell. Captain Joppich was to be charged with various offenses for the purpose of revoking his master's license. This action came less than a month after similar proceedings against Captain Albert Olson of the freighter *J. E. Upson*, which ran into the lighthouse at Gray's Reef.

Standing before the board, Lieutenant Commander Arthur Gove, a stout Coast Guard officer clad in dress khakis, read the charges. "Captain Martin Joppich is hereby charged with negligence for failure to navigate his vessel at a moderate speed in the fog; failure to reduce speed to bare steerage way on hearing almost dead ahead, the fog signals of another vessel; failure to sound the danger signal after getting no response to his passing signal; and failure to reduce speed to bare steerage way or stop or reverse, upon approaching within half a mile of another vessel, the intentions of which were not known as required by the inland rules of navigation."

Without hesitation, Keenen stood and cleared his throat. "Captain Joppich pleads not guilty to all charges," he said curtly before returning to his seat.

Ironically, Captain Hoagland was also present, though the Coast Guard had no authority to proceed against his license. Squirming in his chair, he dreaded his turn on the stand, where he would soon be called upon to condemn his colleague's actions on the morning of the collision.

Much of the ground had been covered during the previous testimony of Len Gabrysiak and the *Topdalsfjord* bridge crew. It was well established that *Cedarville* was traveling at full speed in excess of twelve knots and that Joppich had ordered three erratic course changes in the minutes before the collision. The evidence weighed heavily against Joppich.

With the captain scheduled to appear next, the board recessed for lunch.

Foregoing a quick meal in the cafeteria below, Keenen, Parilla, and Joppich huddled in a smaller office down the hall.

The situation did not look good for United States Steel. The company could be cited on at least four major violations of navigational rules, and their own log books supported the charges. Furthermore, Joppich, their key witness, was falling apart. Shaking visibly, he had bitten his fingernails beyond the quick.

Opting to cut their losses, the executives huddled quickly to break the news to Joppich. He would be their scapegoat, but they would continue to back him and hope for some leniency on the part of the board. Perhaps they would only recommend a short suspension of his license.

Several minutes later, the board was stunned when, rising unexpectedly, Roman Keenen placed his hand on Joppich's shoulder and said, "At this time Captain Joppich wishes to change his plea to guilty on all counts."

Taking the stand thereafter, Joppich admitted that his ship was traveling in excess of twelve knots before the collision and that he could not explain such high speed through the fog. He also denied Captain Parilla's involvement in the decision to beach the vessel.

Parilla breathed a sigh of relief. Joppich would take the fall.

CLEVELAND, OHIO—
1245

Ned Mann sauntered past the imposing statues of "Jurisprudence" and "Commerce" on his way to the desk of the clerk of court. Retained by Victor Hanson as local counsel, Mann was dispatched to file claims against U.S. Steel on behalf of several of the survivors and widows. Soon, four other legal teams would appear for the remainder of the crew, including Captain Joppich. Their goal: to defeat the company's limitation bid.

Hanson was well aware of the implications of a successful limitation. Given the relatively low scrap value of the vessel, liability would hinge on the weight of the vessel, calculated at sixty dollars per ton. As *Cedarville* weighed in at approximately 8,575 gross tons, United States Steel could be held liable for no more than $514,500. Unless. . . .

Once asserted, the best way to trump the right to limitation under maritime law was to prove gross negligence or intentional misconduct. As the investigation of the plaintiffs' committee gathered momentum, counsel began to consider the various elements of negligence or misconduct contributing to the casualty. Did U.S. Steel refuse to make hull repairs as mandated by the Coast Guard? Was the company negligent in systematically overloading the vessel? Was United States Steel remiss in encouraging its captains to maintain high speed and deviate from recommended courses through the fog? Was Captain Joppich negligent in failing to sound danger signals and reduce speed in the face of impending danger? Did management refuse to abandon ship when *Cedarville*'s loss was imminent?

As Hanson suspected that the company would be less than forthcoming on these issues, he convinced the committee to pool its resources and hire a private investigator to canvass Rogers City for information. His name was Osgood.

July 22, 1965
M/V Weissenburg—

In a quiet ceremony on the forecastle, Admiral Charles Khoury, accompanied by U.S. Steel photographers, presented an award for courageous action to the German ship and twenty of her crew who participated in the rescue.

In an obvious public relations pitch, photos and an account of the awards ceremony would soon be released to newspapers throughout the Great Lakes region.

August 25, 1965
CLEVELAND, OHIO—
1330

Roman Keenen appeared on behalf of Captain Joppich to reiterate his guilty plea. Joppich was confined to a Cheboygan hospital, undergoing treatment for a newly diagnosed nervous condition, and was unable to attend the fifteen-minute hearing.

The senior examiner had taken Joppich's earlier admission under advisement and now stood ready to issue his decision. "It is the finding of this Board," Carroll began, "that on May 7, 1965, Captain Joppich failed to operate his ship at the safe speed warranted by the low visibility and failed to take proper action when *Cedarville* detected the approaching fog signal of the other ship.

"Furthermore, throughout the emergency, Captain Joppich poorly judged the peril to his crew and vessel. Had he decided to beach the ship on the nearest shoal rather than the south shore of the Straits of Mackinac, the ship and crew would have been saved.

"Accordingly, it is the recommendation of this Board that the

Great Lakes master's license of Captain Martin Joppich be suspended for a period of one year, at which time Captain Joppich may apply for reinstatement and reissuance of his license.

"This Board is adjourned," Carroll concluded with a rap of the gavel.

STRAITS OF MACKINAC, MICHIGAN

Meanwhile, the collision had indirectly claimed yet another life. Diving on the unguarded wreck, a local youth drowned while trying to recover the nameplate from *Cedarville*'s inverted and partly buried bridge. His dive partner survived but was hospitalized with the bends. The incident would be remembered by the community as just another unnecessary tragedy stemming from the *Cedarville* incident.

October 13, 1965
ROGERS CITY, MICHIGAN—
1110

"Mr. Osgood . . . Yes, I have it right here." The manager of the Rogers City Motel on Highway 23 ran his stubby finger down the short reservation list. "You'll be in room 12. All the way down at the end."

"Thanks," Osgood said as he peeled off a few bills on the narrow counter.

A few minutes later, he dropped his bag on the bed and considered the tiny room. "Oh well," he thought. "I won't be spending much time in here anyway. There's work to be done."

Having invested in a few drinks at Greka's, Osgood had the lead that he needed.

Word around town was that the wife of a Bradley Fleet engineer, one Louella Jane Brege, "Lou" for short, had listened to communications between *Cedarville* and management from beginning to end on her husband's ham radio.

Tipping the bartender, he strode past the Galaxy 200 jukebox and into the gravel parking lot. Minutes later, his late-model car labored up the hill at the end of Third Street. Checking the address against the page he had torn from a telephone directory along the way, he stepped from the car. His eyes adjusted quickly in the gathering October dusk.

Lou Brege was alone in the kitchen when the doorbell rang. Her husband was out on another run.

"Yes, can I help you?" she asked politely as she opened the door, still wiping her hands on her apron.

"Mrs. Brege, my name is Osgood," he offered. "I am investigating some of the circumstances surrounding the recent *Cedarville* tragedy. Could I trouble you for just a moment of your time?"

17

Troublemaker

April 21, 1966
Mercywood Hospital
YPSILANTI, MICHIGAN—
1547

"Where the heck am I?" Gabrysiak wondered as he struggled against the drug-induced fog. A nurse walked into the room, checked his chart, and quickly left. Len laughed out loud. "Why do they wear those funny hats?" he wondered. "They look like wings on the top of their heads." Giggling at the thought of the whole lot of them flying away like a gaggle of geese, he was jerked back to the present by a scream from down the hall. "Wh . . . what's that?" he asked out loud, increasingly confused. "What kind of place is this?"

He was trying to remember. Yes. He was having trouble at home. The company wasn't paying compensation benefits like Mr. Hanson said he was due under the law. They owed him six dollars a day, and his bills were stacking up. He had to go back to work. But what was he doing here?

Drifting off, he started suddenly, as if he were falling. "Oh, yeah," he thought. It was coming back. He had returned to work as a materiel handler at Port Calcite in October 1965. But he really wanted to get back out on the lakes.

That spring he was assigned to another one of the Bradley Fleet's self-unloaders. Which one? Len just couldn't remember the name—but other things were coming back to him. His legs. They kept hurting. Yeah, he couldn't do it. He couldn't stand watch at the wheel. His legs were hurting. When the ship pulled in, he spoke with Captain Parilla.

Captain Parilla was very understanding. He suggested that Len check into Mercywood Hospital in Ypsilanti. Wasn't that a sanitorium, Len wondered? No, they treat all work-related injuries for the company in this area, Parilla assured him. Len agreed. But only for a few days. He was desperate to have his legs examined.

"Wait a minute," Len thought. "No one has asked me about my legs once since I got here." The door to his room opened, another shriek piercing the quiet. A nurse he vaguely recognized walked in with a small tray containing two white cups. "How long have I been here?" he asked.

"About ten days," she answered. "Now be a good boy and take your medicine."

She handed Len the cups, one containing water and the other a small white pill.

Then it occurred to him. He had sued the company. More precisely, he had filed a claim in the limitation action. What were they trying to do here? Turn him into a nutcase? Smiling at the nurse, he placed the tablet under his tongue and drank the water, settling back into his bed. When she was gone, he spit the pill into the toilet in the adjacent bathroom. He needed to clear his head.

April 22, 1966
0921

The next morning, Gabrysiak was itching like crazy. He had developed a case of psoriasis a few years before and was out of his medicine. "Yeah," he thought. "This may be my ticket out of here."

When the nurse returned for mid-morning rounds, he feigned grogginess. "Where's the medicine I brought with me?"

"You ran out of them a couple of days ago," she answered sweetly.

"Oh. Well, I need to refill my prescription," he replied. "My doctor is in Ann Arbor. Could I take a taxi to see him and then come back?"

"I'll see what I can do," she responded with little interest. But within the hour, Len found himself being wheeled to a taxi with instructions to come right back when he had obtained his prescription.

Ann Arbor, Michigan—
1622

As his general practitioner wrote out a prescription for his psoriasis, Gabrysiak casually interjected, "Hey, doc, did I tell you that the company has me in the hospital?"

"Oh yeah, where?" his physician asked.

"Mercywood." This brought a cold stare.

"What's wrong?" the doctor asked cautiously.

"My legs. They have been hurting since the *Cedarville* collision. But nobody there seems to care anything about it. The company told me the folks at Mercywood would treat my legs, but all they do is dope me up."

"Hmm," his doctor replied. "Do you have time?"

"Doc, I've got all the time in the world," Len laughed.

A few minutes later, he was seated on a table in the office of the physical therapist down the hall. The metal was cold, and he missed his pants, but Len was happy that someone was finally examining his legs.

"Mr. Gabrysiak, could you please lift your left leg," the therapist gently instructed. "OK, now your right. Lie down. Lift your left leg again. Your right again. OK. You can sit up now."

The therapist crossed the room to a small metal stool. Pulling a prescription pad from his desk drawer, he spoke over his shoulder. "Mr. Gabrysiak, you have reduced circulation in your lower extremity, and both of your legs have atrophied. I recommend that you begin a home therapy regimen. Tie a half pound weight to each leg, lift ten times, then increase by another half pound, until you can't lift any more. Do this three times a day and see me next month."

Folding the prescription, he tucked it in his shirt pocket and returned to Mercywood to pack his bags.

April 23, 1966
Mercywood Hospital
YPSILANTI, MICHIGAN—
0835

Gabrysiak was ready to go. He had packed his bags the previous evening and hidden them under his bed. Now, as he walked to the nurses' station, fully dressed and carrying his belongings, he caused a stir.

"I'm checking out," he said to the pretty young duty nurse with a smile.

Her eyes like saucers, she stammered, "I don't know about that."

"Well, I do," he retorted. "I'm checking out."

By then the head nurse had joined the conversation. "Now, Mr. Gabrysiak," she said with a condescending voice, "you just can't do that."

"Sure I can," he said, turning from the desk. "Just watch me."

"Wait, wait," the head nurse pleaded, searching for his file. "Let me make a call first."

Not wanting to cause a scene, Len waited.

"Yes, Mr. Parilla, this is Mercywood Hospital. Mr. Gabrysiak insists on checking out. Are we cleared to release him?" she asked into the receiver, glancing sideways at the rebellious patient. "Yes. OK. Thank you, sir." Obviously relieved, she looked up at Len. "You're free to go, sir. We just have a few papers for you to sign."

"So, Parilla's behind this all the way," Len mused as he signed the discharge sheets. "Should have known."

April 25, 1966
PORT CALCITE, MICHIGAN—
1230

Parilla had not heard so much as a peep from Gabrysiak since he had checked out and decided to give him a call. "Hello?" the deep familiar voice answered from the other end of the line.

"Len, it's Joe Parilla. Haven't heard from you in a while. Why haven't you checked in with the office?"

A pause. "I was kind of expecting you to check in with me, seeing as how I'm the one that's hurt and all."

"Fair enough," Parilla blustered. "Say, why don't you come down to the office and we'll talk about it?"

"Alright. I'll be there in a few minutes," Len agreed.

Half an hour later Len was surrounded and definitely outnumbered. Parilla's office was packed. Norm Haslin from safety, company lawyer Glen Cook, Parilla, Keenen, and George Jones from personnel were waiting when he arrived.

"Look, Captain Parilla, I have yet to receive maintenance and cure or any of the other benefits to which I am entitled for my injuries. You still owe me five hundred dollars for all my lost clothing and personal belongings," Len boldly accused.

"He's right," Cook added, drawing an instant glare from both Parilla and Keenen. "This man hasn't received any compensation for the time he was out following the incident."

"Thank you, Glen. That's quite enough," Keenen shot authoritatively.

"Len, what are your intentions here?" Parilla asked, changing the subject in a fatherly tone.

"Well, for starters I need physical therapy," Len offered.

"It's your word that you need physical therapy," Parilla countered, his demeanor increasingly aggressive.

"Not just my word. I went to see my doctor while you had me locked up at Mercywood," he said, handing over the prescription. Noting the look of astonishment, he added, "Didn't know that, did you?"

Parilla examined the prescription. "Well, then, you've obviously lied to this fine doctor," he said, smugly tossing the paper back at Gabrysiak.

"Lied?" Len roared as he came out of his seat and over the desk. Before he knew it, Cook and Jones were pulling him back. Parilla was leaning back in his chair, obviously shaken. A sly smile crossed Len's face as he shook off Parilla's protectors. Laughing, Gabrysiak straightened his shirt. "I'll see you in court, gentlemen," he challenged before turning for the door.

March 23, 1967
DETROIT, MICHIGAN—

Hanson had been informed of Gabrysiak's commitment to the sanitorium at Mercywood shortly after his release. Angered by the development, he was more determined than ever to pierce U.S. Steel's defenses and had spent much of the next year picking and poking into the ever increasing irregularities surrounding the sinking and the curious treatment of the survivors. In October he had even hired a team of divers to inspect the wreck, render an independent report, and obtain photos. Unfortunately, given the season, the bottom was silty and conditions were not good for photography. Nevertheless, his efforts were consistently paying off, and each day brought new information to support the case. This day was no different.

"Whoa," Hanson shouted, settling into his high-backed chair to reread the report. "They took long enough, but this is good stuff."

He ignored the cover letter from the Treasury Department and focused again on the March 7, 1967, report of the board of inquiry concerning the sinking of the SS *Cedarville,* duly approved by Captain W. C. Foster, chief of the Coast Guard's Merchant Vessel Inspection Division. Scanning the factual findings of the board of inquiry, he came to the real clincher.

> *The testimony of Helmsman Gabrysiak and Captain Joppich differs in several vital respects as to speeds and maneuvers before collision. The version as related by Gabrysiak is considered correct and that as related by Captain Joppich is considered self-serving and false and is accordingly rejected. Hence it is concluded that the* Cedarville *was operated at full speed almost up to the jaws of collision.*

"It just gets better and better," he said, lacing his fingers behind his head as he kicked his feet up on the desk.

18

Intimidations

March 29, 1967
ROGERS CITY, MICHIGAN—
1116

Robert Jason, Hanson's associate in Alpena, had spent much of the morning preparing Gabrysiak for his deposition. Now it was show time, and Len was already tiring of the questions.

After some relatively benign preliminary queries concerning his own personal injury claim and his position aboard the ship, counsel for the defense attacked his story. How could he be sure as to the exact courses ordered by the captain? Didn't the ship actually slow long before the collision? Joppich didn't actually speak with Captain Parilla, did he? Weren't you mistaken when you testified before the Coast Guard board of inquiry?

But Len wouldn't waiver. Finally, exasperated, he shoved his arms toward his interrogators. "You want blood?" he challenged. "Here are my wrists. I've told this story four times. I'm not changing my testimony."

"Thank you, Mr. Gabrysiak, that will be all," his questioner concluded. With that, he was dismissed, knowing that he had testified for the last time.

May 10, 1967
ROGERS CITY, MICHIGAN—
0935

"Of course I never spoke with Captain Joppich," Parilla said from the witness stand. "I would not have wanted to interfere with his decisions. He was in command. He was there. Not me."

"But you spoke with Captain Ursom aboard *Munson*?" he was asked.

"Yes. WLC had a tie line to Pittsburgh. When I received word of the collision, I contacted Captain Ursom and asked him to proceed to the scene and render assistance. . . . but I never tried to call *Cedarville*."

"Why not?"

Crossing his arms, he assumed an air of confidence and eyed his inquisitor. "I didn't want to interfere," he said, leaning back in his chair.

Cliff Buehrens would later corroborate his testimony.

May 14, 1967
PORT CALCITE, MICHIGAN—
1855

Parilla smiled contentedly. Although the case could be going better, he and Roman Keenen had interviewed Joe Hassett, and it was clear that he would toe the party line. The weeks before trial were passing in a flurry of last-minute discovery as most of the claimants and witnesses were subpoenaed to testify as to their respective claims.

Buehrens and Joppich had each done their part to protect Parilla and the company. Now Hassett was on board. Under careful prompting from Keenen and Parilla, the radioman agreed that, of the five tapes he had made of the event, the second apparently fouled and the fourth, tragically, didn't record at all. Furthermore, although the damaged tapes would likely have recorded key segments of communications between *Cedarville* and management, Hassett just couldn't remember the substance of anything that was said on that day.

Two years had passed since the tragedy that led the Coast Guard to revoke the captain's master's license. Unemployed for most of that time, Joppich had only recently taken a job with the University of Michigan as a seismic testing assistant. He would never sail again. Gabrysiak returned to the Bradley Fleet, but his injured legs never fully recovered, and he was soon forced ashore permanently. Sometime seminarian Stan Mulka worked the remainder of the summer of 1965 as a plumbers helper and returned to school in the fall. As a student, he became engaged and was planning a teaching career with his new family. Raphael Przybyla returned to work in his father's auto agency with a pay increase. In his estimation, he would soon be taking over the business. Of the twenty-four *Cedarville* survivors, thirteen returned to the lakes, including the Piechan brothers, Billy Holley, and Mike Idalske. In fact, Idalske did not miss a single day of work due to the tragedy.

Now, with the trial looming large on the horizon, United States Steel was preparing its witnesses.

"Who's next?" Parilla asked, kicking his feet up on his desk.

"Louella Jane Brege," Keenen replied, referring to his notes. "Her husband is . . ."

"Yeah, I know. Dick Brege. He's the chief engineer on *Rogers City*."

"Right. Problem is, the claimants' committee has a statement from her that makes us look really bad. There's no telling what she'll say on the witness stand." Seeing the look on Parilla's face, Keenen continued. "It seems an investigator named Osgood got ahold of her a few months after the accident. She claims to have heard the entire incident played out on her marine band radio."

"That means . . ." Parilla stammered, his face flushed.

"That means we need to have a little talk with Mrs. Brege," Keenen concluded.

Parilla sat silent for a moment, his fingers laced below his chin. "*Rogers City* is headed toward Gary right now," he offered.

"Well, then," Keenen answered, "there's no time like the present."

Flipping through the company directory, Parilla found the listing for Richard Brege. Dialing quickly, he relaxed when Lou's gentle voice answered on the other end.

"Hello, Mrs. Brege? Yes, good evening. This is Joseph Parilla at the port."

Keenen sat across from Parilla, taking in the one-sided conversation.

"No, I know Dick is not at home . . . That's right . . . I understand that you have been subpoenaed to testify in a few days. . . . Yes, I understand. . . . Would you mind if we came by to speak with you?" Parilla paused to check his calendar. "Tomorrow evening? That will be fine. I'll see you then."

Turning to his associate, Wendell Lang, Keenen spoke. "Pull Dick Brege's personnel file and see what you can find on our chief engineer."

May 17, 1967
Presque Isle County Courthouse
ROGERS CITY, MICHIGAN—
1703

Lou Brege was obviously terrified as she took the stand. It seemed as though everyone was there. Counsel for both sides stared from around the room as she raised her right hand for the court reporter.

"Do you swear to tell the truth, the whole truth, and nothing but the truth?" he asked.

"Yes," she answered, glancing furtively at Keenen.

After establishing name, address, and personal information, Robert Jason, representing the Hanson group, launched into the deposition.

"Have you discussed your testimony today with any counsel, Mrs. Brege?" he asked.

"No. But I asked them what I should do. See, Dick wasn't home, and I didn't know what to do," she mumbled.

Straining to hear, Abraham Freedman, counsel for several of the other claimants, interjected, "Will you speak up, please?"

Glancing at Freedman, Jason continued. "Mrs. Brege, let me be clear. Did you talk to counsel?

"Yes."

"Who?"

"Mr. Elmer Radke," she replied.

Probing, Jason continued. "Have you talked to any other lawyer?"

"No."

"You have not talked to Mr. Keenen at any time?"

"Oh, I am sorry," she said, looking to Keenen. "I didn't realize he was a lawyer."

"Right here," Keenen offered from behind the bar, raising his hand with a smile.

"OK," Jason continued. "You recognize Mr. Keenen in the courtroom?"

"Yes."

"Mrs. Brege, when did you talk to Mr. Keenen?"

"On the fifteenth. Just a few days ago. We spoke in my home," she volunteered.

"How did that meeting come about?" Jason asked.

"Oh, Mr. Parilla wanted to see me."

"Would you keep your voice up, please?" Freedman interrupted again.

"I am sorry," Brege offered. Turning back to Jason, she continued. "He called me on a Sunday evening and asked if he could see me."

"Who was present at the meeting?"

"Mr. Parilla, Mr. Keenen, and I believe it is Mr. Lang," she said, pointing to the young attorney seated beside Keenen.

"May I ask you if they discussed testimony that you were to give today?" Jason queried.

"Somewhat," she responded as the claimant's counsel exchanged glances.

Stepping back from the witness stand, Jason considered his notes. "What is your husband's employment?" he asked, changing direction.

"He is with Bradley Transportation," she whispered.

Freedman reacted once again. "Speak up, please," he barked curtly. All eyes turned his way as he pretended to brush lint from his dark blue jacket.

Waiting several seconds, Jason continued. "What is his occupation with the company, if you know?"

"He is chief engineer of the *Rogers City*. He has been in that position since this spring."

"Does he own a marine ham radio set?"

"Yes, sir," Brege affirmed.

Jason crossed the floor to lean against the wooden partition. "Do you ever use this set?"

"I only listen. I'm not licensed, so I can't talk on it."

"There are periods when you leave it on and listen to it, is that correct?" Jason asked.

"Yes."

"Where is this set located in the house?" he asked.

"In the basement. I turn it on every morning and leave it on until seven o'clock at night," she mumbled.

Cupping his ears, Freedman nearly stood. "I'm sorry. I am having trouble hearing you. Could you keep your voice up, please?" His colleagues chuckled quietly as Brege nodded from the stand.

"Getting specifically to the day that we're concerned about here, the morning of May the seventh, do you recall listening to your radio that morning?"

"Yes," she admitted.

"What time did you get up and turn on the radio, if you can recall?"

Thinking for a moment, Brege responded. "I got up at six a.m. and turned on the radio at seven. I wanted to listen because my husband was out on a trip."

"Tell me, if you can, Mrs. Brege, what did you do from seven a.m. on?"

"Well," she paused, "I had breakfast, took the boys to school, and came home to start baking."

"What time did you return home after taking the boys to school?"

"I had to get groceries, so I didn't get home until nine-thirty."

"Did you listen to the radio at any time that morning?" Jason asked.

"Not until after eleven," she said, glancing at Keenen.

Eyeing Brege suspiciously, Jason tried a different approach. "Mrs. Brege, did you ever discuss this disaster, this *Cedarville* incident, with anyone?"

"No."

"Is it your testimony under oath that you did not tell anybody at all?"

"I don't think I did," she said meekly.

"Mrs. Brege," he persisted, "specifically did you ever tell anyone that you overheard any of the conversations between *Cedarville* and WLC on the marine band?"

"Objection," Keenen said, standing at his seat.

"Well," she hesitated, "I might have talked to a few."

"Who?"

"Mrs. Clarence Solisky and I. We discussed what we had heard on the standard radio."

"Did you discuss this with an investigator by the name of Mr. Osgood that I sent to talk to you?" he asked.

"Yes, but—"

"Is he a person?" the attorney chided.

"Yes, he is," Brege mumbled to Freedman's continued frustration.

Taking a moment, Jason rechecked his notes. "Did you tell Mr. Osgood that you were listening at nine thirty that morning?"

"No, I couldn't have," she responded, her eyes glued to the floor.

"I have no further questions," Jason said as he gathered his notes from the podium and took his seat behind the bar.

Next up, Ned Phillips continued the pursuit. "Mrs. Brege," he began, barely out of his seat, "how long have you been married?"

"Eighteen years."

"Do you love your husband?"

"Yes," she answered warily.

"And I suppose as a dutiful wife you would do anything reasonable to help your husband and his work and his career? Yes?"

"Well, I think he does pretty well on his own," she bristled.

"Mr. Parilla is his boss at U.S. Steel, isn't that right?" he asked, ignoring her tone.

"Yes, sir."

"And you know, of course, that Mr. Keenen and Mr. Lang represent U.S. Steel, don't you?"

"Yes, sir," she repeated.

"And the three of them visited your home to talk with you on May fifteenth, isn't that right?"

"Yes, sir."

"No further questions," Phillips concluded as he turned from the witness.

"Well, I might have one or two little questions here," Freedman said, addressing the room as he swaggered to the podium.

"Mrs. Brege, I am a little puzzled. Why did Mr. Keenen and Mr. Lang and Mr. Parilla want to talk to you?"

"Objection," Keenen said, obviously weary of the continued line of questioning.

Ignoring the U.S. Steel attorney, Freedman pressed on. "When Mr. Parilla called you on the telephone, did he tell you what he wanted to talk about?"

"He said he would like to see me about Mr. Osgood," she admitted, smoothing the hem of her skirt as she crossed her legs.

"Did he tell you that he heard that you had said something about listening to the radio during the period immediately following the collision? Isn't that what he said to you?"

"He asked if I had listened to the radio and what time," she allowed.

"He said that is what he heard, and he said that is what he wanted to talk to you about? Is that right?"

"I believe so."

"When he came over, did he want to talk about Mr. Osgood's visit?" Freedman continued, pursuing her testimony.

"No. We discussed different things."

"Like what?" Freedman probed.

"How can you answer that?" Brege shot back.

"I can't, but you can. Just tell us what they said."

Settling back into her seat, Brege glared at Freedman. "Well, I don't know when they asked about Mr. Osgood, if that is what his name is," she finally said. "They started by asking questions about my husband's woodworking around the house. Then we started discussing this."

"Started discussing what?"

"What I heard. Or what time I started listening. Excuse me."

"What did you say to them?" Freedman asked.

"Eleven o'clock."

"Mrs. Brege, you have stated that you have the set turned on all day every day. Why didn't you listen to it then?"

Speaking slowly at first, Brege crafted a response. "Because my son had a thesis to write, and I had to help him spell a few words."

"Hmm. Does your son go to school?" Freedman asked.

"High school."

"Oh, high school," Freedman repeated as he stepped up to the witness stand. "What time does he go to school?"

"He has to be there at eight, but I take him at seven thirty," she replied, sensing a trap.

"And what day of the week was this?" he queried, suppressing a smile.

"Friday," she muttered.

"May I suggest to you, Mrs. Brege," he pronounced boldly, turning to face Keenen, "that you made a mistake? That he was in school that day?"

"Yes," she admitted grudgingly.

"So that at that time you were as free to listen as you were every other day, isn't that right?"

"Yes."

"And yet you did not listen between nine thirty and eleven a.m.?"

"No, I did not. I was making a cake and cookies," she said as forcefully as before.

Surprised with the audacity of her statement, Freedman merely repeated it. "Cake and cookies?"

"Yes," she said confidently. "And when you run the mixer you cannot hear on the radio."

Taking a moment to collect his thoughts, Freedman continued. "How long does the mixer run?"

"Not too long," she admitted. "But I was not going to run down in the basement to turn up the volume."

"Mrs. Brege, did you tell all of these things to Mr. Keenen and Mr. Lang?"

"No. You mean about baking cookies? They weren't interested," she replied as laughter filled the room.

"I see," Freedman said, waiting for the laughter to die down. When quiet had returned, he continued. "Mrs. Brege, are you afraid that your husband will lose his job if you tell us what happened on that day?"

"No," she said, suddenly apprehensive.

"Mrs. Brege, if you are not afraid that your husband will lose his job, why are you concerned about telling us what happened on that day?"

"Objection," Keenen barked, standing once again.

"You keep the door open to the basement, don't you?"

"Yes," she said.

"So you can hear the radio coming up without too much trouble?"

"No," she said slowly. Then after a long pause she said, "We were having trouble with the furnace, and I had been listening to that."

Sensing a stalemate, Freedman changed his tack. "Mr. Osgood came to see you because he said that he knew you had listened to a conversation immediately following the collision of the *Cedarville,* is that right?"

"Yes."

"So the word was around that you had listened in on the radio and heard some things immediately following the collision, is that right? The word was around?"

"Yes," she admitted.

"Mrs. Brege, what did you hear over the radio that morning?"

"All I can remember hearing was the central radio asking the position of the *Cedarville.* They wanted the Coast Guard to stand by until the *Munson* got there."

"You heard that over the radio?" Freedman asked.

"That is right," she allowed. "But I didn't hear anything else. I had to make lunch for my boys."

"Oh, but you know you listened that day, don't you, Mrs. Brege? It was exciting and very important news, wasn't it?"

"Right."

"As soon as you heard the news, you would have been immediately attracted to the radio and you wouldn't have left it, would you?"

"I guess not."

"You said before that WLC was asking the Coast Guard cutter for its position so that *Munson* could go to the scene of the collision and give assistance," Freedman summarized.

"Yes."

"And then I assume that you followed the subsequent broadcasts about the pickup of bodies from the water?"

Nodding her head, she answered, "That is right."

"Then you must have heard the Mayday call."

"No, I didn't," Brege protested. "I . . . I was at my neighbor's house returning an egg."

"When was this?"

"Around a quarter till eleven.

Smiling, Freedman stepped back to the podium. "Mrs. Brege," he continued, "I would like to remind you that the calls on WLC to the Coast Guard cutter came before eleven o'clock. The records will prove that Mrs. Brege."

"Objection," Keenen blurted, turning red in the face.

Adopting a softer tone, Freedman stepped back to the witness stand. "Mrs. Brege, are you scared that your husband will lose his job if you tell us what happened?" he urged gently.

"Oh, look, please," she whined, wringing her hands and looking to Keenen. "I didn't start listening on the ham radio until eleven."

"Why didn't you tell this to Mr. Osgood?"

"Because I figured it was none of his business," she said defiantly.

Feigning a shocked look, Freedman waited. "Your knowledge was very important. Why wouldn't it be the business of the people who were involved in the accident? He was an investigator. He was trying to help people out. Why wouldn't it be his business?"

"I have no answer for that," she said, averting her gaze.

Crossing his arms, he turned slightly. "You weren't trying to conceal information, were you?" he asked suspiciously.

"No. I couldn't remember that day what had happened. I . . . I thought Dick might be trying to get in touch with me for my birthday. That is why I made an appointment to be at home at eleven. My birthday is the fifth. No, the third . . . and Dick was going to try to contact me on the post office net."

"What did that have to do with May eighth?"

"May seventh," the other attorneys sang out en masse.

"Thank you, gentlemen," Freedman allowed.

"You're welcome," responded a sarcastic Mr. Lang.

"What did your birthday have to do with May seventh?" he continued after a pause.

"Because my husband did not make it home for my birthday. I was listening for him on the radio."

"If you expected a message, it would be on the day of your birthday, wouldn't it? Did you get a message from him on your birthday?"

"No."

"Did you get it on May fourth?"

"No. He forgot."

"Did you get it on May fifth?"

"He forgot."

"Did you get it on May sixth?"

"No," she answered with a trace of anger as the listeners around the room squirmed in sympathy for Dick Brege.

Disregarding the melodrama, Freedman went on. "Then why would you expect it on May seventh?"

"I don't know," she responded. "I was just kind of hoping."

Taking a moment to check his notes, Freedman hovered beside the podium. "Mrs. Brege, you know you are under oath now, don't you?" he asked sharply.

"Yes."

"And you are not giving us the whole story, are you? You heard WLC talking to the Coast Guard before *Munson* was dispatched to the scene? How long were you plugged in prior to the *Munson* call?"

"I would say about twenty-five minutes," she allowed.

"The Mayday call was placed during that period," Freedman nearly shouted. "We have that established in the record. The collision happened at nine forty-five, and Captain Parilla testified at his deposition that within a very, very short time after that he called the *Munson*."

Pausing, he paced before the bar. "Do you understand what I am saying? It had to be somewhere close to ten o'clock that he called the *Munson,* and that is the call that you heard. Do you understand this, Mrs. Brege? This is what the record establishes."

Keenen and Lang objected simultaneously.

"I don't care. I didn't hear it," she pleaded.

"What else *did* you hear?" he prompted.

Considering for a moment, she finally answered. "Where the men were."

"The men were not yet in the water, Mrs. Brege," Freedman quipped.

"I don't care," she barked, instantly regretting the outburst.

Freedman adopted a more concerned tone. "You don't care?" he asked gravely.

"I am sorry that sounded that way. I didn't mean it that way. I could not always hear the signal. We are by the hospital, where they have an X-ray machine."

Laughing, Freedman pounced. "Are you saying now that the hospital had something to do with it?"

"Y-Yes," she stammered. "Whenever they turn on their machines it is very hard to hear anything."

"How long was it noisy that day?"

"The noise from the X-ray machine comes in spurts. It goes 'bzzzz bzzzz'."

"Do you know how long an X-ray machine is on?" he queried.

"Yes. A fraction of a second," she said, realizing the flaw in her story.

"Are you saying that this prevented your hearing the broadcast?" Freedman asked incredulously.

"Well, maybe another kind of machine. I don't know what they use."

"So, then," he postured, "you were *trying* to listen but couldn't hear anything behind the static?"

"That's right. There may have been something said, but I couldn't hear it."

Approaching the witness, Freedman laced his fingers and leaned on the oak partition. "Mrs. Brege, you don't have to be concerned," he assured. "Your husband belongs to the union, doesn't he?"

"I think so. I've never asked him that," she said.

"You don't know whether he does or not? Do you know what salary your husband makes from United States Steel?"

"No," she asserted firmly.

Rolling his eyes, Freedman stepped away. "Doesn't he turn the money over to you when he gets paid?"

"Yes."

"Who deposits the money in the bank?"

"I do."

"And you are telling us that you have no idea how much he makes?"

"N-No," she stammered. "It varies with overtime."

Considering his next question, Freedman was distracted by laughter from the defense table. "What's so funny?" he barked.

"I think it's pitiful the way you are carrying on with this witness," Lang jeered.

Ignoring the comment, Freedman turned back to the witness. "I suppose it was quite an achievement for your husband to become chief engineer after only a few years as first assistant engineer. Is there a large difference in pay?"

"We haven't received a chief's pay yet."

"How come?" he asked.

"Because they have too many chiefs for the appointed positions."

"I see," he said suspiciously. "But yet they appointed him chief even though they didn't need a chief, is that what you are saying?"

Brege did not respond.

"Mrs. Brege," Freedman continued, "you know that it is the rumor around town that you heard the broadcast between *Cedarville* and U.S. Steel, isn't it?"

"No."

"Mrs. Brege, Mr. Osgood didn't come out of the clear blue sky, did he?"

"I swear he did," she said, raising her right hand.

"Thank you, Mrs. Brege," he concluded abruptly. "That is all I have."

Looking across the room, Freedman pointed to Ed Silber, counsel for Den Norske Amerikalinje, who merely shook his head. "I do not care to ask this witness anything," he said with apparent contempt.

With that, Freedman returned to his seat.

Finally, rising from the defense table, Keenen approached the witness. "Mrs. Brege, is it a fair statement to say that the majority of our conversation related to your husband's hobbies? His train set, his models, antique gun, and his woodworking shop? Is that correct?"

"Yes," she said flatly, glaring at Keenen.

"Thank you," he smiled. "That is all. This witness is dismissed."

19

Closure

May 15, 1967
DETROIT, MICHIGAN—

It wasn't fair. Pure and simple. In fact, Hanson was willing to argue that it may have been unconstitutional. A violation of the equal protection clause. The Limitation of Liability defense was a statutory protection available to powerful and wealthy shipowners to the detriment of the poor, unsophisticated seamen in their employ.

Hanson had seen it often enough, but that didn't make it any more palatable. His disgust grew with each new case—each new attempt to cheat some pitiful widow and her children out of a little money just because their father's ship was now a worthless piece of rusting metal far beneath the waves.

"Limitation" was an anachronism. Admitting that the statute may have been necessary when it was enacted to protect the burgeoning merchant marine of the time, he would also adamantly argue that the need for such draconian protections had long since passed without anyone broaching the subject.

Merchant navigation was no longer the perilous adventure it had been in the days of sail. Today, Hanson reasoned, most fleets were owned and operated by large and prosperous corporations. Even smaller companies, owning less magnificent vessels, were well insured against any eventuality. But most outrageous of all—their insurers were afforded the same protections under the act. They were untouchable. The corporate fat cats were getting off easy, leaving the families of their employees holding the bag.

Hanson was attacking the issue from all sides. He had unsuccessfully filed motions to have the protection set aside on the ground that the company knew that *Cedarville* was unseaworthy and was not entitled to protection from their own negligence. He had even tested the political approach. In a letter to Representative Thomas Ashley of Ohio, he pleaded for legislation to repeal the act, arguing that "the existence of this statute and the shipowner's reliance on it can only encourage and promote a more careless and irresponsible attitude in their operations." All to no avail. The shipowners were too strong—their lobby too influential. Too much money was involved for politicians to turn against their greatest benefactors.

Undaunted, Hanson vowed to get the unjust law abolished, no matter how long it took. But in the meantime, the claimants' committee had one more trick up its sleeve.

With the June trial date fast approaching, attorneys representing seaman and shipowner alike gathered for a mandatory settlement conference before the magistrate judge assigned to the case. Guided by the judge, the parties agreed that *Weissenburg* bore no responsibility in the collision and released Hamburg-Amerika Linje from the lawsuit. That left United States Steel and Den Norske Amerikalinje to split the pecuniary damages already established by the widows and survivors.

Earlier in the litigation, Judge Connell had appointed a commissioner to assess the pending claims and to issue a recommendation as to the validity of each. With the damages calculated, the commissioner determined that the combined claims totaled $436,000. Split two ways, the remaining shipowners agreed to pay more than $200,000 each—far less than their anticipated exposure in Limitation of Liability. Even so, this did not completely put the issue to rest.

Anticipating U.S. Steel's move to settle out on the issue of liability, the claimants' committee petitioned the court for additional punitive damages in the amount of $4 million. Asserting gross negligence and active complicity in the tragedy and subsequent cover-up, the claimants continued to pursue the company through Judge Connell's courtroom—and with the dismissal of the other shipowners, U.S. Steel would have to go it alone.

Penned by Abe Freedman and Harry Traverse, and coordinated with Vic Hanson, Ned Phillips, and the constellation of other attorneys working the case, the claimants' committee's brief on punitive damages spun a tale of intrigue and deceit, detailing the company's role in causing *Cedarville*'s collision and the deaths of nearly one-third of her crew.

Why, the committee pondered to the court, did U.S. Steel do nothing more than provide a small and ineffective collision mat to protect the aging freighter against the threat of flooding? Why, although apprised of wastage in the ship's hull, did the company defer repairs for more than five years? Perhaps more importantly, why did the Bradley Fleet deliberately overload its vessels, avoid established shipping lanes, and require its captains to maintain full speed at all times, in violation of navigational safety rules? Of course, the questions had no legitimate answers, except to suggest a pattern of imprudence and misconduct that could exist only with corporate complicity.

Worse yet, the claimants continued, was U.S. Steel's willful and reckless disregard for the safety of the crew. Unbelievably, facing the imminent loss of the vessel, Captain Parilla refused to release the men to a position of safety aboard *Weissenburg*. This indifference and contempt for human life, they urged, permeated the highest ranks of the company. On this point, Freedman wrote that, "following the collision, Captain Joppich's 'May Day' call immediately reached Admiral Khoury and Captain Parilla. Although there appears to be a conspiracy of silence with regard to Parilla's communications with Joppich, the evidence establishes quite conclusively that United States Steel deliberately and willfully subjected the *Cedarville* crew to such great danger as to risk death and substantial injury to the crew."

Continuing, Freedman argued that the hand of U.S. Steel was also clearly visible in the subsequent developments that closed the mouths or clouded the memories of adverse witnesses. Joppich, Parilla, and Buehrens were evasive, and Hassett could not explain gaps in the recordings he had made. But the bizarre and often disjointed testimony of Louella Jane Brege was most demonstrative of United States Steel's perfidy.

Brege, whose husband had been promoted to chief engineer under extremely peculiar circumstances, was visited shortly before her scheduled deposition by Captain Parilla and two company attorneys. From this visit, she concluded that she had not been listening to her radio at any time between the collision and the sinking of *Cedarville*. Her confused testimony, however, quite clearly established that she must have been listening, as she described several key events that occurred during that span of time.

This testimony, the claimants concluded, was particularly illustrative of the intimidation and obfuscation tactics U.S. Steel employed to conceal the truth from the court.

In response, counsel for U.S. Steel parried that the claimants' case was unfounded supposition and innuendo. There was absolutely no evidence, Keenen noted, to support the assertion that United States Steel officers influenced Captain Joppich in the handling of the emergency. Rather, the testimony at hand demonstrated that Parilla was not involved. Citing statements by Parilla, Buehrens, Joppich, and Brege denying contact, he argued that it was clear that the claimants could offer no proof in support of their outlandish conspiracy theory.

Without evidence, the pending claim for punitive damages must fail, he reasoned. Joppich had admitted that the decisions to navigate recklessly through the fog, to beach the vessel, and not to allow the crew to escape were his and his alone. United States Steel should not be exposed to punitive damages for one captain's negligence.

October 26, 1967
CLEVELAND, OHIO—
1635

Starting from his reverie, Judge Connell returned his attention to the task at hand.

This had been no easy case to try. In fact, it was quite a long haul. In opening arguments, the claimants painted the company as a corrupt, money-hungry institution more interested in profits than the welfare of its employees. U.S. Steel opened the defense by attempting to cast doubt upon the conspiracy theory. Then the real work began.

For twenty-four days in June, the parties presented their cases. Connell did not hear any live witnesses but considered the investigation reports and mountains of deposition testimony as selectively narrated by teams of attorneys for both sides.

By the time the defense rested, the outcome was decided. The judge found the company's arguments meritless and discounted the testimony of Joppich, Parilla, and Buehrens as self-serving. He also suspected coercion and witness tampering and gave no weight to the tainted testimony of Lou Brege and Joe Hassett.

In his written opinion, Connell hammered the United States Steel Corporation relentlessly for thirty-six pages. Finding complicity and institutional negligence on the part of United States Steel, Connell concluded that the decision to beach was not that of Captain Joppich alone. Rather, it was obvious that Captain Parilla and Admiral Khoury were closely involved from the outset. "Today," Connell reasoned, "the lake captain's first call is to the ship owner. Thus, the highest officers of United States Steel were not only cognizant of the effort to beach the fully manned ship as she was sinking, but did not intervene to prevent the inevitable consequences."

Blasting the company's conduct throughout, Judge Connell adopted nearly every assertion set forth by the claimants' committee, rendering judgment against United States Steel for nearly $3 million.

Satisfied with his decision, Connell turned the page. Removing the cap to his fountain pen, he closely examined the italic nib, signed the opinion with great judicial flourish, and turned his attention to the next case.

October 30, 1967
ROGERS CITY, MICHIGAN—

News of the decision spread quickly among the survivors, but it would ultimately be a hollow victory. The company was already planning its appeal. Asserting one technicality after another, U.S. Steel would drag the case through court for so many years that the matter would be forgotten by many in the community as those involved got on with their lives. Nevertheless, for the time being, justice had been served.

Epilogue

July 3, 2000
ROGERS CITY, MICHIGAN

On a slate-gray summer morning, Len Gabrysiak took a few minutes to meet with a curious author from New Orleans to relive the incident once again over coffee and cinnamon rolls. Long since retired, his mind was clear and his memory of the tragedy razor sharp. After talking for hours, he abruptly ended the story with an invitation. "You really need to go out and see the monument," he said.

"The monument?" the author asked.

"Yeah. Down by the marina. It's a big stone monument. You can't miss it."

A few hours later, having already visited a hundred other Rogers City landmarks, the author found himself standing before the monument. Beyond, sailboat masts swayed and the waters of Lake Huron glowed a deep blue as the freshening wind parted the thinning clouds to reveal the sun. Constructed of white granite with black inlaid marble, the monument paid tribute to the seamen of the Bradley Fleet who had perished on the lakes. From the top, the inscription read:

STR CEDARVILLE
May 7, 1965

William Asam Wheelsman   Eugene Jones Stokerman
Wilbert Bredow Steward   Eugene Jungman Watchman
Charles Cook 3rd Mate   F. Donald Lamp Chief Engineer
Arthur Fuhrman Deckwatch   Reinholdt Radtke 3rd Ast. Engineer
Stanley Haske Wheelsman   Hugh Wingo Oiler

. . . Dedicated August 9, 1987

As the author considered the memorial, Gabrysiak returned to his backyard garden, where Pat was already hard at work harvesting an early crop of sugar snap peas.

THE END

Author's Note

The reader will note an abundance of dialogue in the telling of the *Cedarville* story. The reader may then justifiably inquire as to the source of this dialogue, as the events portrayed in this book are quite serious in their implications. This section is intended to satisfy that curiosity; but first it is important to understand that the *Cedarville* story presents itself in distinct elements—though in the telling, those elements are interspersed.

At the story's core are the documented specifics of the various ships' movements during *Cedarville*'s last season, her sinking, and the rescue of the surviving crewmen. The incident and its causes were examined and reported in detail by Coast Guard and civilian investigators, and nearly everyone involved was interviewed and reinterviewed at length. Most of the surviving *Cedarville* crew, several *Topdalsfjord* and *Weissenburg* officers, Bradley Fleet officials, company radiomen, widows, and other witnesses were questioned or deposed under oath. The transcripts of these interviews detailed ship movements and crew statements made during *Cedarville*'s last few runs and in the hours following her collision. Cited directly, these disclosures, along with statements made by key witnesses interviewed by the author, served as the framework upon which this narrative was built.

Then we have the conspiracy. In fairness, none of the participants to the conspiracy have ever admitted to their roles—or even that there was a conspiracy. Rather, evidence of a conspiracy begins with *Cedarville*'s helmsman, Len Gabrysiak, who testified as to the company's directive to keep the men aboard the doomed ship. This testimony—combined with the destruction of pertinent tape recordings, the company's apparent efforts to improperly influence witnesses, *Cedarville*'s long-standing deterioration, the apparent refusal of the company to make repairs mandated by the Coast Guard and its insurers, the undisputed overloading of the vessel, and the fleet's history of disregarding navigational safety rules—raised the suspicions of the trial judge. But Louella Jane Brege's nervous and disjointed testimony completed the picture. Although circumstantial, her flimsy, nonsensical account cast the company in a bad light and sealed the judge's (and the author's) opinion.[1]

Even so, there were still no confessions. At the time of this writing, Charles Khoury, the only surviving company official, was confined to a nursing home and was unable to grant an interview. Mrs. Brege, still living in Rogers City, refused to speak further of the matter. Thus, the author turned to the one who weighed the testimony of the participants—Judge James Connell.

Scattered throughout the story are passages addressing the statements and motives of company officials necessary to portray the conspiracy. These actions have been reconstructed from the recorded findings of the trial judge; the testimony of witnesses such as Gabrysiak, Parilla, and Joppich; and the author's deductions from the available evidence. As noted in the preface, there are two sides to every story. Perhaps in the future some lost diary or memoir will surface to shed new light on the incident and the participation of company officials. But in the meantime, this narrative ultimately reflects the author's opinion on how the play was acted out.

Returning then to our initial query—How can the reader distinguish actual quotes from reconstructed dialogue?—the following notes are provided to assist the reader to that end.

1. *Return to Rogers City*

This chapter initially follows the Gabrysiak family as they return to Rogers City. The specifics of this journey, including dialogue, were reconstructed from information provided by Len Gabrysiak.

Cedarville's arrival at winter layup was recounted, to a large

---

1. *In re: Petition of Den Norske Amerika-Linje A/S, for Exoneration From or Limitation of Liability, et al.,* 276 F.Supp. 163 (N.D. Oh. 1967).

extent, from press reports heralding the end of the shipping season. Dialogue of the *Cedarville* crew was reconstructed from those accounts and confirmed by Mr. Gabrysiak, who was the third mate on watch during *Cedarville*'s arrival.

2.   *Headquarters*

In the opening sequence of this chapter, Admiral Khoury arrives at U.S. Steel headquarters in Pittsburgh. It is unclear whether he actually arrived at that time on the date specified. Rather, the sequence was crafted to introduce the reader to this figure and to explain his position at U.S. Steel.

Later in the chapter, Admiral Khoury places pressure on the fleet captains, who in turn pressure the ship captains to increase their deliveries. The communications depicted in this segment are the first of the statements to portray conspiratorial conduct on the part of company officials. As noted previously, the participants never admitted to these events. Accordingly, they are reconstructed by the author in the spirit of the findings of the trial court concerning corporate wrongdoing.

3.   *Fit-Out*

The depositions of engineers Harry Bey and Walter Tulgetske clearly reflect that, during the first few days of fit-out, Chief Engineer Lamp examined every inch of *Cedarville*'s engineering spaces and reported his findings to Captain Joppich. Whether Lamp was engaged in the specific activities portrayed at the times depicted is unclear from those accounts, but it is certain that he exercised due diligence in preparing his ship to get underway. This segment was intended to summarize those preparations and to introduce the reader to the environment in which he and his fellow engineers labored.

The record is also clear that Captain Joppich spent several days during fit-out roaming the ship, inspecting her gear, and supervising the crew in their efforts to revive the aging freighter. Though the exact sequence of his activities during fit-out is unknown, the captain's musings about *Cedarville*'s weather decks are depicted in such a manner as to acquaint the reader with the pressures facing the captain as he prepared his aging ship for another season of service.

Finally, Joppich's ascent to the captain's chair is recounted from historical accounts identified in the bibliography and by the eyewitness Len Gabrysiak.

4. Icebound

The initial segment of this chapter, depicting Captain Parilla's frustration with weather conditions, is derived from press reports indicating that the departure of the Bradley Fleet was delayed by inclement weather and frozen passages. Reasonably inferring the officer's displeasure with his inability to put his fleet to sea, the author chose to report this occurrence as written.

The story of *Cedarville*'s stranding and rescue from ice floes in the Straits of Mackinac was related by Third Mate Gabrysiak to the author. Likewise, the adjoining segment portraying Pat Gabrysiak waiting for the ship's return was reconstructed from information provided by Mrs. Gabrysiak.

5. Topdalsfjord

The Norwegian vessel *Topdalsfjord* departed Denmark, transited the North Sea, and entered the North Atlantic on her voyage to the Great Lakes. The historical records reflect that the SOSUS watch center in Keflavik, Iceland, monitored those sea lanes at that time using the technology described in the chapter. It is, therefore, reasonable to believe that *Topdalsfjord* was monitored by U.S. Navy and Soviet assets as it entered the North Atlantic. This chapter paints the cold war in the North Atlantic in an effort to give the reader a better understanding of the times in which the story takes place.

6. Arrivals

In this chapter Gabrysiak reflects on Rogers City and his experiences aboard the Bradley Fleet vessel *Carl D. Bradley*. These experiences were written as recounted by Mr. Gabrysiak to the author.

As for Przybyla's tour upon reporting aboard, such tours are standard for new hands and is included to introduce the reader to the technical aspects of the engineering spaces. For the most part, the details cited were provided by engineers Bey and Tulgetske.

Well documented and commented upon by the trial judge, the

overloading of *Cedarville*'s holds was also related by the crew interviewed and is depicted in the manner described.

The segment in which Mrs. Brege listened to the marine band
radio is adapted from her deposition testimony, to the extent that she
testified to routinely monitoring fleet radio traffic to keep tabs on the
movements of her husband's ship, the M/V *Munson*.

Finally, *Topdalsfjord*'s passage through the St. Lawrence Seaway,
though not recorded in detail, was reconstructed from press reports
concerning other ships' passages and mishaps in the Seaway at the
time. Channel conditions, pilotage requirements, and communications and docking procedures were recounted from applicable St.
Lawrence Seaway passage guidelines.

7. *Passages*

Topdalsfjord's passage through Welland Canal is recounted in accor-
dance with Welland Canal passage guidelines as promulgated by the St.
Lawrence Seaway Authority. Although the specific orders of the compulsory pilot were not recorded, his supervision of the *Topdalsfjord*
crew in their passage of the Welland Canal was crafted to illustrate the
seamanship necessary to navigate the waterway. To the extent that
interactions with other vessels and the responses of the crew to the
pilot's orders are depicted, they are done so as envisioned by the author.

8. *Turnaround*

The first segment in this chapter deals with Captain Parilla's departure for a meeting in Pittsburgh with U.S. Steel vice president Charles
Khoury. As Parilla's deposition testimony reveals, the purpose of the
meeting was to discuss fleet conditions with his supervisor. This segment was included to explain Parilla's absence from fleet headquarters during the ensuing emergency and to acquaint the reader with the
topic of the scheduled meeting. As Parilla's exact words are lost to
history, the segment is recounted as envisioned by the author.

Topdalsfjord's departure from Milwaukee was reconstructed from
crew testimony to Coast Guard investigators, bills of lading, and
shipping records.

The circumstances and actions of the *Cedarville* crew (Joppich,
Fuhrman, Haske, and Gabrysiak) before sailing are recounted from
their deposition testimony or that of their survivors.

9. Fog

The circumstances and actions of the *Cedarville* crew (Rygwelski, Bredow, Haske, Brewster, and Joppich) as they set sail on their final cruise are recounted from their deposition testimony, the testimony of other witnesses, and that of their survivors.

Topdalsfjord's passage was reconstructed from the ship's navigational log and testimony of the crew before the Coast Guard board of inquiry.

The account of the allision of the freighter *J. E. Upson* with a Coast Guard lighthouse was taken from press reports of the incident.

Cedarville's passage and the actions of her officers were reconstructed from the ship's log and the testimony of the survivors before the Coast Guard board of inquiry.

Mrs. Brege's actions on the morning of the collision were coaxed from her confused and conflicting deposition accounts of the day.

10. Approaches

The passage, positions, bridge communications, convergence, and words and actions of the crew of the *Cedarville*, *Topdalsfjord*, and *Weissenburg* are reconstructed from Coast Guard and trial testimony, log books, shipping records, and interviews. Captain Parilla's meeting with Admiral Khoury was reconstructed from Parilla's deposition testimony, with some dialogue as suggested by the trial decision and envisioned by the author.

11. Collision

The collision of the *Cedarville* and *Topdalsfjord* and the words and deeds of their crews were retold from the accounts of the survivors as recorded in their testimony and interviews.

12. Miscalculation

The actions of *Cedarville*, *Topdalsfjord*, and *Weissenburg* officers and crew are recounted from the exhaustively detailed accounts provided by the survivors in their Coast Guard and trial testimony and subsequent interviews with the press and the author. Segments concerning the notification and reaction of family members are retold from their individual depositions and interviews with the author.

Although the portions of this chapter concerning Mrs. Brege reflect the contents of her troubled deposition testimony, her monitoring of the Bradley Fleet radio frequency is depicted as determined to have occurred by the trial court in support of its findings of conspiracy.

The story of U.S. Steel employees who monitored and facilitated communications between *Cedarville* and company officers is reported from the deposition of Bradley Fleet radioman Joe Hassett. But to the extent that its officers guided and instructed the *Cedarville* captain, that dialogue reflects the observations of Third Mate Gabrysiak, the factual findings of Judge Connell, and the investigative findings of the author.

13. *Capsize*

The actions of the *Cedarville* officers and crew are crafted from the accounts provided by the survivors in their Coast Guard and trial testimony and subsequent interviews with the press and the author.

14. *Rescue*

The positions, bridge communications, and actions of the *Topdalsfjord* and *Weissenburg* crews in rescuing the survivors are recounted from Coast Guard and trial testimony, log books, interviews, and the various statements provided by the survivors.

Cedarville crew survival efforts are recounted from the accounts provided by the survivors. Segments concerning the notification and reaction of family members are retold from their individual depositions and press reports.

Although the local press canvassed the area to report on search-and-rescue efforts, most of the material addressing this topic came from another authoritative source. Chuck Marsh, dive team foreman for Durocher & Van Antwerp, kept a detailed log of his team's activities during the incident. This he was gracious enough to share with the author. Accordingly, dive team and recovery accounts are taken straight from his records.

Miscellaneous community reactions were recorded in various press accounts and retold throughout the chapter.

Again, at no time did U.S. Steel officials admit to a conspiracy. Nevertheless, based on the evidence, the trial judge (and the author) concluded that one was hatched during the early stages of the search and rescue operations. Accordingly, the actions and conversations of those officers in the aftermath of the collision are recounted in a manner consistent with the factual findings of Judge Connell and the investigative findings of the author.

15. Damage Control

Press reports concerning the search and rescue efforts, community tributes, and the conduct of Coast Guard investigative hearings were plentiful. These references are scattered liberally throughout the chapter.

As before, Durocher & Van Antwerp recovery efforts are chronicled as per Chuck Marsh's detailed work logs.

The segment in which some of the bed-ridden crew were visited by Marsh and Parilla is based on information reported to the author by Gabrysiak and Marsh.

The segment in which company officials plot to obtain control over the witnesses and the evidence, though not specifically documented, is based on the trial court's factual findings concerning the conspiracy and the destruction and disappearance of tape recordings of communications between *Cedarville* and those officers.

The Mother's Day card given to Elizabeth Haske by her husband, Stan, was entered into evidence at the trial and is a part of the record maintained by the National Archives in Chicago.

Finally, the chapter closes when Len Gabrysiak is approached by an ominous attorney claiming to represent Den Norske Amerikalinje, owners of the *Topdalsfjord*. This incident is recounted as told by Mr. Gabrysiak.

16. Limitations

Again, Coast Guard hearings on the incident were well documented in the press. Together with the reports of the hearing officers, this segment details the conduct of those hearings.

Another key player was an investigator named Osgood. The record, including Mrs. Brege's deposition, reflects that Mr. Osgood met with Mrs. Brege to discuss the rumors that she had monitored the entirety of the incident by radio. This segment is reconstructed from those fragmentary records.

17. *Troublemaker*

Len Gabrysiak's involuntary hospitalization and escape from Mercywood Hospital in Ypsilanti, Michigan, were related by Mr. Gabrysiak, as were his subsequent confrontations with company officials.

18. *Intimidations*

This chapter consists almost entirely of excerpts and summaries of the depositions of Len Gabrysiak, Joe Parilla, and Lou Brege. Scattered among the testimony are the conspiratorial plottings of fleet officials. As noted previously, though expressly denied by those speakers, these discussions are recounted in a manner consistent with the factual findings of the trial judge and the investigative findings of the author. Nevertheless, Parilla's call to Mrs. Brege is reconstructed from admissions made in their depositions.

19. *Closure*

The author coordinated with claimants' attorney Victor Hanson to chart the thought processes of the claimants' committee's counsel. To a large extent, the evidence and theories put forth by the committee were detailed in the volumes of pleadings on file with the National Archives. Mr. Hanson graciously provided the rest in the form of his notes and correspondence on the subject of the *Cedarville* claim and of Limitation of Liability in general.

The chapter closes with the completion of Judge Connell's written opinion concerning the conspiracy as recorded at *In re: Petition of Den Norske Amerika-Linje A/S, for Exoneration From or Limitation of Liability, et al.*, 276 F.Supp. 163 (N.D. Oh. 1967).

Bibliography

AFL-CIO. "United States Coast Guard Powerless in S.S. Carl D. Bradley Disaster." *Maritime Trade Department News Report,* March 12, 1959.

Bey, Harry. "Deposition Transcript." In *In re: Petition of Den Norske Amerika-Linje A/S, for Exoneration From or Limitation of Liability, et al.,* March 28, 1967.

Bingle, Robert. Interview. In *Cedarville Remembered.* VHS. Lexington, MI: Out of the Blue Productions, 2000.

———. Interview. In *Deep Six, Titanics of the Great Lakes.* Vol. 2. VHS. Midland, MI: Imageworks, 1998.

Blade (Toledo). "Lake Freighter Sinks after Crash; 20 Missing," May 7, 1965.

Blossom, Stephen. "Master of Cedarville Is Charged." *Plain Dealer,* July 10, 1965.

———. "Norwegian Captain to Describe Sinking." *Plain Dealer,* May 11, 1965.

———. "Probe Told: 2 Ships at Right Angles." *Plain Dealer,* May 15, 1965.

———. "Ship Collision Probe in Confusing Turn." *Plain Dealer,* May 13, 1965.

———. "Witness Describes Cedarville's Turn." *Plain Dealer,* May 12, 1965.

Brege, Louella Jane. "Deposition Transcript." In *In re: Petition of Den Norske Amerika-Linje A/S, for Exoneration From or Limitation of Liability, et al.,* May 17, 1967.

———. Telephone interview by author. Rogers City, MI, June 28, 2000.

Brewster, Edward. Interview. In *Cedarville Remembered.* VHS. Lexington, MI: Out of the Blue Productions, 2000.

———. Interview. In *Deep Six, Titanics of the Great Lakes.* Vol. 2. VHS. Midland, MI: Imageworks, 1998.

Buehrens, Clifford. "Deposition Transcript." In *In re: Petition of Den Norske Amerika-Linje A/S, for Exoneration From or Limitation of Liability, et al.,* May 16, 1967.

Bukema, Chris. Interview. In *Deep Six, Titanics of the Great Lakes.* Vol. 2. VHS. Midland, MI: Imageworks, 1998.

Business Week. "How Steel May Save an Old Market," December 5, 1964, 33.

———. "Steelmen Breathe Easier," May 11, 1963, 28.

———. "U.S. Steel Adopts New Corporate Look," September 21, 1963, 29.

————. "U.S. Steel Strips for a Fight," September 21, 1963, 114.

Cedarville Remembered. VHS. Lexington, MI: Out of the Blue Productions, 2000.

Cleveland Press. "Lakes Ship Sinks; 28 Saved, 1 Dead," May 7, 1965.

Commercial Research Service. Correspondence to Victor Hanson, re: SS *Cedarville*, October 4, 1966.

Cook, Jean. "Transcript of Proceedings before Commissioner Oliver Schroeder, Jr." In *In re: Petition of Den Norske Amerika-Linje A/S, for Exoneration From or Limitation of Liability, et al.*, March 1, 1968.

Crawford, M. Correspondence to Victor Hanson, re: wreck survey, November 4, 1966.

Deep Six, Titanics of the Great Lakes. Vol. 2. VHS. Midland, MI: Imageworks, 1998.

Den Norske Amerikalinje. "Answers to Interrogatories Propounded by Marion Jones." In *In re: Petition of Den Norske Amerika-Linje A/S, for Exoneration From or Limitation of Liability, et al.*, April 3, 1967.

Detroit Free Press. "Weather Delays Dive to Wreck," August 15, 1995, 2B.

Doran, John. Correspondence to Victor Hanson, re: report on SS *Cedarville*, November 4, 1966.

————. Statement of diver to Victor Hanson, re: SS *Cedarville*, October 4, 1966.

Erickson, David. Interview. In *Cedarville Remembered*. VHS. Lexington, MI: Out of the Blue Productions, 2000.

Evening News (Sault Ste. Marie). "Cedarville Got No Answer to Fog Signal," May 8, 1965.

————. "Two Vessels Collide in Mackinac Straits," May 7, 1965.

Flesher, John. "Bradley Diving Expedition Postponed." *Oakland Press*, August 14, 1995.

Freedman, Abraham, et al. "Brief on Behalf of Marion Jones, et al. sur Punitive Damages." In *In re: Petition of Den Norske Amerika-Linje A/S, for Exoneration From or Limitation of Liability, et al.*, June 27, 1967.

Friedhoff, William. "Deposition Transcript." In *In re: Petition of Den Norske Amerika-Linje A/S, for Exoneration From or Limitation of Liability, et al.*, March 30, 1967.

Fuhrman, Barbara. "Transcript of Proceedings before Commissioner Oliver Schroeder, Jr." In *In re: Petition of Den Norske Amerika-Linje A/S, for Exoneration From or Limitation of Liability, et al.*, December 13, 1967.

Gabrysiak, Leonard. "Deposition Transcript." In *In re: Petition of Den Norske Amerika-Linje A/S, for Exoneration From or Limitation of Liability, et al.*, March 29, 1967.

————. Interview. In *Cedarville Remembered*. VHS. Lexington, MI: Out of the Blue Productions, 2000.

————. Interview. In *Deep Six, Titanics of the Great Lakes*. Vol. 2. VHS. Midland, MI: Imageworks, 1998.

————. Interview by author. Rogers City, MI, July 3, 2000.

————. Interview by author. Rogers City, MI, July 2, 2002.

Gabrysiak, Patricia. Interview by author. Rogers City, MI, July 2, 2002.

Gilbert, Lewis. "Deposition Transcript." In *In re: Petition of Den Norske Amerika-Linje A/S, for Exoneration From or Limitation of Liability, et al.*, April 11, 1967.

Grand Haven Tribune. "I Saw Shadow of Cedarville Go Under," May 10, 1965.

——. "Ship Sinks after Collision Near 'Big Mac'," May 10, 1965.

Green Bay Press Gazette. "Negligence to be Charged against Cedarville Skipper," July 11, 1965.

Griffin, Julian. "Coast Guard Charges Collision to Ship Captain." *Cleveland Press,* July 16, 1965.

Hahn, Peter. Interview. In *Cedarville Remembered.* VHS. Lexington, MI: Out of the Blue Productions, 2000.

Hamburg-Amerika Linje. "Answers to Interrogatories Propounded by Marion Jones." In *In re: Petition of Den Norske Amerika-Linje A/S, for Exoneration From or Limitation of Liability, et al.,* March 27, 1967.

Hanson, Victor. Interview by author. Detroit, MI, July 6, 2002.

Haske, Elizabeth. "Transcript of Proceedings before Commissioner Oliver Schroeder, Jr." In *In re: Petition of Den Norske Amerika-Linje A/S, for Exoneration From or Limitation of Liability, et al.,* December 13, 1967.

Hassett, Joseph. "Deposition Transcript." In *In re: Petition of Den Norske Amerika-Linje A/S, for Exoneration From or Limitation of Liability, et al.,* May 18, 1967.

Holley, Billy. "Transcript of Proceedings before Commissioner Oliver Schroeder, Jr." In *In re: Petition of Den Norske Amerika-Linje A/S, for Exoneration From or Limitation of Liability, et al.,* March 20, 1968.

Idalski, Micheal. "Transcript of Proceedings before Commissioner Oliver Schroeder, Jr." In *In re: Petition of Den Norske Amerika-Linje A/S, for Exoneration From or Limitation of Liability, et al.,* February 15, 1968.

Inouye, Daniel, Senator. Correspondence to Victor Hanson, re: Merchant Marine, February 5, 1996.

In re: Lamp v. United States Steel Corporation, 402 U.S. 987 (1971).

In re: Petition of Den Norske Amerika-Linje A/S, for Exoneration From or Limitation of Liability, et al., 276 F.Supp. 163 (N.D. Oh. 1967).

In re: United States Steel Corporation v. Fuhrman, 407 F.2d 1143 (6th Cir. 1969).

Jarvis, Woodie. "Aftermath of Cedarville Sinking Almost as Confusing as Testimony." *Evening News (Sault Ste. Marie),* June 25, 1965, 1.

——. "Captain Testifies." *Evening News (Sault Ste. Marie),* May 13, 1965.

——. "Cedarville Captain Cites 5th Amendment in Collision Probe." *Evening News (Sault Ste. Marie),* May 13, 1965.

——. "Coast Guard Declines to Release Testimony from Survivors Involved in Straits Sinking." *Evening News (Sault Ste. Marie),* July 9, 1965.

——. "Coast Guard Hearing Opens—It's Captain against Captain." *Evening News (Sault Ste. Marie),* July 16, 1965.

——. "Coast Guard Quiz Shifts." *Evening News (Sault Ste. Marie),* May 17, 1965.

——. "How a Piece of Paper Could Solve Mystery of Sinking." *Evening News (Sault Ste. Marie),* May 18, 1965.

——. "Should Sunken Ship Be Impounded?" *Evening News (Sault Ste. Marie),* July 1, 1965.

——. "Sinking of Cedarville—Second Quiz Appears Likely." *Evening News (Sault Ste. Marie),* July 3, 1965.

———. "Skipper of Sunken Ship Accused." *Evening News (Sault Ste. Marie)*, July 15, 1965.

Jones, Marion. "Transcript of Proceedings before Commissioner Oliver Schroeder, Jr." In *In re: Petition of Den Norske Amerika-Linje A/S, for Exoneration From or Limitation of Liability, et al.*, December 14, 1967.

Joppich, Martin. "Deposition Transcript." In *In re: Petition of Den Norske Amerika-Linje A/S, for Exoneration From or Limitation of Liability, et al.*, May 17, 1967.

Kierzek, Jerome. "Transcript of Proceedings before Commissioner Oliver Schroeder, Jr." In *In re: Petition of Den Norske Amerika-Linje A/S, for Exoneration From or Limitation of Liability, et al.*, March 20, 1968.

Labor's International Hall of Fame. "Victor Hanson Founding Trustee." Pamphlet.

Lamp, Alice. "Transcript of Proceedings before Commissioner Oliver Schroeder, Jr." In *In re: Petition of Den Norske Amerika-Linje A/S, for Exoneration From or Limitation of Liability, et al.*, February 15, 1968.

Lee, John. "U.S. Steel Corporate Reorganization in Effect." *New York Times*, January 1, 1964.

Lietzow, James. Interview. In *Cedarville Remembered*. VHS. Lexington, MI: Out of the Blue Productions, 2000.

Marsh, Charles. Durocher & Van Antwerp search and rescue log, May 31, 1965.

———. Interview by author. Rogers City, MI, June 16, 2001.

May, Wehrner. "Deposition Transcript." In *In re: Petition of Den Norske Amerika-Linje A/S, for Exoneration From or Limitation of Liability, et al.*, April 18, 1967.

McCulla, James. "Quiet Rogers City, Mich., Stunned by 2nd Tragedy." *Milwaukee Journal*, May 10, 1965.

McDonald, John. "Big Steel Wants a Bigger Share." *Fortune*, January, 1965, 136.

Memorial Resolution in the Matter of the Death of the Honorable James C. Connell, 484 F.Supp. (N.D. Oh)

Miller, Al. *Tin Stackers: The History of the Pittsburgh Steamship Company*. Detroit: Great Lakes Books, 1999.

Miller, Ron. Correspondence to Victor Hanson, re: SS *Cedarville*, July 16, 1999.

———. Correspondence to Victor Hanson, re: SS *Cedarville*, November 5, 1999.

Miller, William. "German Crew Tells of Mackinac Rescue." *Plain Dealer*, May 10, 1965, 8.

Morrow, Edward. "Sea Union Scores U.S. Steel Pact." *New York Times*, April 12, 1964.

Mulke, Stanley. Interview. In *Cedarville Remembered*. VHS. Lexington, MI: Out of the Blue Productions, 2000.

Newsweek. "The Change at U.S. Steel," December 30, 1968, 42.

———. "Captain Declines to Give Testimony," May 14, 1965, 17.

———. "Door Defect Cited on Doomed Vessel," January 27, 1965, 70.

———. "Dutch Ship Reaches Chicago," April 21, 1965, 89.

———. "Freighter Captain Enters Guilty Plea," August 25, 1965, 76.

———. "Ice Blocks the Soo," April 3, 1965, 58.

———. "Lake Captains Fight Ship Whistle Rule," January 29, 1965, 57.

———. "News of Shipping: A Seaway First," April 4, 1965, 78.

———. "Shipping Events: 1964 Tonnage Up," December 2, 1964.

———. "Trial of Captain in Sinking Begins," July 17, 1965, 22.

———. "U.S. Steel to Build Pittsburgh Offices," September 12, 1966, 71.

———. "Wreck Is Blocking St. Lawrence River," April 12, 1965, 9.

Parilla, Joseph. Correspondence to Barbara Fuhrman, May 12, 1965.

———. "Deposition Transcript." In *In re: Petition of Den Norske Amerika-Linje A/S, for Exoneration From or Limitation of Liability, et al.,* May 10, 1967.

Piechan, Ronald. "Transcript of Proceedings before Commissioner Oliver Schroeder, Jr." In *In re: Petition of Den Norske Amerika-Linje A/S, for Exoneration From or Limitation of Liability, et al.,* March 20, 1998.

Plain Dealer. "Cedarville Survivors Still Sought," May 9, 1965.

———. "Fog Delays Search for 7 Lake Sailors," May 9, 1965.

———. "Third Captain Tried to Avert Collision," May 9, 1965.

Presque Isle Advance (Rogers City). "Bradley Ships Begin Fit-out for Shipping Season," March 18, 1965.

———. "Bradley Ships Buck Ice to Open Navigation Season," April 1, 1965.

———. "Bradley Vessels Go into Winter Layup," December 24, 1964.

———. "Challenges Ahead for Growth at Calcite Plant," January 7, 1965.

———. "Small Boat Harbor Shows Promise for the Future," December 24, 1964.

Przybyla, Raphael. "Transcript of Proceedings before Commissioner Oliver Schroeder, Jr." In *In re: Petition of Den Norske Amerika-Linje A/S, for Exoneration From or Limitation of Liability, et al.,* March 18, 1968.

Radke, Rita. "Transcript of Proceedings before Commissioner Oliver Schroeder, Jr." In *In re: Petition of Den Norske Amerika-Linje A/S, for Exoneration From or Limitation of Liability, et al.,* December 18, 1967.

Ratigan, William. *Great Lakes Shipwrecks and Survivals.* New York: Galahad Books, 2000.

Richard, Larry. Interview. In *Cedarville Remembered.* VHS. Lexington, MI: Out of the Blue Productions, 2000.

Rubin, Larry. "Tragedy Strikes Area as Ships Collide." *Evening News (Sault Ste. Marie),* May 8, 1965.

Shoenbaum, Thomas. *Admiralty and Maritime Law.* 2d ed. St. Paul, MN: West Publishing, 1994.

Staten Island Advance. "Hope Dims for 7 Seamen Lost in Mackinac Crash," May 8, 1965.

Time. "Steel," August 27, 1965, 74.

———. "U.S. Business," June 19, 1964, 83.

Trafelet, Ivan. "Deposition Transcript." In *In re: Petition of Den Norske Amerika-Linje A/S, for Exoneration From or Limitation of Liability, et al.,* March 30, 1967.

Tulgetske, Walter. "Deposition Transcript." In *In re: Petition of Den Norske Amerika-Linje A/S, for Exoneration From or Limitation of Liability, et al.,* March 27, 1967.

United States Coast Guard. Correspondence to Victor Hanson, re: SS *Cedarville,* March 15, 1966.

United States Coast Guard. Correspondence to VADM W. D. Shields, re: SS *Cedarville*, March 22, 1966.

United States Coast Guard. "Commandant's Action on Marine Board of Investigation, re: SS *Cedarville*," February 6, 1967.

United States District Court, Northern District of Ohio. "Civil Docket Sheet." In *In re: Petition of Den Norske Amerika-Linje A/S, for Exoneration From or Limitation of Liability, et al.*, undated.

White, Stoddard. "Lake Crash Widow Granted $452,000." *Detroit News*, May 8, 1969, 3.

Index